A

TREATISE

OF

Feme Coverts:

OR, THE

LADY's LAW.

CONTAINING

All the Laws and Statutes relating to WOMEN, under several HEADS:

VIZ.

I Of Discents of Lands to Females, Coparceners, *&c.*
II. Of Consummation of Marriage, stealing of Women, Rapes, Polygamy.
III. Of the Laws of Procreation of Children, and therein of Bastards or spurious Issue.
IV. Of the Privileges of Feme Coverts, and their Power with respect to their Husband, and all others.
V. Of Husband and Wife, and in what Actions they are to join.
VI. Of Estates Tail, Jointures and Settlements, real and personal on Women.
VII. Of what the Wife is entitled to of the Husband's, and Things belonging to the Wife, the Husband gains Possession of by Marriage.
VIII. Of Private Contracts by the Wife, Alimony, separate Maintenance, Divorces, Elopements, *&c.*

To which are added,

Judge *HIDE's* very remarkable Argument in the *Exchequer-Chamber, Term. Trin.* 15 *Car.* 2. In the Case of *Manby* and *Scot*, whether and in what Cases the Husband is bound by the Contract of his Wife:

And select

Precedents of *Conveyances* in all Cases concerning Feme Coverts.

THE LAWBOOK EXCHANGE, LTD.
Clark, New Jersey
2003

ISBN 1-58477-286-7

Printed in the United States of America
on Acid-Free Paper

The Lawbook Exchange, Ltd.
33 Terminal Avenue
Clark, New Jersey 07066

Please see catalogue at rear of this volume
or our website
www.lawbookexchange.com
for a selection of our other publications.

Library of Congress Cataloging-in-Publication Data

A Treatise of feme coverts, or, The lady's law: containing all the laws and statutes relating to women, under several heads ... to which are added, Judge Hide's very remarkable argument in the Exchequer-Chamber.

p. cm.

Originally published: London : E. and R. Nutt and R. Gosling, 1732.

Includes bibliographical references and index.

ISBN 1-58477-286-7 (cloth: alk. paper)

1. Married women—Legal status, laws, etc.—England. 2. Husband and wife—England. 3. Marital property—England. I. Title: Treatise of feme coverts. II. Title: Lady's law. III. Clarendon, Edward Hyde, Earl of, 1609-1674. IV. Great Britain. Court of Exchequer Chamber.

KD758 .T8 2002
346.4201 '6—dc21 2002041292

A

TREATISE

OF

Feme Coverts:

OR, THE

LADY's LAW.

CONTAINING

All the Laws and Statutes relating to WOMEN, under ſeveral HEADS:

VIZ.

I Of Diſcents of Lands to Females, Coparceners, *&c.*
II. Of Conſummation of Marriage, ſtealing of Women, Rapes, Polygamy.
III. Of the Laws of Procreation of Children, and therein of Baſtards or ſpurious Iſſue.
IV. Of the Privileges of Feme Coverts, and their Power with reſpect to their Husband, and all others.
V. Of Husband and Wife, and in what Actions they are to join.
VI. Of Eſtates Tail, Jointures and Settlements, real and perſonal on Women.
VII. Of what the Wife is entitled to of the Husband's, and Things belonging to the Wife, the Husband gains Poſſeſſion of by Marriage.
VIII. Of Private Contracts by the Wife, Alimony, ſeparate Maintenance, Divorces, Elopements, *&c.*

To which are added,

Judge *HIDE*'s very remarkable Argument in the *Exchequer-Chamber*, *Term. Trin.* 15 *Car.* 2. In the Caſe of *Manby* and *Scot*, whether and in what Caſes the Husband is bound by the Contract of his Wife:

And ſelect

Precedents of *Conveyances* in all Caſes concerning Feme Coverts.

In the *SAVOY*:
Printed by E. and R. NUTT, and R. GOSLING, (Aſſigns of *E. Sayer*, Eſq;) for B. Lintot, and Sold by H. Lintot, at the *Croſs Keys*, againſt St. *Dunſtan*'s Church in *Fleetſtreet*. M DCC XXXII.

THE

PREFACE.

WHEN *a Man and Woman are join'd in Matrimony, the Woman is called a* Feme Covert, *and the Law regards them but as one Person. And an ancient Author has assur'd us, that all Women, in the Eye of the Law, are either married or to be married; and their Desires are subject to their Husbands, as a Man shall forsake Father and Mother to stick to his Wife.*

The

The Principal Causes of Matrimony are these two; Increase of Children, and the Avoiding of Fornication and Uncleanness; and whosoever marries for Beauty, Riches, or other Motives, rather than those before mentioned, are said to be guilty of a Crime, tho' it be not expresly disallow'd by our Law. And the Church *of* England *is more strict in providing against the Change of Lust, and prohibiting Separations of Man and Wife, than the* Roman Catholick *Church; which in some Countries, indulges both the married Woman and the unmarried, in the full Exercise of their Lustful Pleasures.*

As to the following Treatise it contains, besides the Law of Marriage, the Laws and Statutes concerning Women in general: But some Things of Entertaiment, being writ long ago, are mix'd with the

the Law; and our old Laws and Customs relating to Women, are many of them very merry, though the Makers of them might possibly be grave Men. The fair Sex are here inform'd, how to preserve their Lands, Goods, and most valuable Effects, from the Incroachments of any one; to defend themselves and their Reputations against all unlawful Attacks of Mankind, and to maintain Actions, and carry on Prosecutions in Cases of Violation of their Persons, to the Death of a daring Offender.

Further, the Reader is to be acquainted, that this Work comprehends the Rights and Privileges of Females, as to Discents, Partitions of Lands, &c. Estates-Tail affecting Them; all the Laws relating to Rapes, Polygamy, and stealing of Women; Judge Hide's *learned Argument*

in

in the Exchequer Chamber, and ſelect Precedents of Conveyances concerning Feme Coverts, not ſo much as mentioned in the Treatiſe called Baron and Feme; *which 'tis hoped is ſufficient to recommend it to all Practiſers of the Law, and other curious Perſons.*

THE

A TREATISE OF Feme Coverts: OR, THE LADY's LAW.

Of Females unmarried, and their Rights in Discents, Coparceners, &c.

BY our ancient Laws, Women have divers Ages to several Purposes; as Seven Years for the Lord to have Aid; the Age of Nine Years to deserve Dower; Twelve Years to consent to Marriage; Fourteen to chuse a Guardian, and

One and Twenty Years to alienate Lands, Goods and Chattles. *Co. Lit.* 78.

In Cases of Discent of Lands, a Female may sometimes be preferred in Succession before a Male: As for Example; Land is given to a Man, and the Heirs of his Body, who having Issue two Sons dies, the eldest Son dies also, leaving behind him a Daughter, this Daughter shall inherit by Right of Blood.

A Man is seised of Lands in Fee-simple, and hath Issue a Son and a Daughter by one Venter, and a Son by another Venter, and dies; whereupon the eldest Son enters and dies likewise, but without Issue, the Daughter shall have the Land, and not the younger Son; yet the younger Son is Heir to the Father, but not to the Brother. *Co. Lit.* 14.

And if a Man has Issue a Son and a Daughter by one Woman, and a Son by another; and the first Son makes a Purchase in Fee, and dies without Issue, the Sister shall have the Land by Discent, as Heir to her Brother, and not the younger Brother; for she is of the whole Blood of her elder Brother. *Ibid.*

But where there is a Son and a Daughter by one Venter, and a younger Son by another Venter, if the Father die seised of Lands, an Advowson, Rent, *&c.* and the eldest Son dies before Entry, or before he receives the Rent, the Daughter shall not inherit, but the younger Son, as Heir to the Father. *Co. Lit.* 11.

If a Man has Issue three Daughters by one Venter, and one Daughter by another Venter, and die seised, *&c.* they all enter, and

two

two of the Daughters by the firſt Venter die, the third Daughter, by the ſame Venter ſhall be Heir alone to their two Parts, and the fourth Daughter of the Half Blood gains Nothing therein. 10 *Aſſiſ. p.* 27.

There is a great Difference between Land purchaſed by him that died ſeiſed, and Lands deſcended to the ſame Perſon; for the firſt may go to the Heir on the Father's Side, and for Default of ſuch to the Heir on the Side of the Mother; but Lands deſcended muſt always go to the Heirs of the Blood of the firſt Purchaſor. *Co. Lit.* 12.

And the Caſe may be ſuch, that a Female ſhall carry away Inheritance from a Male, though there be no Difference of Right Line, which *Bracton* calls *Jus ſanguinis duplicatum*; as where a Man purchaſes Lands in Fee, and dies without Iſſue, an Aunt or Uncle's Daughter, on the Father's Side ſhall inherit before an Uncle or Uncle's Son, on the Mother's Side, where they are both Collateral, and the Relation of Blood is alike.

And if the Purchaſor died leaving Iſſue a Son, and this Son dies without any Iſſue; now the Lands ſhall not go to the Heirs on the Part only of the Mother of the Son. To find out who ſhall inherit in this Caſe, we muſt aſcend a Step higher to the Marriage of the Father and Mother of the firſt Purchaſor; where if there be neither Brother nor Siſter of the Purchaſor, a Daughter of the eldeſt Uncle, on the Father's Side, may inherit before any of the Mother's Side; and ſuch Daughter ſhall likewiſe be preferred before a Son of the ſecond Uncle, on the Part of the Father, by the Worthineſs of Blood. *Co. Lit.* 12.

Where there is a Brother and Siſter, and Lands are let for Life to a Stranger, the Remainder to the Right Heirs of the Brother; and if he and the Tenant for Life die, the Siſter may enter and retain the Poſſeſſion and Fee, though the Brother's Wife be afterwards delivered of a Son: But a Remainder veſted, is not like to Fee-ſimple deſcended to a Daughter, where a *poſthumous* Son may enter. 30 *Aſſiſ. p.* 47. If a Man dies Seiſed of Land, and his Daughter enters, a Son born afterwards may enter; it is otherwiſe in Caſe of Purchaſe, &c. *Co. Lit.*

In the Caſe of *Wimbiſh* and *Talbois*, Chief Juſtice *Mountague* gave his Opinion, That if a Man deviſe Land for Life, the Remainder to the Right Heir Male of the Deviſor, and the Heirs of his Body, &c. now if the Deviſee for Life die, and a Woman, which is Heir general to the Deviſor enters, and has afterwards a Son, the Son ſhall never out the Mother, in whom is veſted the Inheritance, for want of other Perſons to take the falling Remainder. 9 *H.* 6.

But if a Man, ſeiſed by Diſcent from his Mother, make a Feoffment with Condition, &c. and die without Iſſue; if a Woman, Heir on the Father's Side, enter for the Condition broken, an Heir, Male or Female, on the Mother's Side, may ouſt her. *Plow.* 56.

As where Lands are given to a Man, and the Heirs Males of his Body begotten, in this Caſe his Iſſue Male ſhall inherit, and the Iſſue Female ſhall never inherit; ſo if Lands

or

or Tenements are given to a Man, and to his Heirs Females of his Body begotten, there his Iſſue Female ſhall inherit by Force of the ſaid Gift, and not his Iſſue Male; for the Will of the Donor ought to be obſerved. *Co. Lit.* 24.

When a Gift in Tail is made to a Man and the Heirs Females of his Body, and he hath Iſſue a Son, who has Iſſue a Daughter, this Daughter ſhall never inherit; becauſe ſhe muſt convey by Diſcent from Females. Alſo if Lands be given to a Man, and the Heirs Male of his Body, and he hath Iſſue a Daughter, who has Iſſue a Son, and dies, and after the Donee dies, in this Caſe the Son of the Daughter ſhall not inherit by Force of the Entail; for the Heir Male muſt convey his Diſcent whole by the Heirs Males. *Co. Lit.* 25.

A Man gives Lands to another, and the Heirs Females of his Body, and dies, having Iſſue a Son and a Daughter, the Daughter ſhall inherit; but in Caſe of a Purchaſe it is otherwiſe. For if a Man have Iſſue a Son and a Daughter, and a Leaſe for Life be made, the Remainder to the Heirs Females of his Body, and he dieth, the Female can take nothing, becauſe ſhe is not Heir; for ſhe muſt be both Heir and Heir Female, which ſhe is not, the Brother being Heir; and becauſe here is no Gift, therefore the Will of the Giver cannot be obſerved. *Co. Lit.* 24.

And ſo it is, if a Man hath a Son and a Daughter, and dies, and Lands be given to the Daughter, and the Heirs Female of the Body of her Father, the Daughter ſhall take nothing but an Eſtate for Life, becauſe there is no ſuch Perſon, ſhe being not Heir. But where a Gift is made to a Man, and to the Heirs Female of his Body, there the Donee, being the firſt Taker, is capable by Purchaſe, and the Heir Female by Diſcent, *ſecundum formam Doni.* Co Lit. 25.

If a Man gives Land to one in Marriage with his Daughter, to hold to them two and the Heirs of their Bodies, they have Iſſue a Daughter, and the Husband dying, the Wife takes another Husband, by whom ſhe has a Son, and dies, the Daughter ſhall inherit *per modum Donationis.* This is an Example given by *Bracton*, with Relation to his general Rule, That a Woman ſhall not inherit when there is an Heir Male, *niſi contrarium faciat modus Donationis.*

When Lands are given to a Man, and the Heirs Males of his Body, who has Iſſue two Sons, and the Eldeſt dies, having Iſſue a Daughter; if he Leaſe the Land for a Term of Years, the Reverſion deſcends to the Son; but if the Leaſe be made for Term of the Life of the Leſſee, the Reverſion and the Fee-ſimple deſcend to the Daughter, the Diſcontinuance is the Cauſe thereof; and here the Daughter is not in, in the *per*, but *contra modum Donationis*, by violating the Will of the Donor. *Lit.*

If a Man give Lands to a Perſon, and the Heirs Male of his Body begotten; Remainder to him and his Heirs Females on his Body begotten; the Donee has Iſſue a Son, who hath Iſſue a Daughter, and this Daughter has Iſſue a Son, this Son is not inheritable to either of theſe Eſtates-Tail, for the

Reaſons

Reaſons already mentioned, That the Male muſt make his Conveyance only by Males, and the Female by Females; but in this Caſe the Land ſhall revert to the Donor. And therefore the ſafeſt Way, when a Man deſigns to intail his Lands to the Heirs Males and Females of his Body, is to limit the firſt Eſtate to him and the Heirs Males of his Body, the Remainder to him and to the Heirs of his Body, and then all his Iſſues whatſoever are inheritable. *Co. Lit.* 25.

John de Mandevile, by his Wife *Roberge*, had Iſſue *Robert* and *Maud*; and *Michael de Morevil* gave certain Lands to *Roberge*, and to the Heirs of *John de Mandevile*, her late Huſband, on her Body begotten; it was adjudg'd that *Roberge* had but an Eſtate for Life, and the Fee-tail veſted in *Robert*; and that when he died without Iſſue, *Maud* the Daughter was Tenant in Tail, as Heir of the Body of her Father, *per formam Doni*; and the *Formedon* which ſhe brought, ſuppoſed, That after the Death of the aforeſaid *Roberge* and *Robert*, Son and Heir of the ſaid *John de Mandevile*, and Heir of the ſaid *John*, begotten on the Body of the ſaid *Roberge*, to the ſaid *Maud*, Daughter of the ſaid *John*, begotten on the ſaid *Roberge*, Siſter and Heir of the ſaid *Robert*, the ſaid Lands ought to deſcend, *per formam Donationis predict'*. And yet in Truth, the Land did not deſcend unto her from *Robert*; but becauſe ſhe could bring no other Writ, it was held good.

In this Caſe, although *Robert* being Heir, took an Eſtate-Tail by Purchaſe, and the Daughter was no Heir of the Body of the

Father, at the Time of the Gift, ſhe recovered the Land *per formam Doni*, by the Name of Heir of the Body of her Father; which notwithſtanding her Brother was, and he was capable at the Time of the Gift; and therefore when the Gift was made, ſhe took nothing, but in Expectancy when ſhe became Heir, *per formam Doni*. Co. Lit. 26.

If a Man hath Iſſue two Daughters, and dies ſeiſed of two Acres of Land in Fee-ſimple, and one Siſter gives her Part to the other Siſter, and the Heirs of the Body of her Father, here the Donee has an Eſtate-Tail in the Moiety of the Donor's Part; for the Donee is not the entire Heir, but the Donor is Heir with the Donee, and ſhe cannot give to the Heirs of her own Body; and the Donee has the other Moiety of her Siſter's Part for Life. *Co. Lit.* 26.

When there is no Heir Male to an Eſtate in Fee-ſimple, &c. but ſeveral Females, either Daughters, Siſters, &c. they are called *Parceners*, and ſhall inherit together. *Co Lit.* 163.

And although they are ſeveral Perſons, yet are they but one Heir, and they have one entire Freehold in the Land, as long as it remains undivided, in Reſpect of any Strangers, but between themſelves, they have in Judgment of Law, ſeveral Freeholds to many Purpoſes; as one of them may execute a Conveyance of her Part to the other, &c.

By the Death of any one of them, the Coparcency is not ſever'd; for in ſuch Caſe, the Part of the Perſon dying ſhall deſcend to her Iſſue; but the Iſſues of ſeveral Coparceners ſhall never join as Heirs to their Mothers,

thers, becauſe ſeveral Rights deſcend; and yet when they have recovered, a Writ of Partition lies between them. *Co. Lit.* 164.

If the Iſſues of two Coparcerners, who are in by ſeveral Deſcents, be diſſeiſed, they ſhall join in Aſſiſe; though in this Caſe, if the two Daughters had been actually ſeiſed, and afterwards diſſeiſed, after their Deceaſes the Iſſues ſhall not join; becauſe ſeveral Rights deſcend to them from ſeveral Anceſtors; but after they have ſeverally recovered, they are Coparceners, and one *Præcipe* lies againſt them. *Ibid.*

A Man hath Iſſue two Daughters, and the eldeſt Daughter hath Iſſue three Daughters, and the youngeſt one Daughter, all theſe four ſhall inherit; but the Daughter of the Youngeſt ſhall have as much as the three Daughters of the Eldeſt, *Ratione ſtirpium*, and not *Ratione capitum*; for in Judgment of Law, every Daughter hath a ſeveral Stock or Root. *Co. Lit.* 164.

Alſo if a Man has Iſſue two Daughters, and the Eldeſt has Iſſue divers Sons and divers Daughters, and the Youngeſt hath Iſſue ſeveral Daughters, the eldeſt Son of the eldeſt Daughter ſhall only inherit; but all the Daughters of the Youngeſt ſhall inherit; and the eldeſt Son is Coparcener with the Daughters of the youngeſt Daughter, and ſhall have one Moiety, *viz.* his Mother's Part; ſo that Men deſcended of Daughters, may be Coparceners as well as Women, and ſhall jointly implead, and be impleaded. *Ibid.*

A Partition may be made of any Estate of Freehold, or for Term of Years, or at Will, of Manors, Lands, Tenements or Hereditaments, whereof the Partition is demanded. But if a Man have Estovers appendant to his Freehold, they are so entire that they shall not be divided between Coparceners; and if a Corody incertain be granted to a Man and his Heirs, and he hath Issue several Daughters, this Corody shall not be divided between them; but of a Corody certain Partition may be made. Homage and Fealty cannot be divided between Coparceners; and a Piscary incertain, or a Common *Sauns nombre*, cannot be divided.

In these Cases, the eldest Daughter shall have the Estovers, Common, Piscary, Corody incertain, *&c.* and the rest shall have Contribution; that is, an Allowance of the Value in some other Part of the Inheritance. And if the Common Ancestor left no other Inheritance, whereof Contribution may be had, then shall one Coparcener have the Estovers, Piscary, Common, *&c.* for one Time, and the others for the like Time; as the one for one Year, and the other for another, or a longer or shorter Space. Or in Case of the Piscary, one may have the first Fish, or first Draught, and the other the second, *&c.* And if it be of a Park, one may have the first Venison, and the second the second, *&c.* *Co. Lit.* 165.

A Rent-Charge is entire, but it may nevertheless be divided between Coparceners; and by Act in Law the Tenant of the Land is subject to several Distresses, and Partition may

may be made before Seisin of the Rent. Likewise an Advowson is an entire Inheritance, and yet in Effect the same may be divided between Coparceners; for they may so divide it, as to present by Turns. *Ibid.*

If Coparceners, Jointenants, &c. be seised of any Estate of Inheritance in the Advowson of any Church or Vicarage, or other Ecclesiastical Promotion, and a Partition be made between them to present by Turns; then every one shall be adjudged to be seized of his or her separate Part of the Advowson, to present in his or her Turn: As if there be two, and they make Partition, each shall be said to be seized; the one of the one Moiety to present in the first Turn, and the other of the other Moiety to present in the second Turn; and so where there are more than two. Stat. 7 *Annæ*.

If an Advowson descends to several Parceners, and they can't agree in the presenting to the same; the Law casts the first Presentation on the Eldest, and the Second shall have the second Turn, &c. every one in Turn according to *Seniority*. And if they enter into an Agreement to present by Turns, the Inheritance is not thereby divided; but in Case of a Usurpation by a Stranger, they may join in a *Quære Impedit*. 2 Part *Co. Inst.* 365.

Partition may be made several Ways: One is, when the Parceners agree amongst themselves to make Partition of the Lands, or Tenements. As if there be two Parceners, they consent to make a Division between them of the Tenements in two Parts; each Part

Part by it self in Severality, and of equal Value: And if there be three Parceners to divide the Tenements into three Parts in Severality, &c. *Co. Lit.* 166.

Another Partition there is, (*viz.*) to chuse by Agreement certain of their Friends, to make Partition of the Lands or Tenements in Manner aforesaid. And then after Partition made, the eldest Daughter shall make the first Choice of one of the Parts so divided, which she will have for her Part or Share; then the second Daughter next after her of another Part, and then the third Sister another Part, & *sic de cæteris*, unless it be otherwise agreed between them: For the Agreement may be made for one to have such Tenements, and another such Tenements, &c. without any *primer* Election.

But if the Parceners agree that the eldest Sister shall make Partition of the Tenements, and she do it accordingly; then it is said, that the eldest Sister shall chuse last for her Part, and after every one of her Sisters, &c. The Rule of Law is *Cujus est Divisio, alterius est Electio.* And the Reason of this my Lord *Coke* tells us is to avoid Partiality,

Ipse etenim Leges cupiunt ut jure regantur.

which might apparently follow, if the Eldest were permitted both to divide and chuse.

There is another Partition made in the following Manner: After Division made of the Lands, every Part of it is written in a small Scroll of Parchment, and cover'd with Wax li e to a little Ball, so as none may inspect what

what is written on the Scrolls; and then the Balls of Wax, being three, or four, &c. are put in a Bag or Hat held by an indifferent Person, and the eldeſt Daughter ſhall firſt put her Hand into the Hat, and take a Ball of Wax, with the Scroll within the ſame Ball for her Part; and then the ſecond Siſter ſhall put her Hand in and take another; the third Siſter, the third Ball, &c. And in this Caſe, every one of them muſt ſtand to their Chance and Allotment. *F. N. B.* 197.

If there be four Parceners, and they will not agree to a Partition to be made between them; then may one of them bring a Writ of *Partitione facienda* againſt the other three; or two of them may have this Writ againſt the other two; or three of them againſt the fourth at their Election. Upon this Writ Judgment ſhall be given that the Sheriff ſhall go to the Lands and Tenements, and by the Oaths of twelve Men, &c. make Partition between the Parties; and aſſign one Part of the Lands and Tenements to the Plaintiff, and another Part to another Parcener, &c. And here no Mention is made in the Judgment, of Preference to be given to the eldeſt Siſter more than the youngeſt, but to make equal Partition. *Co. Lit.* 168.

In caſe there be three Parceners, and the youngeſt is for having a Partition, but the other two are for holding in Parcenary that which to them belongs without Partition, and will not agree with the youngeſt: Now if one Part be allotted in Severality to the youngeſt Siſter, according to that which ſhe ought to have; the others may hold the Remainder

mainder of the Lands in Parcenary, and occupy in Common without Partition if they will; and if afterwards the eldest or middle Parcener will make Partition between them, they may do it at their Pleasure. But where Partition is made by Writ *Partitione facienda*, there it is otherwise; for every Parcener shall have her Part in Severality, &c. *Co. Lit.* 177.

Bracton's Partition, is where a Commission was issu'd to several Persons nominated by the Parties, or appointed by the King as Justices, with Commandment to the Sheriff to cause the Parceners to come before those Commissioners: And when the Division was made, every Part being written by it self was to be deliver'd to a Lay-man unlearn'd; who was to distribute to every Coheir her Part at Adventure, wherewith she should be satisfied: Tho' this might be altered by their Agreement amongst themselves, to elect according to the Prerogative of their Age. *Bract.*

The last Manner of Partition is by Hotchpot: Which is where a Man seised of certain Lands in Fee-simple, hath issue two Daughters, and the eldest being married, the Father gives Part of his Lands to the Husband with his Daughter in Frank-Marriage; and dies seised of the Remainder, which Remainder is of greater Value than the Lands given in Marriage: In this Case, the Husband or Wife are to put their Lands given in Frank-Marriage in Hotchpot, with the Remainder of the Land, with the Wife's Sister. And if they will not condescend to this; then the youngest Sister may hold and enjoy the same Remainder,

Remainder, and take the Profits only to her ſelf. *Co. Lit.* 175.

This Term Hotchpot ſignifies no more than the putting of the Lands in Frank-Marriage and the other Lands in Fee-ſimple together, to the Intent to know the Value of both, and then Partition ſhall be made as follows. If a Man be ſeiſed of thirty Acres of Land of equal Value *per* Acre *per Ann.* and hath Iſſue two Daughters, one whereof is Covert Baron, with whom the Father gives ten Acres in Marriage, and dieth ſeiſed of the Remainder; then the other Siſter ſhall enter into the remaining twenty Acres, until the Husband and his Wife will put the ten Acres with the twenty Acres in Hotchpot, that the Value of every Acre may be known; and then on the Partition, the Husband and Wife ſhall be allotted, beſides the ten Acres, five Acres in Severality of the twenty Acres, and the other Siſter ſhall have the fifteen Acres remaining; ſo as the Husband and Wife may have as much in yearly Value as the other Siſter. *Co. Litt.* 177.

If two Meſſuages deſcend to two Parceners, and one of them is worth 20 *s.* a Year, but the other is in Value no more than 10 *s.* *per Ann.* in this Caſe Partition may be made between them, by aſſigning one Meſſuage to one Parcener, and the other Parcener to have the other: And ſhe who hath the Meſſuage worth 20 *s.* *per Ann.* and her Heirs, ſhall pay a yearly Rent of 5 *s.* iſſuing out of the ſame to the other Parcener, and to her Heirs for ever, becauſe each of them are to have Equality in Value. *Co. Lit.* 169.

A Partition of Lands ought to be made according to the Quality and true Value of the Lands, and not according to the Quantity or equal Number of Acres. *Hill.* 22 *Car. B. R.* And if there be three Coparceners of a Manor who make Partition, every of them ſhall have a Manor and a Court-Baron within her Purparty. *Dav. Rep.* 61.

But if two Parceners of Land in Fee-ſimple, being of full Age (*viz.*) of twenty-one Years, make Partition between themſelves, and the Part of one of them exceeds in Value the Part of the other, this Partition cannot be defeated. But if the partible Tenements are held in Fee-tail, and the Part of one is more in Value than the Part of the other, the Perſons making the Partition are only concluded during their Lives; for if the Parcener which has the leſſer Part leave behind her any Iſſue, ſuch Iſſue may diſagree to the Partition, and enter and occupy in common the other Part which was allotted her Aunt, &c. as if no Partition had been made. *Co. Lit.* 176.

And if Parceners being married, they and their Husbands make Partition, if the Part of the one be leſs in Value than the Part of the other, the Partition ſhall not be avoided during the Lives of their Husbands; but that Woman which has the leſſer Part after the Deceaſe of her Husband, may enter into her Siſter's Part and defeat the Partition.

Partitions made where the youngeſt Coparcener is within Age, may be avoided by ſuch youngeſt, if the Part allotted her be leſs in Value than the Part of the others; and

ſhe

ſhe may, either during her Nonage, or at her full Age, enter into the Part aſſign'd her Siſter, &c. but if ſhe receives the Profits of the Lands allotted her at full Age, ſhe confirms the Partition, and it may not be defeated.

So that tho' the Partition be unequal, yet the ſame is not void, but voidable by Entry, &c. But a Partition made by the King's Writ, *De Partitione facienda*, by the Sheriff on the Oaths of twelve Men, ſhall bind the Infant for ever, tho' his Part be unequal; and 'tis the ſame of Feme Coverts. *Co. Lit.* 171.

If there be two Parceners, and the one takes Husband, and the Husband and Wife have Iſſue between them, and then the Wife dies, and the Husband keeps himſelf in as Tenant by the Curteſy; in this Caſe the ſurviving Parcener and the Tenant by the Curteſy may make Partition between them. And if the Tenant by the Curteſy will not conſent to make Partition, the Parcener which ſurvives may compel him by Writ *De partitione facienda*, &c. But the Tenant by the Curteſy may not have this Writ to oblige a Partition, becauſe he is no Parcener, and ſuch Writs lie for Parceners only.

Partition of Lands of Inheritance by Parceners, Jointenants, &c. muſt be made by Writ or Deed, and cannot be made by Parol. *Dyer* 350. And when there are three or four Coparceners, who make Partition between them; if the Part of one Parcener be defeated, ſhe may enter and occupy the other Lands with all the other Parceners, and compel them to make new Partition, &c. *Co. Lit.* 174.

174. And where Part of one Parcener's Estate is evicted for Life; that shall defeat the entire Partition. 5 *Mod.* 141.

If a Man having Issue two Daughters, dies seized of Lands in Fee-simple, and Lands in Fee-tail, and the Daughters after his Decease make Partition between them, whereby the Fee-simple Lands are allotted the youngest Drughter, and the entail'd Lands assigned to the eldest; if after such Partition made, the youngest Daughter aliens her Land in Fee-simple to another in Fee, and dies, leaving behind her Issue a Son or a Daughter, the Issue may enter into the Lands in Tail, and occupy them in Purparty with the Aunt; for the Issue can have no Remedy for the Land sold by the Mother, it being in Fee-simple; and being Heir in Tail, and having no Recompence from the Lands entail'd, it is but reasonable he should have his Portion of those Lands, when the Partition makes no Discontinuance. *Co. Lit.* 172. But *Anno* 10 *H.* 6. it was adjudg'd that the Heir shall be put to a Writ of *Formedon*, and may not enter upon the Parcener.

And the Eldest Daughter shall not enter into half the Lands in Fee-simple upon the Alienee; for by the Alienation the Privity of Estate is destroy'd. It shall be accounted the Folly of the eldest Sister that she would agree to such a Partition; for if she had brought a Writ of Partition, she should not have been compell'd to take the whole Estate in Tail, by Reason of the Prejudice that might ensue, but should have challeng'd one Moiety of the Lands in Tail, and another Moiety

Moiety of the Fee-ſimple Lands, and this ſhe might do *ex proviſione legis*, and ſo be ſure to have no Loſs. *Co. Lit.* 173.

The Iſſue in Tail ſhall never be barred, without a full Recompence; but a Partition of Lands intailed between Parceners, if it be equal at the Time of the Partition, it ſhall bind the Iſſue in Tail for ever; although the one do alien her Part. *Dyer* 1. *Mar.* 98.

If a Man be ſeiſed in Fee of an Acre of Land, by juſt Title, and he obtains another Acre by diſſeiſing an Infant, he has Iſſue two Daughters, and dies ſeiſed of both Acres, the Infant being then within Age; and the Daughters enter and make Partition; now, if afterwards the Infant make an Entry into the Acre, of which he was diſſeiſſed, upon the Poſſeſſion of the Parcener, then the ſame Parcener may enter into the other Acre, which her Siſter has, and hold in Parcenary with her. *Co. Lit.* 173.

When the Privity of Eſtate remains, and the Part of the one is evicted, ſhe ſhall enter and hold in Coparcenary with her other Coparcener; and ſo it is in the Caſe of an Exchange. But when the whole Privity between Coparceners is deſtroyed, there ceaſes all Expectation of Recompence, either upon the Condition or Warranty in Law, by Force of the Partition. *Ibid.*

If one Parcener make a Feoffment in Fee, and her Feoffee, being impleaded, voucheth the Feoffor, ſhe may have Aid of her Coparcener to deraign a Warranty Paramount, but never to recover *Pro'rata* againſt her by Force of the Warranty in Law upon the

Partition; for by her Alienation, ſhe hath diſmiſſed herſelf from having any Part of the Land, as Parcener; and as Parcener ſhe muſt recover *pro rata*, upon the Warranty in Law. *Hob.* 21, 26.

A Man is ſeiſed of Lands in Fee, and hath Iſſue two Daughters, and makes a Gift in Tail to one of them, and then dies ſeiſed of the Reverſion in Fee, which deſcends to both Siſters, the Donee, or her Iſſue, is impleaded, ſhe ſhall not pray in Aid of the other Coparcener, either to recover *pro rata*, or to deraign the Warranty Paramount, becauſe the other Siſter is a Stranger to the Eſtate-Tail, whereof the Eldeſt was ſole Tenant, and Partition never was, nor could be made thereof. *Co. Lit.* 174.

When one of the Coparceners enters into the whoſe Eſtate generaſly, this does not deveſt the other of her Right, unleſs ſhe that makes the Entry lays Claim to the Whole, and takes the Profits of the Whole; for that may deveſt the Freehold in Law of the other Parcener. *Co. Lit.* 373.

But after the Parceners are actually ſeiſed, the Taking of the whole Profits, or any Claim made by the one, cannot put the other out of Poſſeſſion, without an actual putting out, or Diſſeiſin. When one Coparcener entereth into the Whole, and maketh a Feoffment of the Whole, this deveſteth the Freehold in Law, out of the other. *Ibid.*

If where there are two Coparceners, one diſſeiſſes the other, and the Diſſeiſee brings an Aſſiſe, and Recovers, ſhe ſhall have Judgment to hold her Moiety in Severalty: And if one Coparcener Recover against another in a *Nuper Obiit*, or a *Rationabili parte*, the Judgment ſhall be for the Demandant to Recover, and hold in Severality. *Bract. l.* 4. *Co. Lit.* 167.

A Writ *De Rationabili parte* may be brought where an Anceſtor ſeiſed of Lands in Fee-ſimple, Leaſes the ſame for Life, and dies, having Iſſue two Daughters; and after the Death of Tenant for Life, one of the Daughters enters into the whole Inheritance, and deforceth her Siſter, the Siſter ſo deforced may bring this Writ. It is maintainable by two or three Siſters againſt the Fourth, or by an Aunt or Niece againſt a Siſter; and it lies as well where the Anceſtor died ſeiſed, as where he died not ſeiſed. *F.N.B.* 9.

If a Man ſeiſed of Lands in Fee-ſimple, hath Iſſue two Daughters, and one of the Daughters is Attainted of Felony; the Father dies, both Daughters being living; one Moiety ſhall deſcend to the one Daughter, and the other Moiety ſhall Eſcheat. But if a Man make a Leaſe for Life, Remainder to the Right Heirs of a Perſon, being dead, who had Iſſue two Daughters, whereof one is Attainted of Felony, in this Caſe, ſome have ſaid, that the Remainder is not good for a Moiety, but void for the Whole; for that both the Daughters are but one Heir. *Co. Lit.* 163. 1 *Roll.* 103.

Husband and Wife, Tenants in Special Tail, have Iſſue a Daughter, the Wife dies, the Husband, by a ſecond Wife, has Iſſue another Daughter, both the Daughters enter, (where the Eldeſt only is Inheritable) and

and make Partition; the eldeſt Daughter, during her Life, cannot impeach the Partition; or ſay that the Youngeſt is not Heir, and yet ſhe is a Stranger to the Tail; but in Reſpect of Privity in their Perſons, the Partition ſhall conclude; though the Iſſue of the eldeſt Daughter ſhall avoid this Partition, as Iſſue in Tail. 4 *Co.* 121.

A Partition between mere Strangers, in that Caſe, is void. And if there be three Coparceners, and a Stranger purchaſe the Part of one of them, he and one of the others ſhall not join in a Writ of Partition, neither by the Common Law, nor by Force of the Statute; but one of the Plaintiffs, (*viz.*) the Parcener, may have a Writ of Partition at the Common Law; and the other Parcener, being a Purchaſer, may have it by the Statute; ſo that they ſhall not join in one Writ. *Dyer* 128.

If where there are three Coparceners, the Eldeſt purchaſes the Part of the Youngeſt, the Eldeſt having one Part by Diſcent, and the other by Purchaſe, ſhall have a Writ of Partition at the Common Law, againſt the middle Siſter, and ſo of the others. And if there be three Coparceners, and the Eldeſt taking Husband, he makes a Purchaſe of the Part of the Youngeſt, although the Huſband for his Part is a Stranger, and no Parcener, yet he and his Wife ſhall have a Writ of Partition againſt the middle Siſter, at the Common Law, becauſe he is ſeiſed of one Part in Right of his Wife, who is a Parcener. *F. N. B.* 52.

If

If the eldeſt Siſter be diſturbed in Preſentation to an Advowſon, by the Youngeſt, or other Siſter, ſhe and her Iſſue and Aſſigns, may have a *Quare Impedit* againſt ſuch other Siſter. But if there be four Coparceners, and the Eldeſt and the Second preſent; and the other two preſent Jointly or Severally, the Ordinary may refuſe them all, by Reaſon the Eldeſt did not preſent alone. 2 *Roll.* 346, 355. *Co. Lit.* 186.

None are called Parceners by the Common Law, but Females, or the Heirs of Females, which come to Lands or Tenements by Deſcent; for if Siſters purchaſe Lands or Tenements, they are called Joint-tenants, and not Parceners. *Lit.*

Between Joint-tenants, there is a two-fold Privity, (*viz.*) in Eſtate and Poſſeſſion: Between Tenants in Common, there is Privity only in Poſſeſſion, and not in Eſtate; but Parceners have a three-fold Privity, (*viz.*) in Eſtate, in Perſon, and in Poſſeſſion. *Co. Lit.* 169.

And Parceners ſeiſed in Fee-ſimple, may deviſe and give away their Parts by Will; ſo cannot Joint-tenants. One Coparcener may infeoff another Coparcener; for though their Poſſeſſion be joint, yet their Intereſt is ſevered; but it is otherwiſe with Joint-tenants, whoſe Right is Entire, and goes with the Poſſeſſion by Survivorſhip. Parceners may Releaſe one to the other; and in this they are like Jointenants only: For if one Tenant in Common Releaſe to his Fellow, this Moiety paſſes not, becauſe he to whom the Releaſe is made of ſuch Moiety, has no Poſſeſſion.

But Parceners, whose Right is from one Root, have a more connect Possession than Tenants in Common, and may Release one unto another. And Parceners differ both from Joint-tenants and Tenants in Common in this, that Coparceners were always compellable to make Partition, so was neither of the other two, before the Stat. 31 *H.* 8.

By 8 & 9 *W.* 3. After Process returned upon a Writ of Partition, and Affidavit of Notice made, &c. if an Appearance be not entred in fifteen Days, the Demandant having enter'd his Declaration, the Court may proceed to give Judgment by Default, and award Partition to be made, &c. But if the Party concerned, move the Court in a Year, and shew good Matter in Bar, the Judgment may be suspended or set aside.

Where Lands of Coparceners are held of a superior Lord, the eldest Coparcener is to do Suit for the whole; but the Lord may take a Distress on the other Parceners, as well as the Eldest; and in such Case the others shall have a Writ against the Eldest, to compel her to do the Suit of Court; and if the Eldest, having done the Suit, the others refuse to make Contribution, she shall by Writ oblige them to it. *F. N. B.* 160.

Castles of Habitation for private Use, may be parted between Coparceners, like unto other Houses; but if a Castle, that is used for the necessary Defence of the Realm, descend to two or more Coparceners, this Castle shall not be divided into Chambers and Rooms, because it is *Pro bono publico, & pro defensione Regni.* Co. Lit. 165.

I have

I have been the more particular under the Head of Parceners, as the the great Sir *Edward Coke*, says, The Inheritance by Coparcenership, is the rarest Kind that is in the Law. I now proceed to Matrimonial Contracts, Consummation of Marriage, *&c.*

Of Marriage Contracts, Consummation of Marriage, Forced Enjoyments, Polygamy, &c.

A Marriage Contract is an Agreement between a Man and a Woman, to live together in a constant Society, 'till the Contract is dissolved by Death, or Breach of Faith, or some notorious Misbehaviour, destructive of the Ends for which Matrimony was intended.

And nothing more is requisite to a compleat Marriage by the Laws of *England*, than a full, free and mutual Consent between Parties, not disabled to enter into that State, by their near Relation to each other, Infancy, Precontract or Impotency; for Marriage is of Divine Institution, to which only the Consent of the Parties is necessary, though the Solemnizing of it is a Civil Right, regulated by the Laws and Customs of Nations.

I have already observed, that at Twelve Years of Age, the Female, and Fourteen Years the Male, they may consent to and contract Marriage.

But

But ſtrictly, ſuch a Number of Years, does not ſeem ſo eſſential for contracting Matrimony, as Maturity, Ripeneſs and Diſpoſition of Body; for ſome Females may be fit for Marriage at Eleven Years of Age, when others may have an intire Inability at Thirteen or Fourteen.

If either Party be under their Ages to conſent to Marriage, the Contract is voidable; and if the Female be under Seven Years of Age, ſuch Contract is abſolutely void: But Marriages of Princes, made by the State in their Behalf, at any Age are held good; though many of theſe Contracts have been broke through. *Swinb. Matrim. Contr.*

In Contracts of Matrimony, the Perſons contracting ought to be of ſound Mind, and Lunaticks may not marry. But a Perſon who is Deaf or Dumb, may contract Matrimony; and ſo may an Idiot, and it ſhall bind him. 1 *Roll. Abr.* 357.

Perſons, who, by Coldneſs of Nature, or other Means are Impotent, are forbid to contract Marriage. And in other Perſons, if after Matrimony is contracted, ſome evil Diſeaſe (as Leproſy, &c.) renders one of the Parties unfit for Generation, the other may *repudiate*, and abandon him or her ſo diſeaſed. But when a Man and Woman are married, they are ſo unpartable, that they may not entirely omit the Marriage Duty, altho' one of them have the Leproſy. And St. *Paul*, ſays, *That the Husband has not Power over his own Body*, &c.

And though Impotency before Marriage, will invalidate a Contract of Matrimony and

Marriage itſelf; yet when Diſability happens after Marriage, he or ſhe that remains Potent, ſhall not be permitted to quit the impotent Perſon, but be compelled to bear the Diſcommodity, as well as any other ill Fortune in Life.

A Promiſe of Matrimony muſt be mutual; and therefore if the Man ſay to the Woman, I do promiſe that I will marry thee, but the Woman makes no Promiſe to the Man; or contrariwiſe, the Woman doth promiſe, but not the Man, this is a lame Contract, and not of any Force in Law, neither is the ſilent Party, in this Caſe, preſumed to Conſent, without ſuch Conſent appear, or the Father or Mother promiſe Marriage for the Child; for the Child's Silence in this Caſe (being preſent and hearing the ſame) is taken for a Conſent and Approbation; but it is otherwiſe if any other Perſon than the Parents promiſe for the Child. *Swinb. Matr. Cont. p.* 5.

Yet if neither the one Party nor the other utter the Contract, but ſome third Perſon pronounces the Words; as if he ſay to the Man, Doſt thou take this Woman to be thy Wife, *&c.* and he anſwers Yes, or I do, or any thing elſe amounting to a Conſent, is of the ſame Efficacy, as if the Parties themſelves had with their own Mouths declared the Words of the Contract. *Swinb.* 86.

There is a Difference between a Promiſe *de præſenti*, and a Promiſe *de futuro*. A Promiſe *de præſenti*; as, I do take thee to my Wife, and I do take thee to my Husband; cannot by any Agreement be diſſolved or re-

leaſed,

leaſed, but they are reputed Husband and Wife, in Reſpect of the Subſtance and indiſſoluble Knot of Matrimony. Therefore if either of them ſhould marry with any other Perſon, conſummating the ſame by carnal Copulation, and Procreation of Children, this Matrimony is to be diſſolved, as unlawful, the Parties marrying to be puniſhed as Adulterers, and their Iſſue in Danger of Baſtardy. *Swinb.* 9, 10, 11. See *Mod. Ca.* 155.

By Promiſe *de futuro*, as, I will take thee to my Wife, *&c.* the Parties are not very Husband and Wife; for by mutual Agreement they may diſſolve thoſe Spouſals, and match themſelves elſewhere; and ſo they may if but one of them renounce; for by the Words, *will do*, the Thing is not thereby done indeed; as in Caſe of the other *Ibid.* But on a Promiſe of future Marriage, if the Parties afterwards lie together, the Contract paſſes thereby into a real Marriage, in Conſtruction of Law. *Swinb.*

If a Man ſay to a Woman, I do promiſe to marry thee; and if thou be content to marry me, then kiſs me, or give me thy Hand; and the other Party do kiſs or give her Hand accordingly, Spouſals are contracted. *Swinb.* 69.

A Ring is ſolemnly delivered and put on the Woman's fourth Finger, by the Party himſelf, and ſhe willingly accepts the ſame, and wears it, the Parties are preſumed to have mutually conſented to be Man and Wife; and ſo have contracted Matrimony, altho' they uſed not any Words. *Swinb.* 210, *&c.*

When

When it is demanded of a Man, whether he will take the Woman to his Wife, and he anſwers, I will; and it is demanded of the Woman, if ſhe will take the Man to her Husband, and ſhe anſwers, I will; by this Marriage, and not Spouſals, is ſaid to be contracted. And the Words, I will take thee from henceforth, *&c.* are as much as I do take thee, and an abſolute Marriage. *Swinb.*

In Contracts of Marriage, it is not neceſſary that both Parties uſe the ſame Expreſſions; but if one Party ſays I will marry thee, and the other anſwers I am content, *&c.* hereby Spouſals are contracted. And where the Man's promiſe is proved, but no actual Promiſe on the Side of the Woman; if ſhe carries herſelf as one conſenting, and approving the Promiſe of the Man, it is Evidence that the Woman likewiſe promiſed. 3 *Salk. Rep.* 16.

And though there be ſome Diſtance of Time betwixt the Promiſe of the Man and the Woman, the Contract may be good, if the Party firſt promiſing continue in the ſame Mind, until the other Party hath promiſed; but where the Words of the Contract are only Conditional on one Side, and on the other Side abſolute; or if they are ſpoken in Jeſt, they are not Obligatory. *Swinb.* 210.

Contracts of Marriage may be by Mediation of Proctors, when the Parties are abſent from each other; and when it is by *Proxy*, it is by Special Power of Attorney to contract Matrimony for the Party in his Name, with ſuch a Woman, *&c.* In which Caſe, both

both Parties are to continue in the ſame Mind 'til the Contract is finiſhed; for before that the Proctor may be revoked, and then the Contract will be void. A Promiſe or Contract of Marriage is good by Meſſenger or Letter, except it appear that the Party diſſents before the other conſents to the ſame; and the mutual Conſent of the other Party ought to be ſent immediately, *&c. Ibid.*

On a Promiſe of Marriage, Damages may be recovered in an Action at Law, if either Party refuſes to marry; but the Promiſe and Remedy muſt be mutual on both Sides. And by the Stat. 29 *Car.* 2. no Action ſhall be brought upon any Agreement or Conſideration of Marriage, unleſs it be put in Writing, and ſigned by the Party to be charged. 1 *Salk.* 24. By *Holt*, Ch. Juſt. a Man is bound, in Reſpect of the Woman's Promiſe; and her Promiſe muſt be good, to make his ſignify any thing to her, in an Action to be brought upon it. 5 *Mod. Rep.* 412.

Where Jewels, *&c.* are given as a Pledge of future Marriage between two Perſons, there is an implied Condition annex'd, that if Matrimony do not enſue, the Things may be demanded back and recovered. Though according to our old Books, if the Man had a Kiſs for his Money, then the one Half of what was given could only be recovered, and the other Half was to be the Woman's own Goods; but the Female is more favoured, for whatſoever ſhe gave, were there kiſſing or no kiſſing in the Caſe, ſhe may demand and have all again.

A Perſon

A Perſon of Quality intending a Marriage with a Lady, preſented her with a Jewel; and the Marriage not taking Effect, he brought an Action of Detinue againſt her, and ſhe taking it to be a Gift, offered to wage her Law; but the Court was of Opinion, That the Property was not changed by this Gift, being to a Special Intent, and therefore would not admit her to do it. 2 *Mod. Rep.* 141.

Although Spouſals are always made with an Intention that Matrimony ſhould enſue, yet the Contractor cannot be compelled thereto (neither are the Parties obliged to marry, though an Oath accompanied the Promiſe) unleſs it were made pure, and without Condition; for in Conditional Contracts the Bond of Performance is ſuſpended in the Condition, till that be performed, except there follow a Relinquiſhment of it, by Copulation of Bodies.

If a Promiſe of Marriage be made without any Limitation of Time, then (if there appear not any weighty Cauſe of Stay) if both the Parties are reſident in one Province, the Woman may after two Years marry to whom ſhe pleaſes; but if the Man does not reſide in the ſame Province, it is ſaid ſhe muſt tarry three Years.

And by the Eccleſiaſtical Laws, if any having abſolutely contracted Spouſals, afterwards refuſe to have the Marriage ſolemniſed, he or ſhe ſo refuſing, are liable to be Excommunicated, and to be committed to Priſon; and there to be kept without Bail or Mainprize, until he or ſhe ſubmit to the Monition

of

of the Ordinary, and agree to the Celebration of the Marriage. *Swinb.*

The Degrees of Consanguinity, and of Affinity and Alliance, prohibited Marriage by the *Levitical* Law, are as follow:

A Man may not marry,

His Mother,——His Father's Sister,——His Mother's Sister,
His Sister,
His Daughter,
The Daughter of his Son or Daughter,
His Uncle's Wife, Father's Wife, Father's Wife's Daughter.
His Brother's Wife, Wife's Sister,
His Son's Wife, or Wife's Daughter,
The Daughter of his Wife's Son or Daughter.

A Woman may not marry,

Her Father,—— Her Father's Brother,—— Her Mother's Brother,
Her Brother,
Her Son,
The Son of her Daughter,
Her Aunt's Husband, her Mother's Husband,
Her Sister's Husband, her Husband's Brother,
Her Daughter's Husband,
The Son of her Husband's Son or Daughter.

Marriages between Cousin Germans, and all Marriages onwards, are by the Statute 32 *H.* 8. declared lawful. One married the Widow of his Brother's Son, and it was adjudged lawful. *Lit. Rep.* 356. *William*'s Case.

But

But where a Perſon married his Wife's Siſter's Daughter, Sentence of Divorce was given. *Cro. Eliz.* 299.

On a Libel exhibited againſt a Perſon for marrying his Wife's Siſter, the Eccleſiaſtical Court annulled the Marriage, and baſtardiſed the Iſſue. But a Prohibition was granted, as to annulling the Marriage, and baſtardiſing the Iſſue, and giving Leave to proceed to puniſh the Inceſt. *Note*; here the Wife was dead, and an Eſtate deſcended to her Son. 2 *Salk.* 548.

A Man marrying his Siſter's Daughter, being ſued in the Eccleſiaſtiaſtical Court, prayed a Prohibition, becauſe out of the *Levitical* Degrees; but it was denied. *Raym.* 464. Though if a Man marry his Mother or Siſter, they are Husband and Wife until a Divorce.

Affinity prohibits Marriage only to the Perſons contracted, *&c.* for the Couſins or Conſanguinity to my Wife, are of Affinity only to me, and not to my Brothers, or Children by a former Wife; and my Blood and Conſanguinity are Kindred, and of Affinity only to my Wife, and not to her Brothers, or former Children. Hence it is, that the Father and the Son may marry the Mother and the Daughter, and two Brethren may marry two Siſters in another Family.

Marriage is defined to be a Conjunction of Man and Woman; an inſeparable Connection and Union of Life; but it is not accounted Conſummated until, with the Conſent of Mind, there is a Conjunction of Body. And it was said in the Beginning, *That Man and Wife shall be one Flesh.*

In Construction of the *Civil Law*, the Wife is *Uxor*, before the Spousals by Contract; for if they have carnal Copulation after Contract, they shall not be punished for Fornication, only for Contempt against an Edict of the Church, which has prohibited Bedding before the Spousals are solemnised *in Facie Ecclesiæ*. See 2 *Salk*. 438.

But before the Time of Pope *Innocent* the Third, there was no Solemnization of Marriages in the Church; for then it was first ordained. Before that Time, the Marriage was solemnised thus; The Man came to the House where the Woman resided, and in the Presence of her Friends and Relations, took the Woman to his own House; and this was all the Ceremony. *Moor* 170.

A *Dissenter* was married to a Woman, by a Minister of the Congregation, who was not in Orders; it was held in this Case, that when a Man demands a Right to him, as a Husband, by the Ecclesiastical Law, he ought to prove himself a Husband by that Law; and he shall not be entitled by the Reputation of the Marriage, unless he hath a substantial Right. But this Marriage is not a meer Nullity; because by the Law of Nature, the Contract is binding; for tho' the positive Law of Man ordains Marriages to be made by a Priest, that Law only makes this Marriage irregular, and not expresly void. 1 *Salk. Rep*. 119.

A Marriage *De facto*, or in Reputation among *Quakers*, &c. hath been allowed to be ſufficient to give Title to a Perſonal Eſtate. 1 *Leon.* 53. *Wood's Inſt.* 59. But Popiſh Recuſants, who are not married according to the Orders of the Church of *England*, ſhall be diſabled, the Husband to be Tenant by the Curteſy; and the Wife to have Dower, &c. and they are alſo liable to further Penalties, by Stat. 3 *Jac.* 1.

By the Ordinances of the Church, before Perſons are to be married, the *Banns* of Matrimony ſhall be publiſhed in the Church where they dwell, three ſeveral *Sundays* or *Holidays*, in the Time of Divine Service. And if at the Time appointed for their Marriage, any Man do alledge any lawful Impediment, why they ſhould not be married, and become bound with ſufficient Sureties to prove his Allegation, then the Solemnization muſt be put off till ſuch Time as the Truth is tried. *Rubrick.*

And no Miniſter ſhall celebrate Matrimony between any Perſons, without a Faculty or Licence, except the Banns of Marriage have been firſt publiſhed, as directed by the Book of *Common Prayer*, upon Pain of Suſpenſion, *per triennium. Can.* 62. And on the granting of Licences, Bond ſhall be taken that there is no Impediment of Pre-contract, Conſanguinity, &c. nor any Suit depending in any Eccleſiaſtical Court, touching any Contract of Marriage of either of the Parties with any other; that the Marriage be celebrated in the Pariſh Church, where one of the Parties dwelleth; and that between the Hours of Eight and Twelve in the Morning. Oath ought likewiſe to be made of there being no Impediment; and two Witneſſes to teſtify the Conſent of Parents, &c. Licences to the contrary are void; and the Perſons marrying may be puniſhed, as for clandeſtine Marriages. *Can.* 102.

But notwithſtanding this Proviſion by the *Canons* of our Church, Perſons of Quality are often married at their own Houſes, and out of Canonical Hours, in the Evening; and other Perſons are married in other Churches than where one of the Parties lives, and out of Time of Divine Service, &c. And on the granting of Licences for Marriage, the Teſtification of Witneſſes of the Conſent of Parents, &c. is diſuſed. All theſe Things are diſpenſed with, in regard to the Subſtance of the Marriage.

In *Lent*, and on Faſting Days, Marriages are prohibited; for the Mirth attending them is not ſuitable to the Devotion of thoſe Times; but Perſons may marry with Licences in *Lent*, (and thereby turn the Faſt into a Feaſt) although the Banns of Matrimony may not then be publiſhed. *Can.*

By the Stat. 7 & 8 *W.* 3. if any Parſon, Vicar or Curate, marry any Perſon in any Church, &c. without publiſhing the Banns of Matrimony, according to Law, or without Licence, he ſhall forfeit 100*l.* And Parſons knowingly employing others ſo to do, are liable to the like Penalty; one Moiety to the King, and the other to the Informer.

And every Man ſo married, without Licence, or publiſhing the Banns, ſhall forfeit 10 *l.* and Pariſh Clerks, *&c.* 5 *l.*

Before this Stat. an Information was exhibited againſt a Perſon for an unlawful Combination, in procuring a clandeſtine Marriage in the Night, between a Maid Servant and a young Gentleman, who was Heir to an Eſtate, without Banns or Licence; and the young Gentleman being Drunk, they were fined an hundred Marks, and committed till paid. But it doth not appear that the Marriage could be made void. *Cro. Car.* 557.

A Licence for Marriage.

SAlutem & gratiam. Cum vos uti aſſeritur ad ſolemnizationem Matrimonii veri & legitimi de & cum conſenſu parentum vel gubernatorum veſtrorum & utriuſque veſtrum procedere decreveritis illudque in facie Eccleſiæ ſolemnizari facere & obtinere magnopere deſideratis; nos volentes ut honeſta hæc veſtra deſideria debitum celerius conſequantur effectum, ut igitur Matrimonium hujuſmodi in Eccleſia de, &c. per Rectorem Vicarium vel Curatum ejuſdem Eccleſiæ abſque aliquibus Bannis Matrimonialibus editis & proclamatis quocunque anni tempore libere & licite ſolemnizari facere & obtinere poſſitis & valeatis. Dummodo vobis ratione præcontractus conſanguinitatis affinitatis, vel alterius cauſæ cujuſcunque nullum legitimum in ea parte obſtiterit impedimentum nec ulla controverſia ſeu querela mota ſit vel pendeat coram aliquo judice

Ecclesiastico vel Civili de Matrimonio aliquo contracto vel allegato cum alterutro vestrum ac modo Matrimonii hujusmodi celebratio publica in Ecclesia predict' fiat inter horas octavam & duodecimam ante meridiem absque tamen præjudicio Ministri Ecclesiæ ubi dicta mulier Parochiana existit licentiam & facultatem tam vobis contrahentibus quam Rectori, Vicario vel Curato Ecclesiæ predict' designato Matrimonium hujusmodi inter vos solemnizand' sub modo & forma superius specificatis juxta ritus libri publicarum precum authoritate Parliamenti in ea parte editi ex causis legitimis benigne concedimus & gratiose dispensamus. Proviso tamen semper quod si aliquid fraudis in hac parte imposterum appareat vel falsitatis nobis suggestæ vel suppressæ veritatis tempore hujus licentiæ obtentæ tunc hæc licentia nostra irrita sit ad omnem juris effectum ac si omnino concessa non fuisset. Et eo casu inhibemus quibusvis ministris modo præmissorum aliquid eis innotuerit, ne ad celebrationem dicti Matrimonii procedant nisi nobis prius consultis.

Dat' sub sigillo, &c.

The

The Condition of the Bond given, on taking out a Licence.

THE Condition of this Obligation is ſuch, That if hereafter there ſhall not appear any lawful Let or Impediment, by Reaſon of any Pre-contract, Conſanguinity, Affinity, or any other lawful Maans whatſoever; but that the above bound A. B. *and* E. F. *Daughter of,* &c. *may lawfully ſolemnize Marriage together; and in the ſame afterwards remain and continue for Man an Wife, according to the Laws in that Behalf provided. And alſo if there be not, at this preſent Time, any Action, Suit, Plaint,* &c. *moved or depending before any Judge Eccleſiaſtical or Temporal, for or concerning any ſuch lawful Impediment before the ſaid Parties; nor that either of them be of any better Eſtate or Degree than to the Judge, at the granting of the Licence is ſuggeſted by the ſaid* A. B. *and that the ſaid Marriage be openly ſolemniſed in the Church, according to the Form of the Book of* Common Prayer, *and between the Hours appointed in the Conſtitutions Eccleſiaſtical. Then,* &c. *or elſe,* &c.

By our Law, Marriage being once lawfully ſolemniſed, and without Impediment, by one in Holy Orders, all the World cannot diſſolve it, let it be at what Time and Place it will. *Sid. Rep.* 64.

But if a Man at Fourteen, marry a Woman at the Age of Ten, at her Age of Twelve Years (her Age to conſent to Matrimony) he he may disagree, as well as she may. And if a Man marry a Woman who is within the Age of Twelve Years, and afterwards the Wife disagrees to the Marriage, within her Age of Twelve Years also, and at the said Age of Twelve Years marry with another, now the first Marriage is absolutely defeated, so that he may take another Wife; for although the Disagreement within the Age of Consent, was not sufficient, yet her taking another Husband at the Age of Consent, and cohabiting with him, affirms the Disagreement, and so the Marriage is void *ab initio*. *Babington*'s Case. *Moor* 575, 764.

Though if a Man marry a Woman within the Age of Twelve Years, and after the Wife at Eleven Years of Age Disagrees to the Marriage, and then the Husband takes another Wife, and has Issue by her, this is a Bastard; for the first Marriage continues notwithstanding the Disagreement of the Woman, as she may not Disagree within the Age of Twelve Years. 1 *Roll. Abr.* 341.

A Woman marries a Man within Twelve Years of Age, and before the said Age of Twelve Years disagrees, and then marries with another, the second Marriage resolved to be good. But if a Man within the Age of Fourteen takes a Wife of Twelve or more, this is a Marriage, and they are Baron and Feme, *de facto*; and the Husband may have Trespass, *de muliere abducta cum bonis viri*, *Trin.* 12 *Jac. B. R. Bradshaw* and *Fletcher*.

But where a Man is at the Age of Consent, and the Woman not; or the Woman of Age, and the Man not, he or she may disagree to the

the Marriage at the other's coming of Age to consent, as well as the other; for there is a mutual Power of Disagreement. 3 *Inst.* 88. 1 *Danv. Abr.* 699.

And if Persons are married before the Age of Consent, they may at that Age Disagree, and marry again, without any Divorce. But if they once give their Consent when they are at that Age, they cannot afterwards disagree; and when they are married before, there needeth not a new Marriage, if they agree at that Age. 1 *Co. Inst.* 33. 2 *Inst.* 182.

And if after Disagreement of the Parties, at the Age of Consent they agree to the Marriage, and live together as Man and Wife, the Marriage hath Continuance: Though if the Disagreement had been before the Ordinary, it is said they could not after agree again to make it a good Marriage. 1 *Danv. Abr.* 699, 700.

If Persons married are *infra annos nubiles*, the Ecclesiastical Judges are to judge as well of the Assent, whether sufficient, *&c.* as of the first Contract. And Loyalty or Lawfulness of Marriage, is to be tried by the Bishop's Certificate, on Inquisition taken before him, and Examination of Witnesses, *&c.* But in a Personal Action, where the Right of Marriage is not in Question, whether a Woman is married, or is the Wife of such a Person, is triable by a Jury at Common Law. 7 *Rep.* 23. *Dyer* 303. 3 *Salk.* 64.

If a Feme Obligee take the Obligor to Husband, this is a Release in Law of the Debt. And if a Woman be *Warden* of the *Fleet*, and one that is in Prison there marry her, the

Law

Law adjudges him to be then enlarged; for it is repugnant, that he, as her Husband, ſhould have the Cuſtody of her, or ſhe, as a Gaoler, have the Cuſtody of him; unleſs it be conſtrued in a ludicrous Senſe. 2 *Vent*.19.

Agreements between a Man and a Woman, who afterwards marry, are commonly by the Marriage extinguiſhed. *Hob*. 216. But this has been ruled, where ſuch Agreements are to have Execution during the Coverture, and not afterwards; as where a Man promiſes a Woman, That if ſhe will marry him, and he dies before her, he will leave her worth ſo much Money, &c.

A Man deviſes to his Daughter one thouſand Pounds, upon Condition that ſhe marries with the Conſent of *A*. and *B*. and it was held, that altho', by the Eccleſiaſtical Law, ſuch a Condition annexed to a Legacy is void; becauſe the Marriage ought to be free, without Coertion; yet it is not ſo at the Common Law. *Poph*. 58, 57.

By 4 & 5 *P*. & *M*. it is enacted, That if any Perſon ſhall take away a Woman Child, under the Age of Sixteen Years, out of the Cuſtody, and againſt the Will of the Father or Mother, or of the Perſon to whom the Father deviſed the Child; the Puniſhment in ſuch Caſes, is two Years Impriſonment, without Bail, or a Fine impoſed in *B. R*. If he marry or defile ſuch Child, he ſhall be impriſoned five Years. And if the Child is above Twelve, and under Sixteen Years of Age, and conſenting to the Marriage, then the next of Kin, to whom her Inheritance would deſcend, ſhall enjoy it during her Life; but after her Deceaſe, it ſhall go to the Heir at Law, and never to the Husband.

A Freeman of *London* deviſed the Cuſtody of his Daughter to *A.* and died, the Daughter being then in the Country; *A.* procured a Warrant from the Lord Chief Juſtice to take her, and by Virtue thereof, took her accordingly, but ſhe was then married to *B.* this was held to be out of the Statute, becauſe the Female was never in the Poſſeſſion of the Guardian. *Sid.* 363.

The ſtealing or taking away a Woman that hath an Eſtate in Lands or Goods, or is Heir apparent, by Force and againſt her Will, and marrying or defiling her, is Felony without Benefit of Clergy. 3 *H.* 7. 39 *Eliz.* And Aiders and Aſſiſters are Principals. *Mich.* 1 *Annæ.*

The Indictment on the Stat. 3 *H.* 7. is expreſly to forth, that the Woman taken away had Lands or Goods, or was Heir apparent; and alſo that ſhe was was married or defiled, becauſe no other Caſe is within the Statute; and it ought to alledge, that the Taking was for Lucre. And it is no Excuſe that the Woman at firſt was taken away with her Conſent, if ſhe be afterwards forced to ſtay againſt her Will; or that ſhe be after married with her Conſent, if ſhe were under the Force at the Time. 3 *Inſt.* 61. *H. P. C.* 119. 1 *Hawk.* 109, 110.

A Man enticed the only Daughter of her Father, who would be worth 5000 *l.* to ſee a Ship; and when he had her on the *Thames*, carried her by Force and Threats into the Country, and there married her; but this

was

was held not to be within the Statute, ſhe having a Brother; for by the Statute ſhe muſt be Heir-apparent, &c. and ſhe had not a preſent Eſtate in Lands or Goods, her Father being living. *Hob.* 182.

But admitting a Woman has an Eſtate in Lands or other Subſtance, or is Heir apparent, a Man may force her to make a Contract, and be no Felony; for there muſt be a Taking by Force, and a marrying or defiling. *Sav.* 59.

In the Reign of King *Charles* I. the Lady *Fullwood*, *Roger Fullwood* her Son, and divers others, were indicted for taking away by Force, and the ſaid *Roger*, by Procurement of the ſaid Lady, marrying *Sarah Cock*, a Maid who had a Portion of 1300*l.* It was agreed, in this Caſe, that Taking of a Woman, unleſs ſhe be married or defiled, is not Felony. But here ſhe was married; and whereas they pretended that it was with the Female's Conſent, and therefore not within the Statute; the Court ſaid, that the Taking being unlawful and by Force, tho' the Marriage was with her Conſent, yet it was Felony. In this Caſe, the Lady *Fullwood* was indicted in the County of *Surrey*, and the ſaid *Roger Fullwood*, and others, were indicted in the County of *Middleſex*. Though if a Woman be taken by Foroe in the County of *A.* and married in the County of *B.* the Offender may be tried in the County of *B.* and Judgment was given that they ſhould be hang'd.

Anno 31 *H.* 8. *Henry Sturges* and other Perſons were indicted for taking one *Agnes*

Hobſon,

Hobſon againſt her Will, who was the Daughter and Heir of *John Hobſon*, who was ſeiſed of a large Eſtate in Lands. And they pleaded to the Indictment, that they ought not to anſwer, *pro eo quod non mentionatur*, in the ſaid Indictment, *quod ceperunt ad intentionem maritandi dictam Agnetem vel ad proſtituendam, &c.* and they were diſcharged.

In the Second Year of Queen *Anne*, a Perſon was indicted at the *Old Baily* for ſtealing an Heireſs worth 2000*l.* in Money, and 20*l.* a Year Eſtate in Lands; he procured her to be arreſted, and threatned that ſhe ſhould go to *Newgate*, if ſhe did not marry him, and thereupon out of Fear, ſhe was married to him without her Conſent. He pleaded in his Defence, that ſhe had ſhewn him ſingular Marks of her Love; that ſhe had been on Shipboard with him, was uneaſy if he ſat not next her, had diſcarded her former Lover, *&c.* but the Jury found him Guilty, and he was hanged. *Swanſon*'s Caſe.

On an Information exhibited againſt a Perſon for taking and marrying the ſole Daughter and Heir apparent of *T.* of *Kent*, without the Aſſent, and againſt the Will of her Father; it was proved that he ſecretly contracted himſelf to her; and by Appointment between them, ſhe left her Father's Houſe, and came to *London*, where ſhe was married to him. This was an Offence puniſhable by Fine and Impriſonment at Common Law; and being proſecuted by the Father and Mother, they pray'd the Fine might be moderated, and they were diſcharged out of Priſon, upon Bail. *Sid.* 387. And the Statutes

3 *H.* 7.

3 *H* 7. and 4 & 5 *P.* & *M.* were ſaid to be but an Aggravation of the Puniſhment, and do not create any Offence originally. 2 *Keb.* 432.

A Man ſteals his Wife againſt her Friend's Conſent, and after ſues in Equity for her Portion; but denied Relief by *Egerton* Chancellor, who ſaid, *He that ſteals the Fleſh, let him provide Bread how he can.* Carey's Rep.

It has been lately adjudged, that whenever a Husband comes into a Court of Equity, for his Wife's Portion, the Chancery will oblige him to make a Settlement on her; or to ſecure her a Maintenance, in Caſe ſhe outlives the Husband. And where a Man makes a Settlement equivalent, it ſhall be intended that he is to have her Portion. 2 *Vern.Chan. Rep.* 494, 502.

One *Griffiths*, a mean Perſon, having married a Woman of Fortune, upon Suggeſtion by the Friends of the Wife, of Lunacy, though the Woman was ſenſible enough, it was moved in *B. R.* that the Eſtate might be ſo ſettled, that ſhe might not be wrought on by the Husband, to give it him from her Children, &c. which the Court order'd. *Skin. Rep.* 110.

Action of the Caſe lies for Damages, where a Man married to another Woman, marries a ſecond Wife, whereby her Credit is injur'd, &c. *Ibid.* 119.

By Statute, it is Felony for a Man or Woman, of the Ages to conſent to Matrimony, to marry a ſecond Wife or Husband, the firſt being then living: But if either a Husband or Wife, ſhall be beyond the Seas, or be abſent in *England*, the Space of Seven Years, and the one of them not know whether the other be living within that Time, it is not Felony to marry again. 1 *Jac.* 1. *c.*11.

One was indicted of Felony upon this Statute, for having two Wives; and the Evidence was, that he eſpouſed one beyond the Seas, and another here in *England*; and the Court was of Opinion, that he might be indicted for it here, the latter Marriage making the Crime; but otherwiſe if the ſecond Marriage were beyond Sea. 1 *Sid.* 171.

Rape is alſo Felony, which is where a Man has carnal Knowledge of a Woman by Force, and againſt her Will. And if a Female, under the Age of Ten Years, be deflowered, either with or againſt her Conſent, it is Felony without Benefit of Clergy. Stat. 18 *El. cap.* 6.

But there muſt be *Penetration* and *Emiſſion* to make this Crime; and it muſt be prov'd that the Offender entered her Body, that there was *res in re*, or it is no Rape. For an Attempt to raviſh a Woman, though it be never ſo outragious, is an Aſſault only. 3 *Inſt.* 60. *H. P. C.*

If a Woman raviſh'd, yielded to the Violence, and ſuch her Conſent was forced by Fear of Death, or of Dureſs, this does not work any Mitigation of the Crime in the Raviſher; or if ſhe conſented after the Fact, or was a common Strumpet, for ſhe is ſtill under the Protection of the Law. But formerly it was adjudged no Rape to force a Man's own Concubine; and it is ſaid by ſome to be Evidence of a Woman's Consent, that she was a common Whore. *Dalt. c.* 105. 1 *Co. Inst.* 123. 1 *Hawk. P.C.* 108.

In ancient Times, it was held not to be a Rape to force a Woman, who conceived at the Time; because if she had not consented she could not have conceived; but this Opinion hath been since Questioned, because the previous Violence is no way extenuated by such a subsequent Consent. 2 *Inst.* 190.

A Woman ravished may prosecute, and be a Witness in her own Cause; though a Woman's Oath of a Rape, without concurring Circumstances, is seldom credited; for if a Man can prove that he was in another Place, and in other Company, at the Time she charges him with the Fact; or if she be wrong in the Description, or swears that the Offence was committed in a Place whereto it was impossible the Man could have Access at that Time, being lock'd up, *&c.* this will overthrow her Oath. 3 *Rep.* 37. 1 *H.P.C.*

Anno 22 *Jac.* 1. A Man of Sixty Years of Age, who had a Wife, was arraigned for the Rape of a Girl of the Age of Seven Years, and no more; and by the Evidence of the Surgeon, several Women, and the Damsel herself, he was found Guilty and executed. *Dyer* 304.

In *Michaelmas* Term, 14 *Eliz.* a *Scotchman* was indicted for a Rape upon a Girl of Seven Years old; and upon the Evidence of credible Witnesses, was found Guilty; but the Court very much doubted whether the Fact could be committed upon such a young Girl. And this was the Reason of making the Stat.

18 *Eliz.* declaring it Felony to raviſh a Girl under Ten Years of Age, though conſenting to the Act.

And *Anno* 9 *Car.* 1. *Martin Page* was indicted at the *Old Baily*, for that he *Carnaliter Cognovit* an Infant under the Age of Ten Years. At his Trial the Jury would not find him Guilty, becauſe it was not proved he enter'd the Body of the Child; but he having very much abuſed her, the Court ordered an Indictment of Battery to be exhibited againſt him, which was tried at the Bar, and he was found Guilty, and fined an hundred Marks, and ordered to ſtand in the Pillory. *Cro. Car.* 332.

Anno 1 *Annæ*, one *Simpkins* was tried and found Guilty of a Rape, on the Body of a Girl of Ten Years of Age. He took the Girl backwards upon his Lap, and ſo forced her. It was proved that he entered her Bodo, ſpoiled her Privy Parts, and gave her the Venereal Diſeaſe. He was hanged; as was likewiſe a Perſon 7 *Annæ*, for holding a young Girl whilſt another raviſhed her.

The 1 *Geo.* 1. a Vintner and his Drawer were indicted for the Rape of a Female belonging to the *Hundreds of Drury*, who declared ſhe was as innocent as an Angel in Heaven; but I ſuppoſe ſhe meant *Satan* caſt from thence: She pretended to be a Virgin of Twenty-ſeven Years of Age; but the Jury acquitted both the Priſoners. *Anne Cooper's* Caſe.

A Perſon was found Guilty of a Rape upon a Man's Wife; and that after he had raviſhed her, he thruſt a lighted Torch betwixt her Legs. *Kel. Rep.* 30.

In *Scotland*, the Woman is to complain the ſame Day or Night in which ſhe is raviſhed; and by our Law, Complaint ought to be made in forty Days afterwards, but rather immediately; for Concealing it implies a Conſent before the Fact. *H. P. C.* 117. 3 *Nelſ. Abr.* 45.

A Feme Covert may bring Appeal of Rape without her Husband; but this is where neither before nor after ſhe gives Conſent to the Raviſher; for if ſhe afterwards conſents, the Husband, Father, or next of Blood, there being no Husband, ſhall proſecute the Appeal. 13 *E.* 3. 11 *H.* 4. And by 6 *R.* 2. the Party raviſhed, if ſhe afterwards conſents, as well as the Raviſher, ſhall be diſabled to hold or challenge any Eſtate of Inheritance, Dower, *&c.* and the next Blood ſhall enter on the Land.

In former Times, Rape was Felony, and puniſhed with Death; unleſs the Woman raviſhed were a Virgin, and would accept of the Raviſher in Marriage, in which Caſe ſhe might demand him for her Husband, and ſave his Life. 2 *Inſt.* 180.

This was only in the Will of the Woman, and not of the Man to demand the Female raviſhed for his Wife; for if it had been in the Will of the Man, this Inconvenience would have followed, That a Raſcal Slave might raviſh a Noblewoman, and by Occaſion of one ſhameful Pollution, perpetually defile her, and to her Diſhonour take her to Wife.

But in our Law-Books I find a Caſe where one *Henwick*, having raviſhed *Matilda*, the

Daughter of *Syward de Wharton*, he desired to have her to Wife; and the Court condescended that he should be affianc'd to her. *Hill.* 6 *Ed.* 1.

Bracton tells us, that by the Law of King *Athelstan*, If a Person meeting a Virgin, did touch her dishonestly, he was Guilty of breaking the King's Edict: If against her Will he threw her on the Ground, he lost the King's Favour; If he discovered her Nakedness, and cast himself upon her, he forfeited all his Possession; If he lay with her he suffered Judgment of Life and Member; and if he were a Horseman in the Wars, his Horse lost his Tail and Main. And the Virgin had in Recompence, all his Lands and Money, by the King's Warrant.

The punishing of the Horse, by Loss of Tail, seems a little Extraordinary; but perhaps it was necessary to add to the Disgrace and Infamy of the Rider and his Family, for the foul Act committed. And though the Punishment of the Ravisher hath undergone great Variations, by the Statutes and Ordinances of our Kings, yet by the Common Law it was always Death, at the Election of the Woman ravished.

In the Book *De priscis Legibus*, it is set down for a Law, made by *William* the Conqueror, that a Ravisher should not be hang'd, or otherwise put to Death, but his Eyes were to be pulled out, and his Privy Members, Feet or Hands, cut away, that the Trunk, or mutilate Body, still left alive, might remain as a Testimony of his Prodition and Lewdness.

This was a very mangling Law; and the Statute of *West.* 1. reduced the Crime to Trespass, subjecting the Offender to two Years Imprisonment and a Fine. But this easy Punishment, very much increasing the Offence, it was again made Felony, as it now stands. *Co. Lit.* 123.

A Woman may justify the killing a Person, attempting to ravish her. And a *Monk* had his Privy Members cut off, by a Man who caught him in Bed with his Wife, and the Husband was only tried for *Maihem.*

Buggery with Man or Beast, is Felony in Women as well as Men. The Case of a Lady of Quality, who committed this Crime with a Baboon, and conceived by him, may be read in 3.*Co. Inst.* 59.

Of what Things belonging to the Wife, the Husband gains Possession by Marriage; and what the Wife is entitled to of the Husband's; of Dower, Jointures, &c.

BY Marriage with a Woman, who hath an Estate of Freehold, a Man gaineth such Estate of Freehold, and he may enter, *&c.*

As if a Man take to Wife a Woman seised in Fee of Lands or Tenements, by the Intermarriage, he is entitled to the same in her Right; and yet this Eſtate, the Husband ſo gains, depends upon an Uncertainty, and is ſupported by Privity; for if the Wife be Attainted of Felony, the Lord, by Eſcheat, ſhall enter, and put out the Husband; unleſs the Felony be committed after Iſſue had, when the Husband may be Tenant by the Curteſy. And if the Husband be Attainted of Felony, the King acquires no Freehold, but a Pernancy of the Profits during the Coverture, and the Freehold remaineth in the Wife. *Co. Lit.* 350.

But if a Feme Termor takes Husband, yet the Term continues in her; and if a Feme Sole poſſeſſed of a Chattel real, be thereof diſpoſſeſſed, and then taking Husband, ſhe dies, the Baron ſhall not have this meer Right, but the Executors or Adminiſtrators of the Wife ſhall have it. It is otherwiſe, if the Right accrues during the Coverture: And the Husband ſhall not have by the Intermarriage, Chattels real, conſiſting meerly in Action; albeit he ſurvives his Wife, except he recovered them in the Life of his Wife. *Co. Lit.* 357.

Chattels Real, being of a mixt Nature, partly in Poſſeſſion, and partly in Action, which accrue, during the Coverture, the Husband is intitled to by the Marriage, if he ſurvive his Wife, albeit he reduceth them not into Poſſeſſion in her Life-time; but if the Wife ſurvives, ſhe ſhall have them. As if the Husband be ſeiſed of a Rent-Charge, *&c.* in Right of his Wife, he ſhall have the Arrearages after the Death of the Wife; though if the Wife ſurvive the Husband, ſhe ſhall have the Arrears, and not the Executors of the Husband. But if the Arrearages become due before Marriage, whereby they were meerly in Action before the Marriage, in this Caſe, by the Common Law, he ſhould not have them. But the Statute 32 *H.* 8. gives the Arrearages incurred as well before the Marriage as after, to the Huſband, if he ſurvives the Wife.

A Feme Sole hath a Leaſe for Years, and takes Husband, the Husband hath, by the Marriage, full Power to diſpoſe of it; and if he ſurvives his Wife, he ſhall enjoy it againſt her Executors; but if he makes no Diſpoſition of it, and his Wife ſurvives him, it remains to the Wife. *Hob.* 3. *Co. Lit.* 46.

Chattels Real, as Leaſes for Years, *&c.* are not given to the Husband abſolutely by the Intermarriage, but conditionally, if the Husband happen to ſurvive her; and tho' he hath Power to alien them at his Pleaſure, in the mean Time the Husband is poſſeſſed of the Chattel Real in her Right. *Co. Lit.* 300.

Marriage is an abſolute Gift of Chattels Perſonal in Poſſeſſion, whether the Husband ſurvive the Wife or not. *Co. Lit.* 351.

But a bare Poſſeſſion of Perſonal Goods, is not by the Marriage given to the Husband; for if Goods are bail'd to a Feme Sole, or if ſhe finds Goods, and after marries, the Action of Detinue muſt be brought againſt both Husband and Wife. *Co. Lit.* 351.

If the Wife have Goods, and take an Huſband, the Husband dies, the Executors of the Husband ſhall have the Goods. And where the Wife loſeth Goods, and marries, but the

Husband

Husband dies, the Executors of the Husband ſhall have theſe Goods; becauſe the Property is in him by the Marriage, notwithſtanding the loſing. And if the Goods of a Woman are taken in Diſtreſs, and ſhe takes Husband, the Husband alone ſhall have the Replevin. *Sid.* 174.

A Legacy is deviſed to a Feme, who takes Husband, and the Baron makes a Letter of Attorney to another Perſon to receive the Legacy, and he receives it accordingly, this, by his Receipt, is become the Chattel of the Husband; for by the Receipt, this ceaſes to be a Thing in Action, and is become a Thing in Poſſeſſion; and the Husband or his Executors, after the Death of the Feme, may have Account upon this Receipt againſt the Attorney who received it. *Moor* 452.

If a Feme Sole Obligee marries, and the Husband makes a Letter of Attorney to *A. B.* to receive the Money, who receives it, and after the Feme dies, the Baron ſhall have an Action of Account for the Money. *Moor* 452. And a Baron, poſſeſſed of an Obligation, in Right of his Wife, may give it to a Stranger. *Mich.* 38 & 39 *Eliz.*

Where a Feme Sole has a Patent for the ſole Exerciſing a Trade, *&c.* and after takes Husband, the Husband ſhall have the Advantage of it, becauſe he is Aſſignee in Law. 1 *Jac.*

A Feme poſſeſſed of a Leaſe for Years, takes Husband, and they join in the Grant of a Term upon Condition, that if they, their Executors or Adminiſtrators, pay 10 *l.* at ſuch a Day, it ſhall be lawful for them to re-enter, and after the Wife dies, the Husband pays the the 10*l.* and enters, and dies, his Executors ſhall have the Term, and not the Adminiſtrator of the Wife; for the Intereſt of the Term ſurvives to the Husband. 12 *Jac. B. R.*

If the Husband be poſſeſſed of a Leaſe for Years of Land, in Right of the Wife, and after the Wife dies, the Intereſt of the Leaſe is preſently veſted in the Husband by Law, and he ſhall have it, and not the Adminiſtrator of the Wife. *Dyer* 151.

If a Term be granted in Truſt, the Baron ſhall not have it, after the Death of the Feme. But if a Feme before Marriage grant over a Term to her own Uſe, the Husband ſhall nevertheleſs have the Money, which by his Wife, in her Life-time, was actually received upon this Truſt; becauſe, by the Receipt, the Husband had a Property in the Money. *Lit. Rep.* 147.

Baron and Feme, in the Right of the Wife, are ſeiſed of an Advowſon, and the Church is void, and after the Feme dies, yet the Husband ſhall preſent to this Church; for it cannot be granted over, yet it is not meerly in Action. 1 *Inſt.* 120. But otherwiſe it is of a Bond to the Wife; as if a Man becomes bound to a Feme Covert, and ſhe dies, her Husband ſhall not have this Obligation, without Adminiſtration; for that it is a Thing in Action.

Where a Man marries a Woman ſeiſed of Lands in Fee-ſimple, or Fee-tail general, or ſeiſed as Heir in Tail ſpecial, and hath Iſſue Male or Female, by the ſame Wife, born

born alive, though the Iſſue afterwards, either die or live, the Husband ſhall enjoy the Lands after the Death of the Wife, during his Life, by the *Curteſy* of *England*.

And by *Littleton*, in every Caſe where a Man takes a Wife ſeiſed of ſuch an Eſtate in Lands or Tenements, &c. as the Iſſue which he has by his Wife, may by any Poſſibility inherit, as Heir to the Wife: After the Deceaſe of the Wife, he ſhall have the Tenements by the Curteſy of *England*. *Lit. Sect.* 52.

But if Lands be given to a Woman, and the Heirs Male of her Body, and ſhe taking Husband, hath Iſſue a Daughter, and dies, he ſhall not be Tenant by the Curteſy, becauſe the Daughter, by no Poſſibility, could inherit the Mother's Eſtate in the Land. *Ibid.*

If a Man died ſeiſed of Lands in Fee-ſimple, or Fee-tail general, and theſe Lands deſcend to his Daughter, and ſhe takes Husband, and has Iſſue, and dies before any Entry, the Husband ſhall not be Tenant by the Curteſy; and yet in this Caſe ſhe had a Seiſin in Law; but if ſhe or her Husband had enter'd during her Life, ſhe would have been Tenant by the Curteſy. 1 *Inſt.* 29.

The Wife muſt be actually ſeiſed, or the Heir ſhall not make himſelf Heir to the Wife; and this is the Reaſon that a Man ſhall not be Tenant by the Curteſy of a Seiſin in Law. But if a Man, ſeiſed of an Advowſon, or Rent in Fee, has Iſſue a Daughter, who is married, and hath Iſſue, and dies ſeiſed; and the Wife, before the Rent becomes due, or the Church becomes void, dies,

dies, in this Case the Husband shall be Tenant by the Curtesy, although the Wife had but a Seisin in Law. *Co. Lit.* 29.

A Man shall not be Tenant by the Curtesy of a bare Right, Title, Use, or of a Reversion or Remainder, expectant upon any Estate of Freehold; unless the particular Estate be determined by the Coverture; nor of a Copyhold Estate, if there be not a Custom to warrant it. *Cro. Eliz.* 361.

The Custom of a Manor was, That if any Man takes to Wife any Customary Tenant, and over-live his Wife, having Issue by her, he shall be Tenant by the Curtesy. A Man pleads he took to Wife *Anne*, to whom, during the Coverture, a Customary Tenement did descend, and had Issue, by this Custom he shall not be Tenant by the Curtesy; for *Anne* was not a Customary Tenant at the Time of the Marriage. 2 *Lenn.* Sir *John Savage*'s Case.

A Man seised of Lands in Fee, hath Issue a Daughter, who takes Husband, and hath Issue, the Father dies, the Husband enters, he shall be Tenant by the Curtesy, altho' the Issue was had before the Wife was seised; and so it is, though the Issue had died in the Life-time of her Father, before any Descent of the Land. *Co. Lit.*

If a Woman seised of Lands in Fee, take Husband, and by him is big with Child, and in her Travel dies, and the Child is ript out of her Body alive, he shall not be Tenant by the Curtesy, because the Child was not born during the Marriage, nor in the Life-time of the Wife, but in the mean Time the

the Land descended; and he must alledge that he had Issue during the Marriage, in pleading. *Terms de Ley* 206.

A Man entitled to be Tenant by the Curtesy, makes a Feoffment in Fee upon Condition, and enters for the Condition broken, and then his Wife dies, he shall not be Tenant by the Curtesy; for though the Estate given by the Feoffment, be conditional, yet his Title to Tenant by the Curtesy was inclusively absolutely extinct by the Feoffment, the Condition not being annexed to it. *Co. Lit.* 30.

A Woman takes Husband, and hath Issue, Lands descend to the Wife, the Husband enters, and after the Wife is found an Idiot by Office, the Lands shall be seised by the King; for the Title of the Tenancy by the Curtesy, and of the King, happening at one Instant of Time, the Title of the King shall be preferr'd. *Co. Lit.* 30.

If a Man take a Wife seised of Lands and Tenements in Fee, and hath Issue, and after the Wife is Attainted of Felony, so as the Issue cannot inherit to her, he shall nevertheless be Tenant by the Curtesy, in Respect of the Issue which he had before the Felony, and which by Possibility might have inherited. But if the Wife had been Attainted of Felony before the Issue had, altho' he hath Issue afterwards, he shall not be Tenant by the Curtesy. *Co. Lit.* 40.

And if a Woman Sole seised in Fee, take a Husband, have Issue by him, and he is Attainted of Felony, and pardoned, he shall not be Tenant by the Curtesy, unless he have

other

other Iſſue afterwards. *Keb.* And by *Bracton*, he that ſeeketh the Deſtruction of his Wife, ſhall not be Tenant by the Curteſy.

As to what the Wife may Claim of the Husband's, by Marriage, the Law is not very particular, till after his Deceaſe.

If an Obligation be made to Baron and Feme, the Feme ſhall have it by Survivorſhip. *Roll. Abr.* 911. And if a Leaſe for Years be made to Baron and Feme, the Feme ſhall have the ſame by Survivorſhip. 43 *Ed.*3. But if Goods are given to the Husband and Wife, the Wife ſhall not have them by Survivorſhip, but the Executors of the Husband.

If a Statute be acknowledged to Baron and Feme, they are Jointenants of it; and the Wife ſhall have all as Survivor. And if Baron and Feme recover Damages in a real Action, they may ſue Execution jointly. 28 *Aſſ.* 45.

Baron and Feme make a Leaſe for Years, rendring Rent, if the Feme, after the Death of the Baron, agrees to the Leaſe, ſhe ſhall have the Arrearages incurred duing the Coverture. 7 *Ed.* 4.

If a Feme Leaſes for Years, reſerving Rent, and afterwards takes Baron, who dies, the Feme ſhall have the Arrears accruing during the Coverture, and not the Husband's Executors.

And if a Feme Leaſes for Life, reſerving Rent, and after takes Husband, after the Death of the Baron, the Feme ſhall have the Arrearages incurred during the Coverture, and not the Executor of the Baron, becauſe this Iſſues out of the Freehold. 11 *R.* 2.

But

But if a Feme Leaſes for Life, reſerving a Rent, and takes Husband; and during the Coverture, a Receiver receives the Rent of the Leſſee (it does not appear by whom he was made Receiver; but it ſeems to be intended that he received it for the Baron and Feme) and after the Baron dies, the Executor of the Baron ſhall have the Writ of Account againſt the Receiver, and not the Feme; for this was a Chattel and Duty in the Baron, by the Receipt. 1 *Roll. Abr.* 342.

If a Husband die without making any Will, after his Debts, Funeral and other Expences are paid, the Surpluſage of his Perſonal Eſtate, ſhall go one Third Part to the Wife of the Inteſtate, and the Reſidue be divided amongſt his Children, and their legal Repreſentatives. And if there be no Children nor Repreſentatives, one Moiety ſhall be allotted the Wife, and the Reſidue ſhall go to the next of Kin; and if there be no Wife, but Children, the whole ſhall be diſtributed amongſt the Children. Stat. 22 & 23 *Car.* 2.

By the Cuſtom of *London*, the Wife ſhall have a Moiety of the Goods, whereof her Husband died poſſeſſed; yet the Husband, in his Life-time, may give away all the Goods; but by his Will, he cannot Prejudice her concerning her Part. *Cro. Car.* 345. But ſee Stat. 11 *Geo.* 1.

As to the Husband's Eſtate in Lands, where a Man is ſeiſed of Lands or Tenements in Fee-ſimple, or Fee-tail general, or as Heir in Special Tail, and takes Wife, and dieth, the Wife, after her Husband's Deceaſe, ſhall have her *Dower* therein, *viz.* the Third Part of ſuch Lands or Tenements as were her Huſband's at any Time, during the Coverture, whether ſhe have Iſſue by her Husband or not; but the Wife muſt be Nine Years of Age at the Death of her Husband, or ſhe ſhall not be endowed. *Co. Lit.* 30, 31.

And formerly there were five Kinds of Dower in this Kingdom, *i. e.* Dower *at the Common Law*; by *Cuſtom*; *Ad oſtium Eccleſiæ*; *Ex aſſenſu patris*; and *De la pluis Belle.*

Dower at Common Law, is a Third Part of the Lands or Tenements whereof the Huſband was ſeiſed in Fee-ſimple, or Fee-tail, during the Coverture; and this the Widow is to hold, during her Life. It is aſſigned by the Sheriff, by the King's Writ out of Chancery, called, *De dote aſſignanda*; or by the Heir, *&c.* by Agreement among themſelves. *Lit. Sect.* 37.

Dower by Cuſtom is, that Part of the Huſband's Eſtate, to which the Widow is entitled after his Death, by the Cuſtom of any Manor or Place, ſo long as ſhe lives Sole and Chaſte; which Dower may be more than one Third Part; for in ſome Places ſhe ſhall have Half the Land; as by the Cuſtom of *Gavelkind*; and in divers Manors the Widow hath the Whole, during her Life, called her *Free Bench*: Though, as Cuſtom may enlarge Dower, ſo it may abridge it to a Fourth Part. *Co. Lit.* 33.

Dower *Ad oſtium Eccleſiæ*, was an ancient Dower made and aſſigned by the Husband himſelf, immediately after the Marriage, at the Church Door, *&c.* who named ſuch particular

ticular Lands of which his Wife ſhould be endowed; and it was taken, that a Man could not, by this Dower, endow his Wife of more than a Third Part, but of leſs he might. And, as the Husband openly declared the Certainty of the Land, the Wife, after his Death, might enter into the Land of which ſhe was endowed, without any other Aſſignment. *Lit. Sect.* 39.

Dower *Ex aſſenſu Patris*, likewiſe was of certain Lands named by a Son, who was the Husband, with the Conſent of his Father, and put in Writing as ſoon as the Son was married. And if a Woman, thus endowed, or *Ad oſtium Eccleſiæ*, after the Death of her Husband, entered into the Land allotted her in Dower, ſhe was concluded to claim any Dower, by the Common Law. *Lit. Sect.*41. 1 *Co. Inſt.* 37.

Dower *De la pluis Belle*, was where the Wife was endowed with the faireſt Part of her Husband's Eſtate. But of all the beforementioned Aſſignments and Appointments of Dower, the two firſt are now only in Uſe. *Co. Lit.* 38.

The Husband muſt be ſole ſeiſed of his Eſtate, to entitle Dower, and not in Jointenancy. Father and Son were Jointenants to them and the Heirs of the Son; and being both convicted of Capital Crimes, they were both hanged in one Cart; but becauſe the Son, as was depoſed by Witneſſes, surviv'd, it appearing by ſome Tokens (*viz.*) the ſhaking his Legs, his Wife thereupon demanded her Dower, and had it. *Cro. Eliz.* 502.

And he is to be ſeiſed either in Deed or in Law, during the Coverture, or elſe ſhe ſhall not be endowed, where Lands deſcend to the Husband; now before Entry, he hath but a Seiſin in Law, and yet the Wife ſhall be endowed, although it be not reduced to an actual Poſſeſſion; for it lies not in the Power of the Wife to bring it to an actual Seiſin. *Co. Lit.* 31.

But it is not neceſſary that the Seiſin ſhould continue during the Coverture, tho' the Marriage muſt continue, for altho' the Husband aliens the Lands and Tenements, or extinguiſhes the Rent, *&c.* the Wife ſhall be endow'd.

And if Lands are exchanged by the Huſband, for other Lands, the Wife may have her Dower in which Lands ſhe will, as the Husband was ſeiſed of both; though ſhe may not be endowed of the Lands given and taken in Exchange. 1 *Co. Inſt.* 31, 32.

If a Man, ſeiſed of Lands in Fee, takes a Wife of Eight Years old, and aliens his Land, and after the Wife attains Nine Years of Age, and then the Husband dies, the Wife ſhall be endowed here, though at the Time of the Alienation, the Wife was not Dowable; yet, as the Marriage and Seiſin in Fee, were before the Alienation, and the Title of Dower is not conſummate 'till the Death of her Huſband, ſhe ſhall be endow'd in his Lands. *Co. Lit.* 33.

Of an Eſtate-tail in Lands determin'd, a Woman ſhall be endowed in like Manner as a Man ſhall be Tenant by the Curteſy. She may be endowed of a Caſtle, uſed only for the

the private Habitation of the Owner. She ſhall be endowed of a Principal Manſion or Capital Meſſuage. Of the third Preſentation to an Advowſon; of Tithes; of a Common certain; of a Rent-Service, Rent-Charge, *&c.* And if a Man makes a Gift in Tail of Lands, reſerving a Rent to him and his Heirs, and after the Donor takes Wife, and dies, the Wife ſhall be endow'd of this Rent, becauſe it is a Rent in Fee, and may be perpetual. *Co. Lit.* 31.

But of an Annuity, that charges only the Perſon, and iſſues not out of any Lands or Tenements, ſhe ſhall not be endowed. Alſo if the Freehold of Rents, Common, *&c.* were ſuſpended before the Coverture, and ſo continue during the Coverture, ſhe ſhall not be endowed of them. Of a Mill a Woman ſhall not be endowed by Meets and Bounds, in Common with the Heir; but ſhe may be endowed of the third Toll Diſh, *&c.* and ſhe may be endow'd of the Third Part of the Profits of a Fair, the Third Part of an Office, Piſcary, *&c.*

By *Magna Charta*, 9 *H.* 3. the Wife ſhall have her *Quarentine* (*viz.*) ſhall remain in the Capital Meſſuage of her late Husband (which is not a Caſtle for Defence of the Realm) by the Space of forty Days; within which Time her Dower ought to be aſſigned to her. 2 *Inſt.* 16.

In ſome Caſes of Lands and Tenements, which are diviſible, and which the Heir of the Husband ſhall inherit; yet the Wife ſhall not be endow'd. As if the Husband make a Leaſe for Life of certain Lands, reſerving a Rent to him and his Heirs, and he taketh Wife and dies, the Wife ſhall not be endowed; neither of the Reverſion, though it be within the Word *Tenements*; becauſe there was no Seiſin in Deed or in Law, of the Freehold, nor of the Rent; for the Husband had but a particular Eſtate therein, and no Fee-ſimple. But if the Husband make a Leaſe for Years, reſerving Rent, and takes Wife, the Husband dies, the Wife ſhall be endowed of the Third Part of the Reverſion, by Meets and Bounds, together with the Third Part of the Rent. *Co. Lit.* 32.

A Wife ſhall be endow'd of a Third Part of a Reverſion, Expectant upon a Term of Years; and of the Third Part of the Rent reſerved thereupon. *Lutw.* 729.

Where Lands are limited to the Uſe of *A.* for Life, Remainder to *B.* &c. for Years, Remainder to the Heirs Males of the Body of *A. A.* dies, this intervening Eſtate for Years is no Impediment to the Execution of the Eſtate-tail, nor ſhall be any Bar to the Wife's Dower. *Lutw.* 729.

A Woman recovers Dower of a Manor wherein were ſeveral Copyholds for Life; and the Cuſtom is, that *Dominus pro tempore*, may grant for one, two or three Lives, in Poſſeſſion or Reverſion. She keeps a Court, and grants one of the Copyhold Tenements to three for their Lives; *Habendum* after the Death of *A. B.* the preſent Copyhold Tenant thereof for Life, ſhe afterwards dies, and then *A. B.* dies. And adjudged that this Grant was good, altho' it was not executed in the Life of the Tenant in Dower, who

granted

granted it; for the Grant is warranted by the Custom. *Cro. Eliz.* 661.

The Widow Demandant in Dower, ſhall not recover any Damages, except the Huſband died ſeiſed; and there ſhe ſhall have Damages from the Time of his Death. *Dyer* 284.

A Woman deforced of her Dower, ſhall recover Damages, *viz.* the Value of her Dower, from her Husband's Death, by Stat. 20 *H.* 3. And the Wife is endowable where Lands were recovered againſt the Husband by Default or Covin. 13 *Ed.* 1.

If the Husband be an Alien, his Wife ſhall not be endow'd. *Co. Lit.* 31. And if a Man take an Alien Woman to Wife, and afterwards the Husband aliens the Land, and after that ſhe is made a Denizen, and then the Husband dies, ſhe ſhall not be endowed, becauſe there was an abſolute Diſability; but it is otherwiſe if ſhe be Naturalized by Act of Parliament. 1 *Roll. Abr.* 675.

A *Jew* born in *England*, took to Wife a *Jew*; the Husband was converted to the Chriſtian Faith, purchaſed Lands, and enfeoffed another, and then died; on which the Wife brought a Writ of Dower, but was barred of it. *Co. Lit.* 31, 32.

The Wife of an Idiot, *Non compos mentis*, a Perſon outlaw'd, or one Attainted of Felony, ſhall be endow'd. And though the Iſſue cannot inherit the Lands which the Father had in Fee-ſimple, by the Attainder of Felony, the Wife ſhall be endow'd. But if the Husband alien his Land, and then the Wife is Attainted of Felony, now is ſhe diſabled; though if ſhe be pardoned before the Death of the Husband, ſhe ſhall be endow'd. *Co. Lit.* 31, 33.

Where a Husband is Attainted of Treaſon, ſhe ſhall not be endow'd; for the Attainder of the Husband interrupts the Title of Dower, which ought to be conſummate by his Death; and if the Husband obtains a Pardon, and dies, this doth not help it; as it only extends to the Life of the Offender, but doth not take away the Attainder, by which ſhe is barred to demand Dower; and ſo it is, altho' the Lands be aliened before the Treaſon committed. *Dyer* 140.

If the Wife be divorc'd, *cauſa præcontractus*, *conſanguinei*, or for Impotency, ſhe ſhall not be endow'd. But a Woman divorced a *Menſa & Thoro*, ſhe ſhall notwithſtanding have her Dower, this being but a particular Divorce. *Co. Lit.* 235.

A Wife eloping from her Husband, and continuing with an Adulterer, loſeth her Dower; but if the Husband willingly, without Coercion Eccleſiaſtical, be reconciled to her, and permit her to live and cohabit with him again, ſhe ſhall be endow'd. *Co. Lit.* 32. 2 *Inſt.* 453.

If the Wife commit Adultery with a Man, though ſhe do not continually remain with him, it is a Tarrying within the Stat. *Weſt.* 2 *Co. Inſt.* 2 *Pt.* 436.

A married Woman is taken away againſt her Will, if after ſhe conſents and remains with the Adulterer, without being reconcil'd, *&c.* ſhe ſhall loſe her Dower. And if the Wife go away with the Man, by Agreement of of her Husband, if he commit Adultery with her, and ſhe remain with him, without Reconciliation, ſhe ſhall be barred of her Dower. 2 *Inſt.* 435.

But if the Husband's Friends ſend him away from his Wife, ſo as the Wife knows not what is become of him, and they publiſh that he is dead, and afterwards procure the Woman to Releaſe Marriage, and all Intereſt in him, as an Husband, and after this, by the Perſwaſion of the Friends of the Husband, he marries another Woman, who dies, and ſhe takes another Husband, having no Notice of the firſt Husband's being alive, although the Wife live in Adultery, and tho' the firſt Husband was not out of the Realm, yet inaſmuch as ſhe did not leave her Husband *Sponte*, as the Statute ſays, but by Perſwaſion of the Husband's Friends, that he was dead; and it did not appear that ſhe knew he was alive, this is not any Elopement to bar her of her Dower. 1 *Roll. Abr.* 680.

A Feme may be twice endow'd; as in Caſe of a Recovery by *Eigne* Title. 1 *Roll. Abr.* 684.

But the Wife ſhall not be endow'd of Lands and Tenements, which the Husband held jointly with another, at the Time of his Death; for the Jointenant claims all by Survivorſhip, which is above the Title of Dower; though Tenants in Common have ſeveral Freeholds and Inheritances; and their Moieties ſhall deſcend to their ſeveral Heirs, and therefore their Wives ſhall be endow'd. 1 *Inſt.* 37.

When Lands are redeemed upon a Mortgage, the Wife of the Mortgagee ſhall not have Dower. *Cro. Car.* 191. And if the Husband takes a Fine, *Sur Conuzance de Droit*, and renders again, though it was once the Husband's, yet the Wife shall not have Dower. *Co. Lit.* 31.

If the Widow accepts of Dower of the Heir, against Common Right, she shall hold it subject to the Charges of the Husband; but it is otherwise if she be endow'd by the Sheriff. And by Provision of Law, the Wife may take a Third Part of the Husband's Lands, and hold them discharged. 2 *Danv. Abr.* 672.

Detaining of Deeds and Writings concerning the Lands of which the Widow demands Dower, is a good Plea by the Heir, in Delay of her Dower. But if she delivers up the Evidences, she shall have Judgment. *Hob.* 199. If she denies the Detainer, and it is found against her, she loseth her Dower. *Ibid.*

If a Wife accept and enter upon less Land than the Third of the Whole, on the Sheriff's Assignment, she is barr'd to demand more. *Moor* 679.

A Devise to a Wife, *durante viduitate*, is no Bar to her Dower; unless it be expressed in the Will, That if she claims her Dower, she shall lose the Thing devised to her. *Lutw.* 735.

If an Estate be made to the Wife before Coverture, or afterwards (if after the Death of her Husband, she enter and agree to it) for Term of her own Life, or a greater Estate, this is a Bar of Dower, if it be expressed

preſſed to be for a *Jointure*, or it may be averr'd. 1 *Inſt*. 36.

The Wife had a Jointure made to her after Marriage, and ſhe and her Husband levied a Fine *Sur Conuſance de Droit*, *&c.* and aliened the Jointure, ſhe ſhall not have Dower of the Reſidue of the Lands of her Husband, becauſe her Time of Election is not come till ſhe becomes Sole. *Dyer* 358.

The Husband being Tenant in Tail, the Remainder to his Wife for Life, the Husband made a Feoffment to the Uſe of himſelf and his Wife, for their Lives, for a Jointure, and died without Iſſue; this Jointure was pleaded in Bar of Dower. *Per Curiam*: It is no Bar, becauſe the Wife is remitted, and in her firſt Eſtate, and the Jointure avoided. *Moor* 872.

To the making of a perfect Jointure, within the Statute 27 *H.* 8. ſix Things are required. *Firſt*, The Jointure is to take Effect for the Wife's Life in Poſſeſſion or Profit, preſently after the Deceaſe of her Husband. *Secondly*, That it be of Lands for the Term of her own Life, or a greater Eſtate. *Thirdly*, It muſt be made to herſelf, and no other for her. *Fourthly*, It is to be made in Satisfaction of her whole Dower, and not of Part of it. *Fifthly*, It muſt be expreſſed to be in Satiſfaction of Dower. And *Sixthly*, It may be made either before or after Marriage. *Co. Lit*. 36.

But if the Jointure be made after Marriage, ſhe may wave the ſame, and claim her Dower; except ſhe enters and agrees to her Jointure. But if it be made before Marriage, the

the Wife cannot wave it, and claim her Dower. And a Jointure was no Bar of Dower at the Common Law.

If a Man make a Feoffment in Fee of Lands or Tenements, either before or after Marriage, to the Use of the Husband for Life, and after to the Use of *A.* for Life, and then to the Use of the Wife for Life, in Satisfaction of her Dower, this is no Jointure within the Statute; because by the Limitation, it was not to take Effect in Possession or Profit presently after the Death of the Husband. And where an Estate is made to others in Fee-simple, or for the Wife's Life upon Trust, so as the Estate remains in them; altho' it be for her Benefit, and by her Assent, and by express Words be in full Satisfaction of her Dower, yet this is no Bar of her Dower. The Estate limited, must be either in Fee-tail, or for Term of her own Life; for an Estate for the Life or Lives of any others, or for an hundred Years, *&c.* if she live so long, without such Limitation, is no Bar of her Dower. *Co. Lit.* 36.

A Father made a Settlement of Lands, to the Use of himself for Life, and afterwards to the Use of his Son and his Wife, for their Lives, for the Jointure of the Wife. Adjudg'd, that it was no Jointure to bar the Wife of her Dower; for it might not commence immediately after the Husband's Death, who might die in the Life-time of the Father. 2 *Cro.* 489.

The Duke of *Somerset* purchased Lands to him and the Dutchess his Wife, and to the Heirs Males of their two Bodies; this was a

good

good Jointure within the Intent of the Act. *Dyer* 96. And an Estate to the Wife for Life, upon Condition, is a good Jointure within the Act, if the Wife, after the Death of the Husband, accept it; but if the Condition bind her to any unreasonable Thing, she may wave it. 4 *Co.* 3.

An Estate in Fee-simple, convey'd to the Wife for her Jointure, and in Satisfaction of Dower, is a Jointure within the Equity of the Act 27 *H*.8. for this is a competent Livelihood for the Wife of an Estate of Freehold to take Effect presently after the Death of the Husband, for her Life and more. 4 *Co*.3.*b*. But *Mich*. 28 & 29 *Eliz*. it was agreed that an Estate in Fee, made by the Husband to the Wife, is not a Jointure within 11 *H*. 7. for that any Collateral Heir might inherit it; and the Statute was made for the Benefit of the Issues between them.

Covenant to stand seised to the Use of a Man's Brother and his Wife, for their Lives, is a Jointure within the Statute of 11 *H*. 7. as given by the Ancestor of the Husband; and it is within the Words of 27 *H*. 8. *Plowd*. 307.

The Bishop of *Exeter*, in Consideration of faithful Service done by *A*. *B*. gives Lands to him and *S*. his Cousin, in Tail; and a Marriage was then intended to be had between them, which afterwards was solemniz'd accordingly; this was held no Jointure within the Stat. 11 *H*. 7. for it was not a Gift by the Husband, nor any Ancestor of the Husband; and the Consideration of Service is

not

not what the Law requires. *Yelv.* 101. *Brownl.* 137.

A Conveyance by the Husband, or his Anceſtor, in Conſideration of a Marriage, though it be joined with a Conſideration of Money, is a Jointure within the Statute. As if *A. B.* ſeiſed in Fee, by Indenture, covenants with *C. D.* as well in Conſideration of 500 *l.* paid by *C. D.* as of a Marriage between *L.* his only Son, and *A.* the Daughter of the ſaid *C. D.* to convey the Land to the Uſe of the ſaid *L.* and *A.* and the Heirs of the Body of the ſaid *A.* to be begotten, &c. *Cro. Jac.* 474.

But where a Father of the intended Wife, in Conſideration of Marriage, &c. covenanted to aſſure Lands to the Husband and Wife, his the Covenantor's Daughter, and the Heirs of her Body, &c. this hath been held no Jointure, within the Meaning of the Stat. 11 *H.* 7. *c.* 20. becauſe it is an Advancement of the Woman by her own Father; and not coming from the Husband, or his Anceſtors. 2 *Cro.* 264. 2 *Lill. Abr.* 80.

If Lands are conveyed to a Woman before Marriage, as Part of her Jointure, and after Marriage more Land is conveyed to her, for her full Jointure, and in Satisfaction of all Dower, and after the Husband dies; in this Caſe, if the Woman waves the Land convey'd to her Uſe after Marriage, ſhe ſhall have the Land convey'd to her before Coverture, and her Dower alſo in the Reſidue; for Land conveyed to the Wife, for Part of her Jointure, or in Satisfaction of Part of her Dower, is no Bar for the Incertainty. 3 *Co. Rep.* 1, 5.

Some are of Opinion, that no Estate devised by Will, can be a Jointure within 27 *H.* 8. for by that Act, every Jointure is intended to be made before or during the Coverture; and a Devise takes not Effect 'till after the Death of the Husband. But in *Leak* and *Randal's* Case, it was adjudg'd that if a Man devise Lands to his Wife for her Life, or in Tail, *&c.* for her Jointure, and in Satisfaction of Dower, this a Jointure within the 27 *H.* 8. though a Devise cannot be averr'd in Satisfaction of Dower, if it be not so expressed in the Will. *Co. Lit.* 36.

If a Jointure be made to a Wife, of Lands before the Coverture, and after the Husband and Wife alien those Lands, she shall not be endow'd of any other Lands of her Husband. *Co. Lit.* 36. Acceptance of Dower by Deed indented, shall conclude the Wife of her Right by Jointure.

After the Death of the Husband, the Wife may enter into her Jointure Lands, and is not driven to a Real Action, as she is to recover Dower by the Common Law. And upon a lawful Eviction of her Jointure, she shall be endowed according to the Rate of her Husband's Lands, whereof she was Dowable at Common Law. 1 *Co. Inst.* 37.

A Wife's Jointure shall not be forfeited by the Treason of the Husband. Though Feme Coverts, committing Treason or Felony, incur a Forfeiture of their Jointures. If a Jointress makes any Alienation of the Estate settled on her in a Jointure, by Fine, Feoffment, *&c.* with another Husband, it is a Forfeiture of the same; but if the Lands settled tied are not a Jointure by Law, it is otherwise. Also if she Suffer a Recovery covinously to bar the Heir, the Heir may enter presently on the Lands, where it is a Jointure within the 11 *H.* 7. *Plowd.* 42. 2 *Leon.* 206. 2 *Nels. Abr.* 1040.

By bringing a Writ of Dower for her Thirds, the Wife waves the Benefit of Entry into Lands, so as to hold them in Jointure. And if a Woman conceals her Jointure, and brings Dower, and recovers it, and then sets up her Jointure, she is barr'd thereof. 3 *Rep.* 5. *Cro. Eliz* 128.

A Man enters into Bond to a Woman, with Condition, that if he married her, his Executors or Administrators should pay her 500 *l.* after his Death; he marries her and dies, here this Bond could not be sued during his Life; but the Cause of Action grew only after the Death of the Husband, it being that his Heirs, Executors or Administrators should pay the Wife 500 *l.* if she survived her Husband, which she did, and the Bond remains good to the Wife. *Cro. Jac.* 572.

In Consideration that the Plaintiff would marry the Testator, he promised to leave her worth 500 *l.* and it was mov'd in Arrest of Judgment, that this Personal Contract was determin'd by the Marriage. As if a Release had been made; or as where the Debtor takes the Debtee to Wife, the Debt is determined. But *per Curiam*, It never was a Duty in the Life of the Testator, and therefore could not be released by him. *Hob.* 216.

And

And if a Man and Woman enter into Articles to each other, and the Man gives Bond to a third Perſon to perform the Articles; the Man and Woman afterwards marry, whereby the Articles become void; yet the Bond remains good, and the Husband may be ſued upon it. *Cro. Car.* 376.

A Man and a Woman agree to marry, and they enter into a Deed in Writing, that the Feme ſhould diſpoſe of the Rents of her own Eſtate, during the Coverture; they marry, the Husband receives the Rents, and dies; and the Feme brings her Bill in Chancery againſt the Executors of her Husband, to pay her the Money received by the Baron. But it was decreed that this Agreement, made by the Baron, before Marriage, was by the Marriage determined. *Chanc. Rep.* 21, 217.

A Wife aſſigns her Term before Marriage in Truſt for herſelf; and the Husband, without the Truſtees, mortgages the Term, this is void; neither can the Husband forfeit it by Outlawry or Felony. But if it had been an Aſſignment made by the Husband after Marriage, in Truſt for his Wife; this is a voluntary Settlement, and fraudulent againſt Purchaſors. *Chanc. Rep.* 225.

A Widow being about to marry; to prevent the Husband's Diſpoſal of her Land, conveyed it to Truſtees, who join'd with her Husband in a Sale of the ſame; ſhe commenced a Suit in Chancery, and the Court decreed that the Purchaſor ſhould reconvey to her, though a valuable Conſideration was given for the Eſtate. *Totbil* 43.

Of

Of the Privileges of Feme Coverts, and their Power, in Respect of their Husbands, and all others: Of Husband and Wife, in what Actions they are to join, and how far they are chargeable, &c.

ALTHOUGH a Woman parts with great Powers, as to the Disposition of her Estate, by Marriage, and she is *sub potestate viri*; yet many particular Privileges are belonging to married Females.

In Case of Banishment of the Husband by Parliament, a Feme Covert may act as lawfully as the Husband might, were he not dead in Law. Stat. *Westm.* 2. But my Lord *Coke* makes a Diversity, where the Banishment is Perpetual, and where only Temporary. *Co. Lit.* 133.

Regularly no Laches shall be accounted to Feme Coverts, for not Entry or Claim to avoid Descents; though Laches will be accounted to them for Nonperformance of a Condition annexed to the Estate in the Land; for if a Feme be enfeoffed, either before or after Marriage, reserving Rent; and for Default of Payment, a Re-entry is made; in this Case the Laches of the Husband shall disherit the Wife for ever. 1 *Inst*. 246.

And

And Lapſe ſhall incur againſt a Feme Covert, if ſhe does not preſent to a Church within ſix Months.

A Woman (although the Cuſtom be to elect by Houſes) may not be a Conſtable. *Cro. Car.* 388. And although ſhe is impriſonable for Force, yet Women in Priſon, by Reaſon of their Pregnancy, have been releaſed upon Bail. *Cro. Jac.* 356. *Hob.* 97.

When a Feme Covert dies, no Mortuary ſhall be paid; but if a Woman ſurvive her Husband, and live in a Houſe for a Year ſole, with the Government of a Family, and after dies, ſhe ſhall pay a Mortuary. *Linwood f.* 7.

If the Husband be ſolely impleaded *in Banco*, and he comes with his Wife to the Court to defend the Suit, and both are arreſted, there they ſhall have Privilege; tho' if the Husband have Privilege to be ſued in Chancery, it ſhall not ſerve for his Wife.

A. B. a Clerk in Chancery, married a Feme, who was Executrix to her late Huſband; Debt was brought againſt them in the Common Pleas; *A. B.* brings a Writ of Privilege to have the Action removed into Chancery; the Writ was diſallowed by the Court, and the Defendant rul'd to anſwer over, becauſe the Wife was joined in the Action with the Husband; *aliter*, where the Wife comes in Aid of her Husband to follow the Suit. *Dyer* 377.

A married Woman may make a Teſtament of Goods, and an Executor, by the Aſſent of her Husband. She cannot make an Executor without ſuch Aſſent; and the Adminiſtration

tion of her Goods of Right, appertains to her Husband. 4 *Co.*

But a Feme Covert Executrix, may make an Executor of the Goods which ſhe has as Executrix, without the Aſſent of her Husband; and in ſuch Caſe Adminiſtration appertains not to the Husband; and what ſhe had as Executrix, ſhe had *en auter Droit*, and no other Intereſt in the ſame. *Mich.* 8 *Jac.* ſhe may make her Husband Executor of the Goods which ſhe hath, as Executrix, if he will accept it. 4 *H.* 6.

By Law, the Apparel of the Wife, is called *Bona Paraphernalia.* The Wife by the Common Law, ought to have her neceſſary Apparel after the Deceaſe of the Husband, and not the Husband's Executors. And if the Husband deliver to his Wife, a Piece of Cloth to make a Garment, and dies, altho' it was not made up in the Life of the Husband; yet the Wife ſhall have it, and not the Executor, it being delivered to her to that Intent: But againſt the Debtee of the Husband, the Wife ſhall have no more Cloths than is convenient. *Mich.* 40 & 41 *Eliz.*

A Chain of Diamonds and Pearls, being worth about 400 *l.* uſually worn by a Woman who was the Daughter of an Earl in *Ireland*, and a Baron of *England*, and the Wife of a Knight, and the King's Serjeant at Law, ſhall be *Bona Paraphernalia*; ſo that the Husband cannot deviſe them from the Wife. *Cro. Car.* 343. Lord *Haſtings* and *Dougblas.* Judge *Crook* thought the Wife ſhould not have them as *Bona Paraphernalia*; becauſe they were not neceſſary for her, but only convenient.

A Feme Covert, in our Books, is often compared to an Infant, both being Persons disabled in the Law; but they differ very much: An Infant is capable of doing any Act for his own Advantage, so is not a Feme Covert. A Lease made by an Infant, without Rent, is not void, but voidable: It is void in the Case of a Feme Covert. If a Feme Covert enter into Bond, *Non est factum* may be pleaded to it; but if an Infant enter into Bond, he must plead the special Matter, that he was under Age.

An Infant may bind himself for Conveniencies and Necessaries for himself and Family, and the Law gives him Authority so to do; a Feme Covert cannot do so without the Consent of the Husbaud, because thereby she is to bind another that hath all the Property in her Estate: And yet a Feme Covert is a Favourite of the Law. 2 *Inst.* 18.

And though our Law makes the Woman subject to the Husband, yet he may not beat her, but she may pray the Peace against him; and he shall find Surety that he shall neither do nor procure to be done to her, any Bodily Damage, otherwise than appertains to the Office of a Husband, and for lawful Correction. *F. N. B.* 80. *Dalt.* 284.

Some Authors mention that a Husband may give his Wife reasonable Correction and Chastisement, and by the Common Law she can have no Action; but if a Husband enter into an Obligation for the Duress of his Wife, the Bond shall be void. *Sid.* 123.

A Woman by Marriage with a Nobleman, becomes thereby Noble; and if she be Noble by Descent, she loses not her Nobility by Marriage with a private Gentleman.

If a Queen Dowager marry any of the Nobility, or under that Degree, she loseth not her Dignity. And *Catharine*, Queen *Dowager* of *England*, married *Owen ap Meredith*, *ap Theodore*, &c. and yet she, by the Name of *Catharine* Queen of *England*, maintained an Action of Detinue against the Bishop of *Carlisle*. 2 *Inst*. 50.

But at a Parliament, held 6 *H*. 6. it was enacted, that no Man shall contract or marry himself to any Queen of *England*, without a special Licence or Assent of the King, on Pain to lose all his Goods and Lands. 2 *Inst*. 18.

The Queen Consort, or Queen Dowager, in Case of Treason, shall be tried *per Pares*, as Queen *Anne*, Wife of King *Henry* VIII. was in the *Tower* of *London*, before the Duke of *Norfolk*, Lord High Steward. *Pasch*. 22 *H*. 8.

The Queen of *England* has a certain Prerogative, as she is the King's Wife: She ought not to find Sureties, as a Common Person ought to do. She shall not be amerced; she shall pay no Toll; in Case of a *Quare Impedit* brought by her, *Plenarty* is no Plea. And if the Queen's Tenant alien any Part of the Tenancy to one, and another Part to another, the Queen may distrain any one Part for the Whole, as the King may do. *Co. Lit*. 133.

The Wife of the King of *England*, is an exempt Person from the King, and capable of Lands or Tenements of the Gift of the King, *&c*. and may sue and be sued without the King, as a Feme Sole.

And that the Queen, as Feme Sole, may give and take ſolely without the King, appears by an ancient Charter made before the Conqueſt, which runs thus:

'*I* Ethelſwith, *Queen of the* Mercians, *with* '*Conſent of my Eldermen, do give, by Grant,* '*to* Cawolf, *my moſt faithful Servant, a certain Piece of Land, being Part of my peculiar* '*Power, that he may have and poſſeſs, at his* '*Pleaſure, as long as he lives; and after his* '*End and Limit of his Days, he may leave it* '*to whomſoever he will, for everlaſting Power,* '*and perpetual Inheritance. And We charge* '*all ſecular Powers, in the Name of God the* '*Father, Son and Holy Ghoſt, to obſerve the* '*aforeſaid inviolably. These Witneſſes ſubſcribing and conſenting thereunto.*

Etheldred, *King of the* Weſt Saxons,
Burghred, *King of the* Mercians.

Ethelſwith.

The Queen may inform, by her Attorney, in the Chancery, by *Engliſh* Bill, to have a Decree made in her Court confirmed. But a Protection may be allowed againſt the Queen, though not againſt the King; neither ſhall the Queen be ſued by Petition, but by a *Præcipe*.

Next to Privileges of Feme Coverts, I come to *Actions* brought by Husband and Wife; and in what Actions they are to join.

And *first*, Baron and Feme are to join in Actions due to the Feme before Coverture. *Moor* 422.

For entring and breaking the Wife's Close, or Battery or other Tort done to the Wife, they must join; but if the Wife dies, the Action dies with her. *Trin.* 4 *Jac.*

Trespass, *Quare clausum fregit*, by Baron and Feme. *Pollixfen*, Ch. Justice, was of Opinion, that the Wife ought not to be join'd with him, though it was her Land. *Vent.* 195. But *Brownlow* says, the Action will survive; and they have Election to join, or bring it alone.

In Trespass and Assault, Baron and Feme may say, *Ad dampnum ipsorum*, tho' a Feme Covert can have no Damages. 1 *Sid.* 387.

Baron and Feme bring an Action for the beating of himself and his Wife; the Writ shall abate; for the Wife cannot join for the Battery of her Husband, and the Husband cannot have Judgment alone, because his Wife is join'd with him in the Writ. But the Baron and Feme shall have Judgment for the Battery of the Wife; for this is but one Judgment. *Co. Inst.* 326. 1 *Roll. Abr.* 782.

And Baron and Feme brought Trespass and Battery for beating them both; upon Not guilty pleaded, the Verdict was for so much Damages for beating the Baron, and so much for beating the Wife. On Motion to arrest Judgment, the Court said the Plaintiff might Release Damages for beating of himself, and take Judgment for the other. 1 *Vent.* 328.

Trespass and Assault against Baron and Feme, for the Assault of the Feme, the Ba-

ron

ron and Feme defend the Force, *&c.* and the Baron ſays, that his Wife is not Guilty, this is ill; for the Husband only pleads here, and not the Wife; and it ſhould be *Dicunt*, that ſhe is not guilty. *Cro. Car.* 594.

The Husband ſhall not have an Action ſingly by himſelf, for the beating of his Wife, unleſs he lay a *Per quod conſortium amiſit*, in his Declaration. And if a married Woman be aſſaulted and beaten; if the Husband is thereby deprived of her Converſation, he alone may commence an Action of Treſpaſs. 3 *Co.* 113.

For an Injury done to the Wife only, Action cannot be maintained by the Husband without her; but for a Loſs and Injury done to the Husband, in depriving him of the Converſation and Service of the Wife, he alone may bring an Action; and theſe Actions are laid for Aſſault, and detaining the Wife, *Per quod conſortium amiſit*, *&c.* Cro. Car. 538.

If a Feme Covert ſlander any Perſon, the Husband and Wife are to be ſued for it. But for ſcandalous Words againſt a Man and his Wife, the Husband may proſecute one Action alone for his own Slander, and afterwards join in an Action with his Wife for hers. *Styl. Rep.* 113.

The Husband Sole ſhall have an Action for Words ſpoken againſt his Wife; and if the Wife be joined with him, Judgment ſhall be arreſted. *Sid.* 346. but the Words muſt be ſuch as are Actionable, in Reſpect of Collateral Damages.

Words of a Wife were, That ſhe is a Bawd, and keeps a Bawdy-houſe; upon theſe Words an Action was brought by Baron and Feme, *Ad Damnum ipſorum*. And it was moved firſt, That it is the Husband, and not the Wife, that keeps the Houſe; and therefore the Speaking of the Wife can be no Damage to the Husband. Admit they are actionable, the Husband only ought to bring the Action; becauſe the ſpeaking of the Words is only to his Damage. But by the *Chief Juſtice*, the Wife is to be indicted for the keeping of a Bawdy-houſe, ſhe only being damnified by the Words; and the Husband for Conformity only ought to join in the Action. *March. Rep.* 212.

To ſay another Man's Wife is your Whore, no Action lies at Common Law, but in the Spiritual Court. But to ſay of a Woman ſhe is a Whore, and her Children, which ſhe had by a former Husband, are another Man's Baſtards, the Words are Actionable, tho' the Children cannot be Baſtards in Law, but in Reputation they may; and it is Loſs of Marriage. *Sid.* 61. *Cro. Car.* 322.

To call a Woman, in Communication of Marriage, Burſten Bellied Queen; and ſay her Belly hangs down to her Garters, adjudged Actionable. *Lit. Rep.* 193.

A Man calls another Whore-maſter, or a Woman Whore, no Action lies, unleſs it be in *London*, by the Cuſtom of the City. But to ſay that a Woman is with Child, or that a certain Perſon hath had the Uſe of her Body, *&c.* whereby ſhe loſes her Marriage; for

this

this ſpecial Damage Action lieth. 1 *Danv. Abr.* 81. 2 *Salk.* 696.

And if a Perſon ſay to a Man, Thou art a Whore-maſter, thou haſt lain with ſuch a Woman, and hadſt to do with her againſt a Chair; *per quod, &c.* Judgment *pro Quer. Cro. Jac.* 323.

Thou haſt ſought the Blood of my Huſband, and waſt his Death; for hadſt thou been an honeſt Woman, he had been ſtill alive; and avers *in Facto*, that her Husband was killed; the Words are Actionable. *Cro. Jac.* 306.

The Defendant's Wife ſpoke of the Plaintiff's Wife theſe Words, Thou are a thieviſh Woman, and has ſtolen my Faggots. It was moved that the Words are not Actionable; for a Feme Covert hath not any Goods that can be ſtollen. But *per Curiam*, the Action lies; for ſhe charges her with Felony; and it is no Matter whoſe Goods they are. *Cro. Jac.* 600.

To ſay of a Woman, Thou art a Witch, no Action lies; there muſt be an alledging that ſhe had done ſome Act. But to ſay of a Woman, Thou are a Witch, and I will prove thee a Witch, Action lies. *Cro. Jac.* 478.

In Action upon the Caſe, againſt Baron and Feme, for Words ſpoken by the Wife, the Baron is to be found Not guilty, becauſe nothing is laid to his Charge; and if they are both found Guilty, as to the Husband, the Verdict is void, but good againſt the Wife alone. 3 *Bulſt.* 60.

But when Judgment is given against Baron and Feme, for Words spoken by the Feme, both must be *in mia'*. *Hob.* 127.

The Defendant's Wife said scandalous Words of the Plaintiff's Wife; and he brought his Action against Baron and Feme, and they pleaded *Quod ipsi non sunt Culpabiles*, and good; for the Baron and Feme are charged as for the Wrong of the Wife. *Cro. Car.* 417.

Where Baron and Feme sue for personal Things, they shall not join, unless such Things are in Action; and then it is in the Election of the Husband to join his Wife or not. But where they have a joint Interest, they must join. *March* 47.

In Avowry for Rent, in the Right of the Wife, they ought to join; as if Rent be due to the Wife before Coverture, she and her Husband must join in the Avowry. 4 *H.* 6.

Action of Debt upon the Statute 2 *Ed.* 6. by Baron and Feme, for not setting forth of Tithes, the Baron and Feme may join, if the Baron be seised in Possession of the Rectory, in the Right of his Wife, or in Jointure. *Moor* 912.

Baron and Feme join in Covenant, and the Action was brought against them both, and it abated, because it shall charge the Husband only. 24 *Ed.* 3.

If a Lease be made by Baron and Feme, of the Wife's Land, rendring Rent, the Baron may bring an Action alone for the Rent; and *Quære*, if they may join. 2 *Bulst.* 21.

A Feme having Rent for Life, takes Husband, the Baron shall have an Action of Debt for Rent incurred, during the Coverture, after the Death of Feme; and if the Lessee for Life rendring Rent, takes Husband, and dies, the Husband shall be sued for Rent in Arrear, because he took the Profits of the Lands. 10 *H.* 6.

If a Lease for Life be made to one, the Remainder to Baron and Feme, and to the Heirs of the Baron, Baron and Feme may join in Action of Waste. 17 *Ed.* 3. So if the Baron and Feme, during the Coverture, make a Lease, and Waste is committed.

In Action of Forcible Entry on the Wife's Land, she was joined with her Husband. 2 *Vent.* 195. In *Ejectione firmæ*, the Wife shall join. *Lit. Rep.* 285. Baron and Feme may join in a Writ of *Rescous*; and shall join in *Detinue*, for Charters concerning the Inheritance of the Wife; for the Wife shall have them again when recover'd. 15 *Ed.* 4. 38 *H.* 6.

If Goods are bail'd to a Feme Sole, or if she finds Goods, and after marries, *Detinue* must be brought against both. *Co. Lit.* 351.

Trover before Marriage, and Conversion after, was brought by Husband and Wife; and adjudged good, with or without the Wife; for the Trover gives the Inception of the Action to the Wife, although the Conversion is the Perfection of the Cause. 2 *Lev.* 107. Trover against Baron and Feme held good. *Latch* 126.

Trover was brought against Husband and Wife, and a Possession and Conversion laid in them both, and held to be good; because this Action is not grounded upon any Property

perty ſuppoſed in the Defendants, but in the Poſſeſſion only; and the Point of the Action is in the Converſion, which is a Tort wherewith a Feme Covert may be charg'd; for ſhe may be a Treſpaſſor, and convert Goods to the Uſe of her Huſband, or of a Stranger; although ſhe cannot convert them to her own Uſe. *Yelv.* 165. *Noy* 126. But *Cro. Car.* 254. *contra.*

Trover is brought by Baron and Feme, and laid *Ad Damnum ipſorum*, this is naught; becauſe Huſband and Wife cannot be Jointenants of Goods, the Law transferring, in Point of Ownerſhip, the whole Intereſt to the Huſband, and he muſt bring the Action. *Yelv.* 165.

Trover againſt Baron and Feme, ſuppoſing the Converſion to be to their proper Uſe; and for this Cauſe reverſed, becauſe it is the Converſion of the Baron only, for they are only to his Uſe; and though they may be charged with a joint Battery or Impriſonment, it cannot be ſo for Goods converted. *Cro. Jac.* 161.

Action of Trover was brought by the Huſband, for Money which the Wife had loſt at Cards, and Judgment was for him, tho' ſhe play'd in his Abſence; and yet he may have Action for the Money won by her. *Trin.* 6 *Jac. Ray* and *Stephens.*

An Action lies againſt the Huſband for Goods delivered to his Wife, if ſhe uſually bought Goods, and her Huſband paid for them; or if it can be intended or proved that theſe Goods came to the Huſband's Uſe. 1 *Lev.* 4, 5.

By the Custom of *London*, where the Feme Trades by herself in one Trade, with which her Husband doth not meddle, and buys and sells in that Trade, there the Feme shall be sued, and the Husband named only for Conformity; and if Judgment be given against him, Execution shall be sued only against the Feme. *Cro. Car.* 68.

A Feme buys Things for her necessary Apparel, it shall bind the Husband. 1 *Sid.* 120. So of necessary Diet, Lodging, &c. *Aleyn* 61. And where a Feme makes a Contract to the Use of her Husband, and it comes to his Use, it shall bind him. 20 *H.* 6.

Where Feme Coverts are allowed by their Husbands to be House-keepers, and they have used to buy Things upon Trust for the Houshold, the Husband shall be charged for them; for in such Respect the Wife is as a Servant. 1 *Sid.*109. *Soot* and *Manby*'s Case.

But if a Woman departs from her Husband, without his Consent, and the Husband prohibits several Persons from Trusting her; if afterwards, one who had Notice, trusts her with Necessaries, the Husband shall not be charged: And though after her Departure, she desires to cohabit with her Husband, which he refuses. 1 *Sid.* 109, 110.

Although a Wife is very lewd, if she lives with her Husband, he is chargeable for all Necessaries for her, because he took her *for better for worse*; and so he is if he runs away from her, or turns away his Wife, in which Case he gives her Credit where-ever she goes. But if she runs away from her Husband, then as soon as such Separation is Notorious, who-

ever

ever trusts her doth it at his Peril, and the Husband is not liable, unless he take her again. 1 *Salk. Rep.* 119. *Mod. Case* 171. Case of *Robinson* and *Gosnold.*

By *Holt*, Ch. Justice, while a Man and his Wife live together, the Husband shall answer all Contracts of hers. And if a Wife cohabit with her Husband, and by it gain a Credit, though she depart without Leave of her Husband, and come to *London*, and there become in Debt, the Husband shall be charged till Notice is given of her Elopement; for it shall be intended to be with the Consent of the Husband. But after Notice, the Husband shall not be charged, without his Assent appears. *Mich.* 4 *W.* & *M. Skinn. Rep.* 323.

If a Baron and Feme separate by Consent, and the Wife hath an Allowance for Clothes, &c. Tradesmen that deal with her, Trust her on her own Credit, where it is commonly known; and in such Case a personal Notice is not necessary. And as to Notice on an Elopement, &c. it is said, the putting the Wife in the *Gazette*, or other News Papers, is no legal Notice to Persons in general, not to trust her; though Personal Notice to particular Persons given by the Husband, will be good not to be chargeable to them. 1 *Vent.* 42. 1 *Sid.* 109. 1 *Salk.* 116.

A married Woman runs in Debt to a Tradesman, by taking up divers Goods, and she pawns the Goods before they are made into Clothes, her Husband shall not be compelled to pay for them, because they never came to his Use; but it is otherwise if they were made up and worn, and then pawned

for

for Money, then he ſhall be charged. *Paſch.* 2 *Ann. Etherington* ver. *Parrot.*

If a Feme Sole be indebted to *A. B.* and afterwards marries, this Debt is become by the Marriage the Debt of the Husband and Wife, (*viz.*) the proper Debt of the Wife, and the Debt of the Husband in Right of his Wife; and the Wife muſt be ſued for this Debt jointly with her Husband; and if the Husband die pending the Suit, yet is not the Debt gone; for ſhe may be ſued for it after the Death of her Husband; but if the Husband be not ſued for this Debt, during the Life of his Wife, he can never be ſued for it after her Death. *Trin.* 24 *Car. B. R.*

If there be a Judgment in Debt againſt a Feme Sole, who marries and dies, the Baron ſhall not be charged therewith. But where there is a Judgment againſt a Feme, who marries, and the Judgment is had upon *Scire facias*, againſt Baron and Feme, and then the Feme dies, a *Soire facias* will lie againſt the Baron, to ſhew Cauſe why Execution ſhould not go againſt him upon the firſt Judgment; for upon the Award of the Execution it became his Debt. 3 *Mod.* 186.

A Woman who was married, enters into a Bond, as a Feme Sole, and ſhe is afterwards ſued as a Feme Sole, and pleads *Non eſt factum*, ſhe may give in Evidence, her Coverture at the Time of the Sealing of the Bond, and that ſhall make the Bond void; for a Feme Covert cannot do any Act to oblige herſelf. 5 *W & M.* But a Feme, tho' not bound by her Agreement during Coverture,

yet

yet acting according to the Agreement, when a Widow, is bound by it. *Chanc. Rep.* 255.

If a Feme Sole owe me Money, and takes Husband, I may have an Action of Debt againſt them, and count that they owe me ſo much, without ſaying *Dum ſola fuit, &c.* for by the Marriage this is made the Debt of the Husband, during the Coverture. 1 *Bulſt.* 136.

Baron and Feme cannot be joined in one Action of Debt againſt them for ſeveral Contracts, the one made by the Wife *dum Sola*, the other by the Husband; as was *Revel* and *Gray*'s Caſe. *Revel* brought Action of Debt againſt *Gray* and his Wife, for 3 *l.* 18 *s.* and declared for 39 *s.* upon the Wife's Contract *Dum ſola fuit*, and the other 39 *s.* upon an *Inſimul computaverunt* with *Gray* the Husband, after Iſſue joined, and *Nil debent*, and Verdict *pro Quer'*. Judgment was ſtay'd. *Hob.* 184.

Where a Feme Covert is ſubpœned to give Evidence, and her Charges are tender'd to her, if ſhe neglects or refuſes to appear, an Action lies againſt her Husband and her upon the Stat. 5 *Eliz.* 1 *Leon.* 112.

An Action is brought againſt a ſingle Woman, who pending the Action marries; the Plaintiff ſhall, notwithſtanding the Marriage, proceed to Judgment againſt her, and take her in Execution, by the Name of Single Woman, according as the Action was commenced againſt her. *Trin.* 12 *W. B. R.*

An Action is brought againſt a Feme Sole, pending the Action ſhe married *A. B.* Judgment

ment was given againſt her, and a *Ca. Sa.* ſued out thereupon, upon which ſhe was taken: And reſolved, That where a Woman is found Guilty, and before Judgment takes Husband, the *Ca. Sa.* ſhall be ſued out againſt her, and not againſt her Husband. *Cro. Jac.* 323.

A Man and his Wife (in her Right) recovered in Debt, the Wife being dead, the Husband may ſue out a *Scire facias*, and have Execution; becauſe by the Judgment it became his own Debt. 1 *Mod.* 179. *Cro. Car.* 208.

A Feme Sole recovers Debt, and takes Husband, and Execution is upon that Judgment adjudged to the Husband and Wife; then the Wife dies, and the Husband ſues out a *Scire facias* in his own Name; and the Court ſeemed to be of Opinion that he well might; for that by this Awarding of Execution, the Husband ſhall have the Debt by Survivorſhip; and if the Husband ſhould die before Execution, the Adminiſtrator of his Wife ſhould have it. *Goodyear*'s Caſe. 9 *W.* 3. *B. R.*

Feme Covert Executrix, can do nothing to the Prejudice of her Husband. 5 *Rep.* 27. She cannot ſue without her Husband; and in Caſes as to Matters of Record, the Husband ought to be a Party, but not as to Matters of Fact. 16 *H.* 7. But where a Feme Covert was Executrix, and Judgment againſt the Husband and her, upon a *Scire feci*, it was objected, that the Feme could have no Goods, and therefore the Judgment was void. But it was held good; for the Husband being charged in the Right of his Wife, Judgment

ſhall

ſhall be againſt both. And in this Caſe, if the Husband had ſurvived the Wife, he ſhall be charged. *Cro. Car.* 519.

Action of *Account* was brought againſt a Feme Covert Adminiſtratrix, and her Huſband in *B. C.* and Judgment given againſt the Defendants, *Quod computent*, the Feme dies, and the Baron brings a Writ of Error in *B. R.* to reverſe this Judgment. *Per Curiam*: Writ of Error lies not, becauſe the Record cannot be removed by it; for that would diſturb the Proceedings in the Common Pleas, and the Party would have no Fruit of his Suit, if the Record were removed, nor any Remedy to recover the Money due to him; yet the Original is determined by the Judgment given, *Quod computent*, and a *Scire facias* lies by the Executor, as the Caſe here is. *Stile* 290.

Treſpaſs was brought for mean Profits. The Count was againſt Baron and Feme for Treſpaſs done *cum averiis ſuis*, and ſaith not whether they were their Beaſts after, or hers before Coverture. *Per Curiam*: It is good enough after a Verdict; for ſhe may be Executrix, and ſo by Marriage they may be his Goods; but then the Actions ſhould have been ſeveral, according to their ſeveral Capacities. And if the Goods of an Executrix, after taking Husband be ſtole, the Indictment muſt be for taking of his Goods. 1 *Keb.* 944. *Collingwood* and *Biſhop*.

An Action being brought by a Man againſt Sir *Thomas Pope*, and *A.* his Wife, as Daughter and Heir of Sir *Thomas W.* hanging the Writ, *Pope* died. *Hobart* was of Opinion, that the Writ ſhall not abate. But if an

Executrix

Executrix brings an Action in her own Name, and the Name of her Husband, and pendant the Writ, the Baron dies, the Writ ſhall abate. *Winch p.* 102.

The Feme pending a Writ againſt her, takes Husband, this does not abate the Writ; but the Recovery againſt her upon the firſt Writ is good. Though if after the Original Proceſs ſued, and before the Return ſhe take Huſband, this ſhall abate the Writ. 2 *Roll. Rep.* 53.

A Feme makes a Letter of Attorney to the Plaintiff, to recover a Debt, and then marries, this is not any Countermand or Revocation of the Suit, and the Writ is not abated but only abatable. 1 *Leon.* 186.

A Writ brought againſt Baron and Feme, abates by the Death of the Feme, though after Verdict. *Hob.* 129. And the Writ ſhall abate if the Wife be put before the Huſband. 2 *Leon.* 59.

If a Feme Sole have a Bill depending in the Court of Chancery, and pendent the Suit, takes Husband, by this her own Act her Suit is abated; and if ſhe and her Husband will have the Effect of the Suit, they muſt both join in a Bill of Revivor. But if a Feme in ſuch Caſe be Defendant, and marries, the Plaintiff may proceed in his Suit, for the Marriage is no Abatement where ſhe is Defendant.

The Plaintiff exhibits his Bill againſt a Feme Sole, whereto ſhe makes anſwer, and after marries, the Plaintiff may proceed againſt her and her Husband, without any Revivor, and the Husband ſhall be bound by that Anſwer ſhe made before Marriage, in regard ſhe ſhall not be admitted to take Advantage of her own Act. It is otherwiſe where a Woman Sole exhibits her Bill, to which the Defendant anſwers, and then ſhe marries, her Husband and ſhe cannot proceed againſt the Defendant without Bill of Revivor. *Baron and Feme, p.* 262.

A Man exhibits a Bill in Chancery againſt another Perſon and his Wife, for a Matter which wholly concerns the Wife, and both anſwer, and after the Baron dies, this is an Abatement of the Suit that the Plaintiff cannot proceed againſt the Feme, without Revivor; for the Feme ſhall not be conſtrained to abide by that Anſwer, which ſhe made with her Husband, becauſe ſhe was then under the Power and Coercion of the Husband, and he being dead, and ſhe ſeiſed and poſſeſſed of the Thing in Queſtion, as her former Eſtate, ſhe ought to make a new Anſwer, or ſhe may not be bound in Equity; but if ſhe abide by her Anſwer made with her Husband, then the Plaintiff may proceed, and have a Decree to bind her. *Ibid.* 263.

If a Formedon be brought by Baron and Feme, the Writ muſt conclude to the Feme only. The Caſe was, *Robert* Earl of *Eſſex*, and *Frances* his then Wife, by Fine, gave Lands to *W. G.* and *F. M.* and the Heirs of the ſaid *W.* to the Uſe of *Eliz. Sidney*, Daughter and Heir of Sir *Philip Sidney*, Knt. and for Default of ſuch Iſſue, to the Uſe of the ſaid Lady *Frances* and her Heirs; *Et que poſt mortem pred* Eliz. *ad prefat'* Franciſcam *revertere debent per formam Do-*

nationis pred' ac vigore Stat. Et eo quod pred Elizabetha *obiit sine herede de corpore suo exeunt'.* And the Earl and Countess counted accordingly. The Defendant, Viscount *Lisle*, pleaded in Abatement of the Writ, that the said Countess, at the Time of the Death of the said *Elizabeth*, was Covert of the Plaintiff, her now Husband; so that the Right of the said Tenement, *si quod, &c.* to her Husband and her, did Revert; and so by the said Writ it ought to be supposed. The Demandant demurs, and Judgment was given, That the Writ was sufficient. The Differences observed were, If it were a Formedon in Descender upon a Descent to the Wife, there the Descent in the Writ must be made to the Wife alone; for the Descent follows the Blood, and to that the Baron is a Stranger. But in a Formedon in Reverter, wherein already nothing is invested, but the Right only returns; there it may be laid to Return either to the Wife alone, or to the Baron and Feme. See *Hob. Rep.* 1, 2.

In Ejectment against Baron and Feme, if the Baron dies, the Plaintiff may proceed against the Wife. In an Ejectment, the Husband died after the *Nisi prius*, and before the Day in Bank. And *per Curiam*: Because it is in the Nature of a Trespass, and the Feme is charged for her own Fact, the Action continues against the Wife; and Judgment should be entered against her Sole, as the Husband was dead. *Cro. Jac.* 356.

A *Latitat* was su'd against Baron and Feme, the Feme was arrested, but the Baron could not be taken; the Sheriff returned *Cepi corpus* for the Wife, and *Non est inventus* for the

Baron. And the Court held nothing could be done in this Caſe, unleſs there were Bail put in by the Husband; for the Feme without the Husband cannot be ſued, nor can put in Bail; and againſt the Husband, unleſs he be firſt taken, and put in Bail, there cannot be any Declaration; and therefore in regard the Plaintiff could not declare, the Feme was diſmiſſed. It was ſaid, the Plaintiff ought to ſue them by Proceſs of Outlawry, and by that Means he might have Remedy; for it were a great Miſchief that a Feme Covert ſhould intermeddle, and merchandiſe, and procure Goods into her Hands, and the Baron abſenting himſelf, or keeping in his Houſe, there ſhould be no Remedy againſt them. *Cro. Jac.* 445.

An Action on the Caſe was brought againſt Baron and Feme, and the Feme appeared, and the Husband would not; and the Plaintiff's Attorney inſiſted upon ſpecial Bail for her, which ſhe could not procure, and thereupon, on Motion, it was prayed that ſhe might be delivered, giving common Bail only. By *Glin*, if there be Cauſe to have ſpecial Bail, the Wife muſt lie in Priſon until the Husband appear, and put in Bail for her; for ſhe cannot put in Bail for herſelf, ſhe being a Feme Covert. *Stile* 475. The Lady *Baltinglaſs*'s Caſe.

But in the Caſe of *Bart* and *Deſmond*, in Action of Debt againſt Baron and Feme, it was held unreaſonable that the Feme ſhould lie in Priſon 'till the Husband come in; that her giving common Bail was fitting, if another will be bound for her, but it is at the Election of the Wife, whether ſhe will or not;

and

and that she ought to be discharged without Bail, which the Court conceived reasonable, and so awarded here. Though in this Case it was agreed, that where the Feme is in Execution, she shall not be discharged; and if she be sued as a Feme, and only upon Process, she shall put in Bail. 1 *Keb.* 187.

The Husband only, and not his Wife, shall be imprisoned for Want of Bail, to an Action brought for the Debt of the Wife, when Sole; because the Wife cannot find Bail for herself, but the Husband must find Bail for her and himself, or be imprisoned; and before he is discharged, the Court will make him find Bail for himself and Wife. 1 *Lev.* 216.

In Action of Debt against Baron and Feme, if the Baron appears, and the Feme make Default, the Baron shall not be put to answer; but Process shall issue against the Wife, and *idem dies* given to the Husband. *Mich.* 11 *Jac.*

Action of Waste lies not against the Husband for Waste done by the Wife in her Lifetime, after her Death; for he is to be charg'd by Reason of his Wife, and jointly with her, and she being dead, the Action is gone, it being but a Personal Wrong done by her. If a Baron seised for Life of the Wife, and in her Right doth Waste, and after the Wife dies, no Action of Waste lies against the Husband in the *Tenuit*; for he was seised but in the Right of his Wife, and the Freehold was his Wife's. But if the Baron, possessed for Years in Right of his Wife, doth Waste, and the Wife dies, Action of Waste lies against the

the Husband, for that the Law gives the Term to him. *5 Co. 75.*

If a Leaſe for Years be made to Baron and Feme, and the Baron doth Waſte, and dies, and the Wife agrees to the Eſtate, an Action of Waſte lies againſt her, for ſhe is in from the Leſſor; and if the Action had been brought againſt Baron and Feme, the Writ ſhould have been *Quod fecerunt vaſtum*; for it was the Waſte of the Feme, as well as of the Baron. *2 Inſt.* 303.

Obligation is made to Baron and Feme, the Baron may bring the Action on this Obligation alone, in his own Name, or he may join the Wife at his Election. *Stile* 9.

And if a Bond be made to a Feme Sole, who marries, the Husband muſt join with her in the Suit. 1 *Keb.* 440.

In all Caſes where the Wife ſhall not have the Thing when it is recovered, neither ſole to herſelf, nor joint with her Husband, but the Husband only ſhall have it, there the Husband Sole ſhall have Action without the Wife to recover; as the Husband ſhall have Action ſole, *ſur Stat.* 5 R. 2. for entring into the Lands of the Wife. 38 *H.* 6.

If a Feme Sole hath a Rent-charge, and Rent is Arrear, and ſhe marries, and the Baron diſtrains for this Rent, on which a Reſcous is made, this is a Tort to the Baron himſelf, and he may have an Action alone. *Hill.* 38 *Eliz.*

A Feme has Right to have Common for Life, and ſhe takes Husband, and he is hindred in taking the Common, he may have an Action

Action alone, without his Wife, it being only to recover Damages. 2 *Bulst.* 14.

If *A.* demise a House to *B.* for Years, and *B.* covenants to repair the said House, during the Term, and after *A.* grants the Reversion to Baron and Feme, and the Heirs of the Baron, *&c.* the Baron may have an Action alone upon this Covenant; for therein Damages only are recoverable. *Cro. Jac.* 319.

A Lease is made to one for Years, rendring Rent, and to the Reversion granted to Baron and Feme, the Lessee attorns, and then Rent is Arrear, and the Term expires, the Baron may bring an Action alone for this Rent, because his Action is grounded upon the Duty, and not upon the Nature of their Estate, and the Money must accrue to the Baron; and there is no Difference where Baron and Feme are Joint-Lessors and Joint-Purchasors; in which Case it was never question'd but the Baron might bring the Action alone; but when brought by both, it hath been doubted. 2 *Bulst.* 233. *Lit. Rep.* 13.

A Man, in Consideration that a Feme Covert will cure a certain Wound, promises to pay unto her 10 *l.* if she performs the Cure accordingly, she may join with her Husband in an *Assumpsit* for this Money; for the Promise arising upon a Matter of Skill and Performance of the Wife, she is the Cause of the Action, and such an Action will survive to the Wife. *Trin.* 3 *Jac. Brashford* and *Buckingham* and his Wife.

But for a Promise or Personal Duty to the Wife, it has been adjudged that the Baron only may bring the Action; and the Husband is entitled to the Fruits of his Wife's Labour, for which he may bring a *Quantum meruit.* 1 *Lill. Abr.* 227. 1 *Salk.* 114.

A Feme Covert, by the Custom of *London*, shall sue without her Husband, as a *Feme Sole Merchant*; but the Action must be laid within the City. And every Feme which Trades in *London*, is not a Feme Sole Merchant. 1 *Leon.* 131.

Where the Husband is under Abjuration, Feme Coverts have been held able to sue without naming their Husbands. Sir *Robert Belknap*'s Lady, her Husband being in Exile beyond Sea, sued a Writ of Dower in her own Name, without him, and recovered it. *H.* 4.

In the Reign of *Edward* II. in *Weyland*'s Case, it was held, that after the Abjuration of the Husband, his Wife should have her Jointure; and an Action was brought by her alone for a Personal Wrong done to the Estate conveyed to her. 1 *Inst.* 132.

And on the other Hand, in *Assumpsit* for Wages and Money lent, on *Non assumpsit* the Defendant proved she was married, and her Husband alive in *France*. The Jury found for the Plaintiff, upon which, as a Verdict against Evidence, she moved for a new Trial; but it was denied her; for it shall be intended she was divorced. Besides, the Husband was an Alien Enemy. 1 *Inst.* 132.

If Baron and Feme are divorced *Causa Adulterii*, and after the Wife sues Sole without the Husband, for a Defamation, altho' the Divorce does not dissolve the Marriage; yet because the Wife may sue as a Feme Sole, in such Case, by the Course of the Spiritual

Court, no Prohibition ſhall be granted, tho' it be againſt the Uſage of our Law. 2 *Roll. Abr.* 298.

For Felony, *&c.* Wives are indictable without their Husbands. *Sid.* 410. If a Wife takes away her Husband's Goods, it is not Felony; tho' if an Adulterer receives them, it will be Felony in him. 3 *Co. Inſt.*

Baron and Feme bring an Action in the Nature of a Conſpiracy, for falſely indicting of them, *Ad dampnum ipſorum*; and moved that the Wife cannot join with her Husband for the Damages; for it is a ſeveral Damage to either of them: And of that Opinion was *Berkley*; *Croke contra*, becauſe it is grounded upon an entire Record; and they were both prejudiced, where they may join if they will, or the Husband only may have the Action. *Cro. Car.* 553.

In Treſpaſs brought by Baron and Feme, for impriſoning the Wife until a Fine paid; for all the Treſpaſs, except the Fine, they ſhall recover Damages in Common. 11 *H.* 4. But for the Fine the Husband ſhall recover Damages ſole, becauſe it was Chattel.

The Husband ſhall not be impriſoned for the Fine of his Wife, neither ſhall the Fine be levied upon the Goods of the Husband; but a *Capias pro Fine* ſhall iſſue out againſt the Wife; for it is meerly Perſonal. *Mich.* 5 *W. & M. B. R.*

In Aſſiſe by Baron and Feme, if it be found they were diſſeiſed, they ſhall recover Damages of the Iſſues in Common. 11 *H.* 4. Yet where it is found that certain Goods of the Husband's were taken upon the Land, the Husband

Husband Sole shall have Judgment of the Damages for them.

If the Baron be possessed of a Term, in Right of the Wife, and Damages are recovered against him, the Damages shall not affect the Term of the Wife, after the Death of the Husband, in regard she came in Paramount. *Aliter* if an Extent be upon it, or on a Recognisance in the Life of the Husband. 9 *H.* 6.

Baron and Feme join in an Action, and a Verdict is given for the Plaintiffs, and the Jury assess Damages *ultra misas & custagias per ipsum* (which is the Husband) *circa sectam suam exposit'* to so much, and *pro misis & custagiis illis* to so much. And upon this Judgment is given, That the Husband and Wife shall recover the Costs and Damages; altho' it is found that the Husband only expended and disbursed the Money for the Costs of Suit, for as much as the Wife had nothing; yet the Judgment is good that the Baron and Feme shall recover the Costs; for there may not be one Judgment for the Costs, and another for the Damages. 1 *Roll. Abr.* 516.

Where Baron and Feme are sued, the Feme cannot make an Attorney; but the Husband must make an Attorney for himself and his Wife. 2 *Saund.*

A Woman gives a Warrant of Attorney to confess Judgment, and then marries, you may file a Bill, and enter Judgment against both Husband and Wife, by the Practice of the Court. *Show. Rep.* 91. But it has been held, that by the Marriage of the Woman, the Warrant is countermanded; and Judgment

ment ſhall not be entered againſt Husband and Wife. 1 *Salk.* 399.

The Husband being a Priſoner in the King's Bench, a Declaration was filed againſt him and his Wife, and Judgment thereupon obtained againſt them by Default, and a Writ of Enquiry executed, and the Woman taken in Execution; but upon a Motion, the Judgment was vacated, and a *Superſedeas* granted to the Execution againſt the Wife.

If Baron and Feme are outlawed, and the Wife is taken thereon, ſhe ſhall be ſet at Liberty, and the Husband be compelled to appear for his Wife; becauſe he may bring a *Superſedeas*, which ſhe cannot do. *Lit.Rep.*18.

A Man and his Wife are Tenants for Life, and the Baron acknowledges a Recogniſance, the Feme ſhall hold the Land diſcharged after the Death of the Baron. 8 *R.* 2.

But if the Husband be indebted to the King, and he purchaſes Lands for Years, to him and his Wife, and dies, this Land ſhall be put in Execution for the ſaid Debt, becauſe the Baron had Power to diſpoſe of the Term. 2 *Roll. Abr.* 157.

If a Leaſe for Years be made to Baron and Feme, rendring Rent, after the Death of the Baron, if the Feme agree to the Leaſe, Debt lies againſt her for all the Arrears due in the Life of the Baron: But after his Death, ſhe may diſagree to the Leaſe. 2 *H.* 4.

Baron and Feme grant a Rent for Equality of Partition, this ſhall bind the Wife after the Death of the Husband, and ſhall be intended for her Benefit. 50 *Ed.* 3.

A Feme

A Feme Covert borrows Money of a Man, and with it cloaths herself better than doth belong to her Quality, although this comes to the Use of the Baron, because his Feme of Necessity ought to be cloathed; yet because it is beyond her Degree, he is not chargeable with it. 11 *H.* 6.

If the Wife buys any thing for Herself, Children, or Family, and the Husband does any Act precedent or subsequent, whereby he shews his Consent, though he shall not be charged upon an *Assumpsit* in Law, he may be charged by Reason of his *Assumpsit* in Fact. *Pasch.* 15 *Car.* 2. *Manby* and *Scot.*

If a Feme be indebted to another, and takes Husband, and dies, the Baron shall not be charged in Debt for this after the Death of the Feme. 10 *H.* 6.

And if a Judgment in Debt is had against a Feme Sole, and she marries and dies, the Husband shall not be charged; for he is not liable to her Debts before Coverture, unless they be afterwards recover'd in her Life-time. *Hill.* 3 *Jac.*

A Feme Lessee for Life, rendring Rent, takes Husband and dies, the Baron shall be charged in an Action of Debt, for the Rent incurred during the Coverture, because he took the Profits out of which the Rent ought to Issue. 10 *H.* 6.

The Baron in an Account shall not be charged by the Receipt of his Wife, except the Money receiv'd came to his Use. 1 *Danv.* 707.

A Feme Covert cannot submit to an Award, for the Submission is a free Act; and the

Will of a Feme Covert is ſubject to the Will of her Husband, and ſo is not free. But another Perſon may ſubmit to an Award for a Matter which concerns the Feme, and be bound to the Performance of it; and ſuch a Submiſſion is good in Law; for it may be he may receive Benefit by the Submiſſion; yet if he do not, it is of no Signification.

No Feme Covert can be Evidence, either againſt or for her Husband, nor the Baron againſt the Feme, in any Caſe except Treaſon, becauſe it might occaſion implacable Diſſention. 1 *Inſt*. 6.

Of the Laws of Procreation of Children, by a Man and his Wife; and therein of Baſtards or ſpurious Iſſue.

IT hath been ſaid that the chief Buſineſs of Matrimony is to get Children, and ſuch Children ſhall enjoy the Eſtates and Poſſeſſions of their Anceſtors, according to the Rules of Diſcent by the Common Law, or purſuant to Limitations and Settlements made by ſuch Anceſtors in their Lives Time.

And Lands deſcend to the Worthieſt of Blood; ſo that the elder Son and his Iſſue, ſhall inherit before the Younger, or any of his Iſſue; and all the Females of the Part of the Father, before any of the Males on the

Side

Side of the Mother. And if there be no Heirs Male to an Estate, then shall it descend to Females as Parceners, &c. *Co. Lit.* 12, 13.

If a Person marry the Widow of a Man lately dead, who at the Time of her Husband's Decease, was with Child, and the Child is born after Marriage solemnised with the second Husband, this Child it is said shall be Heir to the second Husband, and adjudged his lawful Son.

But by *Thorpe* and *Willoughby*, 21 *E*. 2. if a Man die seised of Land in Fee-simple, and the Wife which is *privement ensient* with a Son, marry again, and after is delivered, this Son shall be Son and Heir to the first Baron, and not to the second. Tho' Justice *Bert* was of Opinion, that the Infant might chuse his Father. And it would be better Reason perhaps, if the second Husband might chuse whether he should be his Son, or no; and by Allowance make him his Heir.

Sir *Edward Coke* tells us, That if a Man marries and dies, within a short Space after, and the Wife marries again, and within Nine Months has a Child, such Child may be Heir to the first or second Husband, at his Election. *Co. Lit.* 8.

In ancient Times, Women used to feign themselves with Child, and impose upon the World borrowed Children, to deprive the right Heir of the Deceased of his Inheritance. And *Bracton* mentions a Writ directed to the Sheriff, by Virtue of which he was to call before him, the Woman pretending to be with Child, to have her examin'd by Tractation and Search of good and lawful Women, whether

whether ſhe were pregnant or not; and if the Matter were found doubtful, ſhe was to be committed to a Caſtle, and there remain without Acceſs of any ſuſpected Perſon. *Bract.*

Anno 4 *H.* 3. *Thomas de Aldham*, of *Surrey*, Brother of *Adam de Aldham*, claimed his Brother's Eſtate, who was then lately dead. But *Joan*, Widow of the ſaid *Adam*, pleaded ſhe was with Child; whereupon the ſaid *Thomas* obtained the Writ *De Ventre inſpiciendo*, directed to the Sheriff, to make Inquiſition, *&c.*

And *Anno* 29 of Queen *Elizabeth*, Sir *Francis Willoughby*, dying ſeiſed of a great Eſtate of Inheritance, left five Daughters and *Dorothy* his Wife, who at the Time of Sir *Francis*'s Death, pretended herſelf to be with Child by him, which, if it were a Son, all the five Siſters would loſe the Inheritance deſcended to them: They prayed a Writ *De Ventre inſpiciendo* out of Chancery, directed to the Sheriff of *London*, that he ſhould cauſe the ſaid *Dorothy* to be viewed by twelve Knights, and to be ſearched by twelve Women in the Preſence of the twelve Knights, *Et ad tractand' per ubera & ad ventrem inſpiciend'*, whether ſhe was with Child, and to certify the ſame into the Common Bench; and if ſhe were with Child, to certify for how long Time, in their Judgments, *Et quando ſit paritura.* Whereupon the Sheriff accordingly cauſed her to be ſearched, and returned that ſhe was twenty Weeks gone with Child, and that within twenty Weeks *fuit paritura.* Upon this another Writ iſſued out of the Common Bench, commanding the Sheriff

riff ſafely to keep her in ſuch a Houſe, and that every Day he would cauſe her to be viewed by ſome of the Women named in the Writ, (ten being named therein) and ſome to be preſent at the Delivery, and to view the Birth, whether it were Male or Female; and the Sheriff returned, that ſuch a Day ſhe was delivered of a Daughter. *Cro. Eliz.* 566.

In the Reign of King *James* I. a Caſe happened with the like Circumſtances and Proceedings as in the preceding, on this Difference. The Lady *Willoughby* was a Widow, but this was of a Feme Covert, who married within a Week after the Death of her firſt Husband, who is ſuppoſed to get the Child; and they did not take ſuch a Courſe, as in the Lady *Willoughby*'s Caſe, of delivering her into the Sheriff's Cuſtody, but left her with her Husband, he entring into a Recogniſance that ſhe ſhould not remove from the Houſe wherein they inhabited; and that one or two of the Women ſhould ſee her every Day, and two or three be preſent at her Travel; for this Iſſue might well be ſaid to be the Child of the firſt Husband, and ſhould inherit the Land. And after this Courſe obſerved ſhe was delivered of a Female Child, who was afterwards, by Inquiſition on Office, found to be the Daughter and Heir of the firſt Husband. *Cro. Jac.* 685. *Thecar*'s Caſe. *Winch. Rep.* 71.

A Petition

A Petition *for a Writ* De Ventre inſpiciendo.

To the Right Honourable *P.* Lord *K.* Lord High Chancellor of *Great Britain.*

The humble Petition of A. B. *of*, &c.

SHEWETH,

'THAT whereas *T. B.* being in his Life-'time ſeiſed in his Demeſne as of Fee, 'of and in certain Lands and Tenements in 'the County of, *&c.* lately died ſeiſed, ha-'ving, at the Time of his Death, no Iſſue of his 'Body lawfully begotten. And whereas *K.* late 'Wife and Relict of the ſaid *T. B.* ſince his 'Death, hath and ſtill doth pretend and give 'out Speeches, that ſhe is impregnate by the 'ſaid *T. B.* to the Diſheriſon of your ſaid 'Petitioner, who is next of Kin, and Heir 'to the Deceaſed *T. B.* and to whom the ſaid 'Lands and Tenements by Right of Inhe-'ritance do deſcend, the ſaid *T. B.* dying 'without Iſſue of his Body lawfully begot-'ten. And leaſt the ſaid *K.* out of a Deſign 'to deprive your Petitioner of his Inheri-'tance, impoſe upon your Petitioner a Sup-'poſititious Child, as Heir of the ſaid *T. B.* 'declaring the ſame to be born of her Body, 'after the Death of the ſaid *T. B.* to the

'Disherison of your Petitioner, against E-
'quity and good Conscience;

May it please your Lorship to grant to your Petitioner his Majesty's most gracious Writ *De Ventre inspiciendo*, to the Sheriff of, *&c.* directed, returnable, *&c.*

And your Petitioner shall ever pray, &c.

A. B.

Bracton says, That if the Feme hath not an Infant within forty Weeks after her Husband's Death, or if she be not found *Ensient*, she shall be punished by Fine and Imprisonment. But if the Feme hath a Child within forty Weeks, then such Infant shall have the Heritage, if the Heir cannot prove the Infant to be another's, and not the Husband's.

It has been held amongst Physicians, that by the Rules of Nature, the exact Time for the Birth of an Infant is 280 Days from the Conception; that is forty Weeks, which is nine Months and ten Days, accounting thirty Days to every Month: But it is natural, if the Birth be at any Time within ten Months.

In the Case of Doctor *Andrews*, 2 *Jac. B.R.* He died 23 *March*; his Wife *Privment ensient*, which was born 5 *January* after, by Computation forty Weeks and ten Days after the Death of the Husband; and the Physicians, upon Conference, held that twenty Days backwards, or twenty Days forwards, do not take away any Legitimation, though forty Weeks is the *Tempus constitutum*. *Lit. Rep.* 178.

By Accident an Infant may be born after the forty Weeks or before; and in this Case of Dr. *Andrews*, he died of the Plague, so that he was Sick but one Day before his Death; and the Woman's Father-in-Law, used her with great Inhumanity, and caused her to lie in the Streets several Nights: She was in Travel six Weeks, before she was delivered, and then she was delivered within twenty-four Hours after she was taken into the House and well used, which was a good Proof of Legitimation; though it was prov'd at the same Time, that she was a lewd Woman of her Body. And at the Trial of Doctor *Andrews*'s Heir, Doctor *Chamberlain* informed the Court, upon his Oath, that he had known a Woman to be delivered of one Child, and two Weeks after to be delivered of another.

A Woman after forty Weeks and eight Days was delivered of a Daughter. By the Doctors it may be Legitimate; for as *Antenatus* might be Heir in a Child born at the End of seven Months, so might *Postnatus* actually born after forty Weeks; and they said a Child may be Legitimate, though it be born the last Day of the tenth Month, after the Conception, accounting the Months *per Menses solares*, not *Lunares*. *Cro.* 571. *Alsop*'s Case.

If a Man hath a Child by a Woman, and afterwards Intermarries with her, yet the Issue is a Bastard by our Law. *Contra*, if the Woman be with Child by a Man, and after he marries her, and the Issue is born within the Espousals, this is not a Bastard. Nor is it in the first Case by the Civil Law. *2 Co. Inst.* 96, 97.

Though 10 *Ed.* 1. one *R.* being infirm, and in his Bed, was married to *A.* a Woman, by the Bishop of *London* privately, in no Church or Chapel, nor with the Celebration of any Mass, the said *A.* being then with Child by the said *R.* and within twelve Weeks after the Marriage, *A.* was delivered of a Son, and adjudged a Bastard, and so the Land escheated to the Lord, by the Death of *R.* without Heir. *Foxcroft*'s Case.

If a Man, having one Wife, takes another Wife, and hath Issue by her, living the first Wife, this Issue is a Bastard, because the second Marriage is void. *Co.* 7.

But where a Man marries his Sister, or his Cousin, within the Degrees, the Issue between them is no Bastard, 'till a Divorce be had, for the Marriage is not void. 18 *H.*6. 39 *Ed.* 3.

If the Husband be gelt, so that he cannot by any Possibility beget a Child, and his Wife hath Issue several Years after, this will be a Bastard, though it be begotten within Marriage, because it is apparent it cannot be Legitimate. *Hill.* 14 *Jac.* 1 *Inst.* 244.

And if a Woman have Issue, the Husband being but seven Years of Age, at the Birth, this Issue is a Bastard; for it cannot be intended by Law that it was begot by the Baron. It is the same in Case the Husband be Eight or Nine Years of Age at the Time of the Issue. And it is said, that if a Woman hath Issue, her Husband being within the Age of Fourteen, the Issue is a Bastard. 1 & 18 *H.* 6. 38 *Ass.* 24.

If a Feme Covert has Iſſue, and the Huſband hath been ſo long over the Sea, before the Birth of the Child, which his Wife hath in his Abſence, that it cannot be his Child, this is a Baſtard. 18 *H.* 6. See 1 *Salk. Rep.* 122.

By the Law of the Land, a Man cannot be a Baſtard, who is born after Eſpouſals, unleſs it be by ſpecial Matter, as in the Caſes before-mentioned. A Woman is big with Child by one, and another marries her, if the Child is born but three Days after Marriage, it is not a Baſtard. 1 *Danv. Abr.* 729.

And if a Feme Covert hath Iſſue in Adultery, yet if her Husband be able to beget Children, and is within the four Seas, this is no Baſtard. 39 *Ed.* 3.

If a Wife leaves her Husband, and lives with another Man, and during this Iſſue is born in Adultery, this is a Mulier, by our Law; but the Baron ought to be within the four Seas, ſo as by Intendment he may come to his Wife, otherwiſe it is a Baſtard. And by the Spiritual Law ſuch Iſſue is a Baſtard. *Hill.* 14 *Jac.*

By the Common Law, if the Husband be *infra quatuor Maria*, and the Wife hath a Child, it will not be a Baſtard; but he is a Baſtard who is born of a Woman, when her Husband, at and from the Time of Begetting, to the Birth, is *extra quatuor Maria.* 1 *Inſt.* 244. 2 *Salk.* 483.

If the Wife continues in Adultery, and hath Iſſue, this hath been held to be a Baſtard; and Children born in Adultery, are born out of the Limits of Matrimony. 1 *Danv. Abr.* 730.

When a Husband and Wife consent to live separate, the Children born after such Separation shall be taken to be Legitimate; because the Access of the Husband shall be presumed; but if it be found there was no Access, then they are Bastards. 1 *Salk.* 122.

A Divorce, *causa pre-contractus*, bastardizes the Issue; so *causa Affinitatis*, *Frigiditatis*, *&c.*

But if Baron and Feme continue Baron and Feme during all their Lives, the Issue cannot be a Bastard by a Divorce after their Deaths, for the Divorce in the Spiritual Court is *pro peccatis*, which may not be after their Deceases; and therefore such Divorce there is only to disinherit the Issue, which they cannot do. 7 *Co.* 44.

If *A.* marries *B.* and after they are divorced, *causa Frigiditatis* of the said *A.* so that for three Years after the Marriage, she *remansit virgo intacta propter perpetuam impotentiam*, *&c.* and after *A.* marries *C.* by whom he hath Issue in the Life of *B.* this Issue is Legitimate; for by the Divorce, the Marriage was dissolved; and if the second Marriage is voidable, yet it continues 'till it is dissolved, which cannot be after the Death of the Parties. Adjudged upon a special Verdict. *Mich.* 40 *&* 41 *Eliz.* Case of *Webber* and *Bury.*

A Remainder is limited to *A. B.* Son of *E. B.* although he be a meer Bastard, and no *Mulier*; if he is reputed for his Son, it is a good Remainder. But if an Estate for Life be made, the Remainder to the Issue of the Body

Body of *E. B.* or of him begotten on the Body of *K. B.* if he has afterwards illegitimate Iſſue, ſuch Iſſue ſhall never take this Remainder, becauſe he cannot have the Reputation of Iſſue before they are born. 1 *Inſt.*3.

If *A.* makes a Feoffment in Fee, to the Uſe of himſelf for Life, Remainder to the eldeſt Iſſue Male of one *C. D.* of her Body begotten by *A.* the Feoffor, whether he be lawfully begotten or not, if he be the reputed Son of *A.* it is ſufficient for him to intitle himſelf to ſay, That he is Son of the ſaid *A.* begotten on the Body of the ſaid *C. D.* and that he is ſo reputed in the common Fame of the Country, though he was not born, nor *in eſſe*, at the Time of the Remainder granted; and although there are lawful Iſſues between them, which are *puiſne* to the Baſtard; for the Perſon who is to take, is certainly deſcribed, and the Baſtard of a Woman is known to be her Iſſue, and this is limited to the eldeſt Iſſue. *Mich.* 38 & 39 *Eliz.*

By a Deviſe of all a Man's Goods to his Children, a Baſtard *eigne* ſhall take a Portion.

But notwithſtanding a Baſtard be a reputed Son, yet he is not ſuch a Son, in Conſideration whereof an Uſe can be raiſed to him, becauſe in Conſtruction of Law, he is *Nullius Filius.* 1 *Inſt.* 123.

Where a Man hath a Son by a Woman before Marriage, which is a Baſtard, and unlawful; and after he marries the Mother of the Baſtard, and they have another Son, this ſecond Son is *Mulier* and lawful, and ſhall be Heir to his Father; and they are diſtinguiſh'd in our old Books, with the Addition of *Bastard eigne* and *Mulier puisne*. *Co.Lit.*170, 243.

A Man seised of Lands in Fee, and hath Issue *Bastard eigne*, and *Mulier puisne*, and dies, if the Bastard enters, and the *Mulier* dies, his Wife *priviment ensient* with a Son, and the Bastard hath Issue and dies seised, then the Son is born, his Right is bound for ever; but if the Bastard dies seised, his Wife *ensient* with a Son, whereupon the *Mulier* enters and the Son is born, the Issue of the Bastard is barred; for there must be not only a dying seised, but a Discent to his Issue. 1 *Co. Inst.* 244.

And the Case of *Bastard eigne* and *Mulier puisne* differs from the common Cases of Descents; for Descents do only Toll the Entry of him who has Right, and leaveth him to his Action; but if a Man seised of Lands in Fee hath Issue two Sons, *Bastard eigne* and *Mulier puisne*, and the Father dies, the Bastard enters, claiming as Heir to his Father, and occupies the Lands for his Life, without any Entry made upon him by the *Mulier*, and the Bastard hath Issue and dies seised, and the Land descends to his Issue, who enters, in this Case the *Mulier* is barred for ever, both of his Entry and his Action, the Issue being become, in Judgment of Law, lawful Heir. 1 *Inst.* 244.

The Question of Bastardy, or Legitimation, ought to be first moved in the Temporal Courts, and Issue to be there joined, and then transmitted to the Ecclesiastical Court by the King's Writ, to be examined and tried there; and thereupon the Bishop shall

ſhall make his Certificate to the King's Court, which being duly made, the Law gives entire Credit to it. *Dav. Rep.* 52.

Where an Iſſue is joined upon Baſtardy, before it ſhall be awarded to the Ordinary to be tried, Proclamation is to be made thereof in the ſame Court; and afterwards the Iſſue ſhall be certified into Chancery, where Proclamation ſhall be likewiſe made once a Month, for three Months; and afterwards the Chancellor is to certify this to the Court where the Plea is depending; and then it ſhall be proclaimed again in the ſame Court, that all thoſe whom this Plea doth concern, may go to the Ordinary to make their Allegations. 9 *H.* 6.

General Baſtardy ought to be tried by the Biſhop, and not *per pais*, 18 *Ed.* 4. and ſpecial Baſtardy; as whether one was born or begotten before or within the Eſpouſals; or whether a Woman be a Man's Wife or not, or ſhe were married to another before. Theſe Matters being ſpecially alledged, and put in Iſſue, it ſhall be tried *per pais*. *Hard.* 2, 63.

If the Iſſue be, whether born before Marriage; and in an Iſſue againſt an Infant, if Baſtardy be pleaded in the Infant, this ſhall not be tried by the Ordinary, but *per pais*; becauſe the Infant is not compellable to take Iſſue upon it; for then he ſhould loſe the Advantage of the Inquiry of Circumſtances, and ſo no Iſſue can be joined upon this; and if Iſſue be not joined between the Parties, the Ordinary ſhall not try it. 30 *Aſſ.* 45.

But if Iſſue be whether a Baſtard or a *Mulier*, it ſhall be tried by the Ordinary, by Certificate

And no Courts, but the King's Courts of Record, as the Court of King's Bench, Common Pleas, Justices of Assise, and Gaol-Delivery, *&c.* may write to the Bishop to certify Bastardy; for it is a Rule in Law, That none but the King can write to a Bishop to certify; and therefore no inferior Court, as *London*, *Norwich*, *York*, *&c.* can write to the Bishop; in such Cases, the Plea must be removed *in Banco*; and this Court ought to write to the Bishop, and after to remand it again. 1 *Inst.* 134.

In Assise, if the Tenant saith that *A.* the Father of the Plaintiff, took *B.* to Wife, and had Issue the Plaintiff; and after they were divorced, and so the Plaintiff is a Bastard; to which the Plaintiff answers, That he is a Mulier; upon which a Writ is directed to the Bishop, who certifies that the Plaintiff was born in loyal Matrimony, without fully certifying that he is a Mulier; and although the Tenant had acknowledged in his Plea, that there was a Marriage, and that the Plaintiff was born in it; yet because, if there was a Divorce, then this was not a lawful Marriage, the Certificate aforesaid is good, which certifies that he was born in lawful Marriage. 43 *Ass.* 43.

If a Man be certified a Bastard by the Ordinary, he shall be perpetually bound against all the World, to avoid a contrary Certification, and because it is the highest Trial thereof. *Br. Trial* 9.

But if a Man be certified a Mulier, by the Ordinary, this is not any Estoppel, because he may be a Bastard by our Law notwithstanding.

ſtanding. Upon Iſſue of Baſtard, or not, if the Ordinary certify that the Plaintiff was a Mulier, *prout per Inquiſitionem invenit*; this is good without certifying generally *Legitimus*. 3 *H*. 6.

It is only in the Power of the King and Parliament, to make a Baſtard Legitimate. *Dav*. 57.

I ſhall conclude this Chapter with the Laws relating to Baſtardy, where it affects not the Eſtates of Anceſtors; but the Parents are obliged to provide for the Child, or undergo a Corporal Puniſhment.

By 18 *Eliz*. two Juſtices of Peace (one of the *Quorum*) near the Pariſh in which a Baſtard is born, may upon their Examination take Order for the Puniſhment of the reputed Father and Mother; and alſo for the better Relief of the Pariſh; and may charge the Mother or reputed Father with the Payment of Money weekly, for the Relief of ſuch Child. And if the reputed Father or Mother ſhall, upon Notice of ſuch Order in Writing, refuſe to pay the ſame, then the Perſon refuſing ſhall be committed to the common Gaol, until he find Sureties to perform the Order; or elſe to appear at the next General Seſſions of the Peace, and obey ſuch Order as ſhall be made there, *&c*.

An Order of Justices for the Maintenance of a Bastard Child.

Gloucester ss. *THE Order of* A. B. *and* C. D. *Esqs; two of his Majesty's Justices of the Peace for the said County (one whereof is of the* Quorum) *and both now residing near to the Parish of,* &c. *in the County aforesaid, made this Day,* &c. *in the Year of our Lord* 1719. *according to the Form of the Statute in that Case made and provided concerning a Bastard Child lately born in the said Parish of,* &c. *of the Body of* E. F. *single Woman; which Bastard Child ever since its Birth, hath been and is still chargeable to the said Parish, and is likely so to continue.*

FIRST, *Upon Examination of the Cause, and Circumstances of Premisses, taken upon Oath, before us, and due Consideration thereof, we do adjudge* G. H. *of,* &c. *Yeoman, to be the putative Father of the said Bastard Child. And we do Order that as well for the Relief of the said Parish of,* &c. *in Part, as also for a Provision for the said Bastard Child, that he the said* G. H. *shall weekly and every Week, from the Time of the Birth of the said Child, and so long*

long as the same shall be chargeable to the said Parish of, &c. *pay or cause to be paid, unto the Church-wardens or Overseers of the Poor of the Parish aforesaid, for the Time being, the Sum of* 2 s. *for and towards the Maintenance of the said Child; and shall likewise pay or cause to be paid unto the Church-wardens or Overseers of the Poor of the Parish aforesaid, for the Time being, the Sum of* 4 l. *within three Months after the said Bastard Child shall arrive at his Age of Twelve Years, for and towards the placing forth the said Child to be an Apprentice. And farther, we do hereby order, that the said* E. F. *shall every Week, for so long Time thereof as the said Child shall be chargeable as aforesaid, and she shall not keep the same, pay or cause to be paid, unto the Church-wardens or Overseers of the Poor of the Parish of,* &c. *aforesaid, for the Time being,* 1 s. *for and towards the farther Maintenance of the said Child. And lastly, we do order, that the said* G. H. *do, upon Notice of this our Order, forthwith give sufficient Security to the Church-wardens and Overseers of the Poor of the Parish of,* &c. *well and truly to perform so much thereof as doth concern the said* G. H. *and which, on his Part, is hereby ordered to be done and performed.* In Witness, *&c.*

Justices in Sessions have the same Power to do all Things concerning Bastards, that Justices in their several Counties have. 3 *Car.* 1. But if Justices of Peace, in their Sessions, revoke an Order of two Justices, for keeping a Bastard Child, they are liable to keep the Child

Child themselves, if no Father can be found. 1 *Vent. Rep.* 59.

On an Appeal the Sessions will either affirm or quash the Order made by the two Justices. A Motion was made in the Quarter-Sessions to quash an Order made that one should keep his reputed Child, because he had kept him heretofore; but it not appearing by the Order, either that he was his Bastard, or his lawfully begotten Child, the Order was quashed. *Style Rep.* 154.

An unmarried Woman, big with Child, was remov'd from *Westbury* to *Corsham* in *Wiltshire*, and there she was delivered. *Corsham* appealed to the next Sessions, and there the Order was reversed: Afterwards two Justices sent the Child, by Order, to *Corsham*, where it was born; and upon their Appeal, this last Order was confirmed. At last, it being removed in *B. R.* it was adjudged that the Birth did not settle the Child at *Corsham*, because the Mother was there under an illegal Order, procured by *Westbury*, which being reversed, it must now be taken that they unlawfully procured the Woman to go to *Corsham*. *Trin.* 3 *Annæ*, *B. R.* 1 *Salk.*

It is said that the two Justices have no Power to commit a Person for not performing their Order, but they are to bind him in a Recognizance to appear at the next Quarter-Sessions. *Bulst.* 341.

And Justices have no Power, but to indemnify the Parish, (*viz*) only to oblige the putative Father to maintain the Child, as long as it is or may be chargeable to the Parish; for

for the Father may take the Child when he pleaſes, and maintain it himſelf. 2 *Saund.*82.

If the Child dies after the Order is made, and before the next Seſſions, and no Security is given to perform the Order, yet when the Party appears at Seſſions, the Juſtices may order him to pay the Charges, upon Proof of ſerving the Order. And an Order made to pay ſuch Charges as the Pariſh had been at, without ſaying *That the Child was likely to be chargeable*, &c. was held good. 1 *Vent.* 37.

A Baſtard of a Perſon, able to keep it, and not likely to become chargeable to the Pariſh, is not within the Statute 18 *Eliz.* If the Father of a Baſtard Child pay a competent Sum of Money in Groſs, to the Overſeers of the Poor, for Maintenance of the Child, he ſhall be diſcharged. And if the reputed Father, or the Mother have Lands or Goods, the Church-wardens and Overſeers of the Poor, by Order of two Juſtices, may ſeiſe ſo much of the ſaid Goods, and receive the Rents of the Lands, towards the Diſcharge of the Pariſh. 24 *Car.* 2. *c.* 12.

Two Juſtices of Peace may inflict a Corporal Puniſhment upon the reputed Father, not being of Ability to diſcharge the Pariſh, by Whipping, Stat. 18 *Eliz.* And the Juſtices may commit lewd Women to the Houſe of Correction, who have Baſtards that may be chargeable to the Pariſh, there to be puniſhed, and ſet at work for a Year. 7 *Jac.*1.

But if the Woman will diſcharge the Pariſh, ſhe cannot be puniſhed by this Act; though by 18 *Eliz.* ſhe may be puniſhed with

with Whipping; as may likewise the reputed Father, though it is not usually done.

In the Hundred of *Middleton*, in the County of *Kent*, according to ancient Records, he that gets a Bastard shall forfeit all his Goods and Chattels to the King. *MS. Temp. Ed.*3.

And in some Parts of *England*, by the Customs and Tenures of Manors, a Widow that has a Bastard, forfeits her Estate, unless she comes into the Court of the Manor, in the Presence of the Steward and all the Tenants, and pronounces the following Lines, riding on a Ram,

——Here I am,
Riding upon the Back of a black Ram,
Like a Whore as I am;
And for my Crincum Crancum,
I have lost my Binkum Bankum;
And for my Tail's Game
Have done this worldly Shame;
Therefore pray, Mr. Steward, *let me have my Land again.*

Upon this Penance she is restored to the Possession of her Estate, for that Time.

Of Conveyances, Fines and Recoveries, Leases, Wills, &c. made by and to Baron and Feme.

A Feme Covert cannot take any Thing of the Gift of the Husband, but ſhe is of Capacity to purchaſe of others, without the Conſent of her Husband, though the Huſband may diſagree thereto, and deveſt the whole Eſtate; and if he neither agree nor diſagree, the Purchaſe is good; yet after his Death, altho' he agreed thereto, ſhe may, without Cauſe alledged, wave the ſame; ſo may her Heirs alſo, if after the Death of the Husband, ſhe agreed not to it. 1 *Co. Inſt.* 3.

By no Conveyance at the Common Law, a Man could during the Coverture, either in Poſſeſſion, Reverſion or Remainder, limit an Eſtate to his Wife. But a Man, by his Deed, may covenant with others to ſtand ſeiſed to his Wife's Uſe, or make a Feoffment, or other Conveyance to the Uſe of his Wife, and the Eſtate is executed to ſuch Uſes, by the Stat. 27 *H.* 8. Though a Man cannot covenant with his Wife to ſtand ſeiſed to her Uſe, becauſe he cannot covenant with her, and they are one Perſon in Law. 1 *Inſt.* 112.

A Man may deviſe an Eſtate by Will, to his Wife, becauſe the Deviſe doth not take Effect 'till after the Deceaſe of the Deviſor. *Co. Lit.* 112.

One being enfeoffed to the Uſe of a Feme, ſhe takes Husband, who ſells the Land to a

Stranger; the Feme received the Money, the Husband and Wife pray him that was enfeoffed, to the Use of his Wife, to make an Estate to the Stranger; this Sale in Equity ought to be construed the Sale of the Husband alone, and it shall not be esteemed that the Wife did it; for the Deed of the Baron, and the Receipt of the Money by her, is not material, because she cannot have the free Disposal. *Chanc. Rep.*

Baron and Feme join in a Feoffment of the Wife's Land, rendring Rent, the Husband dies, the Feme takes another Husband before any Rent-Day, and the second Husband accepteth the Rent, the Feoffment is affirmed for ever. *Co. Lit.*

Debt on a Bond, conditioned for the Performance of Covenants in an Indenture, made between *A. B.* and *E.* his Wife, of the one Part, and the Plaintiff of the other Part, the Defendant pleads the Indenture as an Indenture of *A. B.* and *E.* his Wife; whereas the Wife never sealed it. The Plaintiff replies, that the Indenture shewed by the Defendant, *Non fuit facta inter A. B.* and *E.* his Wife, on the one Part, and the Plaintiff on the other. The Jury find the Baron sealed it, but the Wife did not: This Verdict is found against the Defendant, who pleaded it as the Deed of the Wife. *Per Curiam*, The Plaintiff is not estopped to say, That the Deed shewed is not the Deed of the Baron and Feme; but he is estopped by the Condition to say, There is not any such Indenture: But if the Baron had sealed and delivered it in the Name of the Feme, it had been

been the Deed of the Wife, during the Life of the Husband; and if they by Indenture, had bargained and ſold the Land of the Wife, rendring Rent, it would have been a good Deed of the Feme's; becauſe ſhe afterwards might have accepted the Rent, and affirmed it as her Deed: And Judgment was given *pro Quer'. Cro. Eliz.* 269.

If the Baron hath a Term in Right of his Feme, he may grant over the whole. But if the Baron makes a Leaſe for Years to another, to the Uſe of his Feme, if ſhe lives ſo long, for the Jointure of the Feme, the Baron cannot Diſpoſe of this Truſt. And if a Baron grants a Term in Truſt, and for the Benefit of his Wife and Children, he cannot Diſpoſe of the Truſt for the Children. *Lane* 55.

A Leaſe is made to Baron and Feme for Years, the Baron cannot deviſe the Term; for the Feme is in by Survivorſhip, before the Deviſe takes effect. And if the Baron hath a Term in Right of the Feme, and he grants a Rent out thereof, and dies, the Feme ſhall hold it diſcharged; for ſhe comes Paramount to the Charge. *Co. Lit.* 351.

If the Baron grants Part of the Term, of which he is poſſeſſed, in the Right of the Feme, and dies, the Feme ſhall have the Reverſion not diſpoſed of. *Co. Lit.* 46. But if the Baron reſerves a Rent upon the Grant, ſhe ſhall not have it; becauſe ſhe comes Paramount the Reſervation.

The Baron grants the Lands which he hath in Leaſe, in the Right of his Feme, except

Part; the Feme ſhall have this Part ſo excepted.

If the Baron poſſeſſed of a Term for Years, in the Right of his Feme, makes a Leaſe for Part of the Years, to commence after his Death, and dies, this is a good Leaſe againſt the Feme, but ſhe ſhall have the Reverſion. *Poph. Rep.* 4.

A Baron poſſeſſed of a Term in Right of his Feme, grants it to *A. B.* if he lives ſo long, and dies, the Feme ſhall have this Poſſibility of a Reverſion, if *A. B.* dies within the Term, and not the Executors of the Baron. *Paſch* 12 *Jac.*

But where a Baron, poſſeſſed of a Term, in the Right of the Feme, grants it over upon Condition, that the Grantee ſhall pay 10 *l.* to his Executors, the Baron dies, the Condition is broke, and the Executors of the Baron enter, the Feme ſhall not have the Term, all the Intereſt being granted over. *Co. Lit.* 46.

If a Feme poſſeſſed of a Term, takes Huſband, and they grant the Term upon Condition, if their Executors or Adminiſtrators pay 10 *l.* then to re-enter, and after the Baron pays the 10 *l.* this is not any Diſpoſition or Alteration, but they ſhall be poſſeſſed in the Right of the Feme; for tho' he paid the Money to redeem it, yet perhaps he received the Money when it was mortgaged. 12 *Jac. Roll.* 345.

But if Baron and Feme are ejected of a Term held in Right of the Feme, and the Baron recovers in an *Ejectione firmæ*, brought by him, in his own Name only, this is an

Altera-

Alteration of the Term, and veſts in the Baron. *Co. Lit.* 46.

Baron and Feme Jointenants for Life, the Baron may ſurrender to him in Reverſion, and this ſhall bind the Husband, though not the Wife; nor ſhall be any Diſcontinuance to her; but this is not a good Surrender, during the Life of the Baron. *Kelw.* 42.

If a Leſſee for Life enfeoff the Baron and Feme in Reverſion, in Right of the Wife, this is a Surrender; (admitting it not to be a Forfeiture) but if Leſſee for Life grant his Eſtate to Baron and Feme in Reverſion, in Right of his Wife, this is not any Surrender for the Benefit of the Baron. 21 *H.* 7.

A. and *E.* his Wife, take a Leaſe jointly for their two Lives, and by new Indenture take a new Leaſe to them two and the Survivor, the Acceptance of the ſecond Leaſe to commence *a die Datus* is a Surrender, becauſe they conclude then that the Leſſor had Power to make a new Leaſe, which he cannot do unleſs the former be ſurrendred. *Moor* 636.

If a Feme Leſſee for Years take Husband, who after accepts a new Leaſe for their Lives, this is a Surrender of the firſt Leaſe. *Plowd.* 199. But Baron and Feme cannot expreſly, nor by Acceptance of a new Leaſe, ſurrender the Wife's Freehold, ſo as to bind her ſurviving. *Hob.* 203, 204.

Baron and Feme make an Exchange with another, this is good, during the Coverture. 39 *Ed.* 3. And if the Husband exchange the Land of the Wife for Lands of leſs Value; if the Wife, after his Death, once agree to the

the Exchange, she shall never avoid it afterwards. 9 *H.* 6.

But if Husband and Wife are seised of Lands in Right of the Wife, they both join in an Exchange of the Lands to a Stranger for other Lands, which Exchange is executed; and the Husband and Wife seised of the Land taken in Exchange, alien the same by Fine. *Per Curiam*, The Wife after the Death of the Husband, may enter into her own Land, notwithstanding the Fine. 1 *Leon.* 285.

And if the Husband alien the Lands of the Wife, she may recover by a *Cui in vita*, after his Decease; but she can have no Remedy so long as he is living. *Co. Inst.* 2 *Pt.* 343.

Two Husbands and their Wives join in a Grant of the Lands of their Wives, and covenant that they have Right to convey, and to make farther Assurance within seven Years, one of the Wives is within Age at the Time of making the Deed, and the Right of the Lands descended to her Son, an Infant; by which the Moiety of the Estate was devested out of the Plaintiff. Adjudg'd, that the Wife being within Age at the Time of the Covenant, (which was made appear on the Verdict) she had not Power then to convey the Estate according to the Covenant, and there was no Request to make the Assurance. And the Death of the Wife in the Infancy of her Son, was the Act of God; and it was the Default of the Plaintiff, that he did not demand Assurance in the Life of the Wife, after her full Age. Sir *Thomas Jones* 195.

Baron

Baron and Feme, and a third Perſon, purchaſe Land to them and the Heirs of the Husband; and the third Perſon releaſeth to the Baron all his Right, &c. without the Word *Heirs*; and afterwards the Baron and Feme make a Leaſe for Years, rendring Rent to them and the Heirs of the Baron; the Baron dies, the Heir ſhall have the Moiety of the Rent, after the Death of the Baron and a Releaſe to the Husband only ſhall enure to him Sole, and not to the Wife. *Dyer* 263.

A Joint Eſtate of Land is made to Baron and Feme, and to a third Perſon; in this Caſe the Baron and Feme have in Law but a Moiety, and the third Perſon ſhall have the other Moiety; for they are but one Perſon in Law. The ſame Law is where an Eſtate is made to Baron and Feme, and two other Men; here the Baron and Feme have but a third Part, and the other two Men the other two Parts. *Lit. Sect.* 291. 1 *Inſt.* 187.

At Common Law, if Land had been given to the Baron and Feme, and a third Perſon, and to their Heirs, and the Baron had made a Feoffment in Fee, this had been a Diſcontinuance of the one Moiety, and a Diſſeiſin of the other, ſo as after the Death of the Baron the Wife had a Right of Entry for one Moiety, and the other Jointenant a Right of Entry into the other. *Co. Lit.* 326.

Lands are given to *A. B.* and *C. D.* a Feme, and the Heirs of the Body of *A. B.* Afterwards *A. B.* and *C. D.* marry, and the Baron ſuffers a common Recovery againſt himſelf, only without naming his Wife; the Recovery is falſyfied for one Moiety, becauſe the Wife who was Jointenant with *A. B.* was not named and made a Party. And this Recovery binds not the Moiety of the Wife. 3 *Leon.* 270.

Baron and Feme are Jointenants, and after they Intermarry, they ſhall take by Moieties; but of Land given to them after Marriage, they take by Intierties; for Baron and Feme cannot take by Moieties, during the Coverture. If Lands are let to a Feme Sole for her Life, who marries, and afterwards the Leſſor confirms the Eſtate of the Baron and Feme, *Habendum* for Term of their Lives; the Husband doth not hold jointly with his Wife, but holdeth in the Right of his Wife, for Term of her Life; for the Wife hath the whole for Life, and Jointenants muſt come in by one Title. But if I let Lands to a Feme Sole for Term of Years, who takes Husband, and after I confirm the Eſtate of the Husband and Wife, to have and to hold for the Term of their two Lives; in this Caſe, they have a Joint Eſtate of Freehold of the Land; for that the Wife had no Freehold before. It is the ſame of a Releaſe, in both Caſes, and the Chattel of the Feme Covert is drown'd. But if Land be let to a Feme Sole for Life, who marries, and a Confirmation is made to the Baron and Feme in Fee, they are Jointenants of the Fee-ſimple; and the Husband is ſeiſed in Right of his Wife, during her Life. *Baron and Feme*, *p.* 176.

If a Man lets Land to the Husband and Wife, *Habendum* the one Moiety to the Husband for Term of his Life, and the other Moiety to his Wife, for Term of her Life;

and

and the Leſſor confirms the Eſtate of both in the Land, to have and to hold to them and their Heirs, by this Confirmation, as to the Moiety of the Husband, it enures to the Husband only and his Heirs; and the Wife has nothing in that Moiety: But as to the Moiety of the Wife, they are Jointenants, for the Husband hath ſuch an Eſtate in his Wife's Moiety, in her Right, as is capable of a Confirmation. 1 *Inſt.* 299.

By Fine levied, &c. on Marriage to the Uſe of the Husband and Wife, for their joint Lives, Remainder to the Heirs of the Body of the Wife, by the Husband to be begotten, Remainder (the Wife ſurviving the Husband) to her for Life, Remainder to the Right Heirs of the Husband; this was adjudged to be an Eſtate-tail, executed in the Wife. *Raym.* 127. 3 *Salk.* 338.

Eſtate-Tail of Land are *general*, where Lands or Tenements are given to a Man and the Heirs of his Body begotten, or to a Woman, and the Heirs of her Body begotten: Or they are *Special*, when Lands and Tenements are given to a Man and his Wife, and to the Heirs of their two Bodies begotten, &c. In the firſt Caſe it is called a General Tail, becauſe whatever Woman the Baron taketh to Wife, or whatſoever Man the Feme takes to her Husband, the Iſſue may inherit the Land; or if ſhe have divers Husbands, and have Iſſue by every of them, they ſhall inherit one after another, as Heir of her Body. But in a Special Tail, no other Perſons can inherit but the Iſſue that are begotten by the Man on that particular Wife; for if ſhe

ſhe die, and the Baron marries a ſecond Wife, by whom he hath Children, they ſhall have no Benefit by it. 1 *Co. Inſt.* 19, 20.

If Lands are convey'd to Baron and Feme, and to the Heirs of the Body of the Man, the Husband hath an Eſtate in General Tail, and the Wife an Eſtate for Life; and if the Eſtates made to the Husband and Wife, and the Heirs of her Body, by him begotten, there the Wife hath an Eſtate in Special Tail, and the Husband for Term of Life only. But if an Eſtate be limited to a Man's Heirs, which he ſhall beget on his Wife, this creates a Special Tail in the Husband, and the Wife will have nothing. 1 *Inſt.* 26.

Where a Feme Covert is Tenant for Life, and the Baron and Feme accept of a greater Eſtate of him in the Reverſion, yet after the Death of the Baron ſhe may wave it, and claim her firſt Eſtate for Life. 2 *Saund.* 386. And if Lands are given to Baron and Feme, and their Heirs, the Baron makes a Feoffment in Fee, the Feoffee gives the Land to the Baron and Feme, and the Heirs of their two Bodies, and the Baron dies; in this Caſe the Wife may elect which of the Eſtates ſhe will. 1 *Co. Inſt.* 357.

Baron and Feme Tenants in ſpecial Tail, upon Purchaſe of the Baron, have Iſſue two Sons; the Husband makes a Feoffment to the Uſe of himſelf for Life, Remainder to the Wife for Life, the Remainder to the ſecond Son and his Heirs; the Baron dies, the Feme enters and makes a Feoffment to the Iſſue of the ſecond Son, and the Eldeſt enters for the Forfeiture within the

Stat.

Stat. 11 *H.* 7. his Entry is congeable; and this Feoffment by the Wife (tho' it be to him who had the Reversion in Fee) is a Forfeiture within the Statute; for by the Entry of the Wife, he was remitted. *Sid.* 63.

Land is given to Baron and Feme in special Tail, the Baron aliens the Land in Fee, and takes back an Estate to him and his Wife for Term of their Lives, this is a Remitter to the Baron and Feme; and it cannot be a Remitter to the Wife unless it be a Remitter to the Husband, they being one Person in Law.

Tenant in Tail before the Statute 27 *H.* 8. made a Feoffment in Fee for the Use of his Wife for Life, and afrer to his Son and Heir in Fee; then the Statute is made, and the Baron and Feme are dead, the Issue shall not be remitted. And if a Feme having Right to Lands discontinu'd, where his Entry was not lawful, if she come to the Land by way of an Use raised out of that Estate, she shall not be remitted, for she must be in of the Estate, as she was of the Use; but the Statute 32 *H.* 8. has chang'd the Reason of this Case, which gives the Wife Entry against her Husband's Fine; so that now by the Use rais'd to her out of such Estate, she is not in of an Estate discontinu'd, but of an Estate; whereupon after the Death of her Husband she might have re-enter'd. Now as upon Re-entry, in case where the Entry is lawful, she is remitted; so where an Estate is convey'd to her, and is in her, tho' by the Statute her Entry being lawful, she shall be adjudg'd in of her best Estate. *Hob.* 255.

If Baron and Feme are Tenants in ſpecial Tail, and the Baron only levies a Fine to the Uſe of himſelf and his Wife for Life; altho' the Entail be barred as to the Baron and the Iſſues, yet the Wife is remitted to the Eſtate-Tail, as ſhe ſhould have been by an Entry, after her Husband's Death; and the Remainders which were depending upon that Eſtate-Tail are likewiſe remitted. *Hob. Rep.* 257.

The Father was Tenant for Life, remainder to his Daughter and Heir Apparent (a Feme Covert) in Fee; the Father makes a Feoffment to divers Uſes, and after levies a Fine with Warranty and dies, the Daughter by Conſent of her Husband enters within the Year after the Fine, claiming the Land as her Inheritance; the Entry by the Feme only by the Conſent of her Husband is good, and the Warranty deſcending upon her during the Coverture, where her Entry is congeable doth not bind her; neither doth it bind the Husband, becauſe it deſcends not upon him, and being void to bind her ſhall not bind him. *Cro. Eliz.* 72.

Husband and Wife Tenants in ſpecial Tail, the Husband levies a Fine and dies; the Eſtate-Tail is barr'd tho' not determin'd, but hath Continuance ſo long as the Wife lives, or the Heirs in Tail remain. 9 *Rep.* 138.

And altho' the Wife hath an Eſtate-Tail, yet ſhe cannot levy a Fine, or ſuffer a Recovery: Becauſe ſhe cannot bar that which was barr'd before by the Priority of the Act of the Husband. 9 *Rep.* 142.

A Wife levies a Fine as a Feme Sole, of Land whereof ſhe was ſeized; this ſhall bar

her

her and her Heirs, if the Husband doth not enter. *Coke* 10. *Rep*. 43. But if the Husband enters and dies, the Conuzee ſhall not have the Land: For by the Entry of the Husband the Conuzee's Eſtate was defeated, and the Wife's ancient Eſtate reveſted in her; and the Husband was ſeized of the whole Eſtate in the Right of his Wife. 7. *Rep*. 8.

Baron and Feme levy a Fine of the Wife's Land, the Husband only declares the Uſes; it ſhall bind the Feme, if her Diſcent doth not appear. 2. *Rep*. 57.

When Baron and Feme levy a Fine of the Wife's Land, and the Baron declares by one Deed the Uſes, and the Wife by another; or where neither of them declares any Uſes which are ſufficient in Law, there the Law doth immediately reveſt the Uſes in the Feme ſolely. 2 *Rep*. 58.

Baron and Feme, the Feme within Age, levy a Fine; and upon Inſpection the Wife was adjudg'd to be within Age; the whole Fine was revers'd. 1. *Leon*. 116.

A Fine is levied by Baron and Feme, the Feme being under Age, and on Error brought the Fine is reverſed for the Non-age of his Wife: The Queſtion in *Worſley* and *Charnock's* Caſe was, if the Fine ſhould be utterly reverſed, or reverſed only as to the Wife, and ſtand good againſt the Husband; and two great Precedents were cited, the one contrary to the other; they who argued that the Fine ſhould be reverſed for the whole, cited *Ely* and *Ford's* Caſe, *H*. 8. A Fine was levied between *R*. *Ely* Plaintiff, and *N*. *Ford* and

Jane

Jane his Wife Defendants; the Wife being within Age, and Judgment was given that the Fine should be reversed, and the Baron and Feme restored; and thereupon a Writ issued to the *Custos Brevium* to bring into Court the Foot of the Fine, and it was presently cancell'd in Court. The other Precedent contrary was 7 *Eliz.* Baron and Feme levied a Fine, the Husband died the Wife being within Age, the Wife took another Husband, and they brought a Writ of Error, and the Wife by Inspection was adjudg'd within Age, and the Fine was reversed as to her and her Heirs only: But in this Case the second Husband was a Stranger to the Fine, and so it might seem absur'd to reverse it as to him; but in the principal Case it was adjudg'd, that the Fine should be reversed as to both; for the whole Estate moved from the Wife, and all pass'd out of her, and Judgment was given *Quod finis predict' reversetur.* 2 *Co.* 77.

At twenty Years of Age a Feme Covert levied a Fine before Commissioners in the Country, and the Wife dying without Issue she had settled the Estate upon her and her Husband, and the Heirs of their two Bodies: The Court was mov'd to set it aside, but they agreed they could not meddle with it; but if the Wife had been alive and under Age, they might bring her in by *Habeas Corpus*, and inspect her, and set aside the Fine upon Motion, for perhaps the Husband would not suffer the bringing of a Writ of Error; and the Commissioners in this Case were not fined, because they could not dis-

cern

cern by the view whether ſhe was of Age, ſhe being twenty Years old: But had it been apparent by Inſpection that ſhe was within Age, or the Commiſſioners had perfectly known that the Feme had been under Age, then they ought to have been fin'd. 2 *Ventr.* 30.

A Feme Covert levied a Fine within Age, ſhe was inſpected by the Court, and adjudg'd within Age; whereupon a *Scire Facias* iſſued to the Tertenants, who pleaded ſhe was of full Age at the Time of the Fine levied; upon which Plea Iſſue was join'd, and a Trial had at the Aſſizes, and Verdict *pro Quer.* who came into Court and now pray'd Judgment. *Per Glyn:* the Court is to judge of her Non-age and not the Jury; and tho' the Proceedings are not duly had yet they do no Hurt, and the Fine was reverſed. *Stile* 472.

Feme Covert of nineteen Years of Age acknowledg'd a Fine before Commiſſioners, ſeveral Judges being in Town who might have examin'd her: She died on *Friday Eaſter* Week, but the Fine and King's Silver were enter'd as of *Hillary Term*, four Days before the Wife's Death: The original Writ of Covenant bore Date 15 *Jan. Ret. Craſt. Pur.* and the *Dedimus poteſtatem* 18 *Jan.* This Fine was ſtop'd the ingroſſing, for undue Means in obtaining it. *Dyer* 220. But in 11 *Co.* the Fine adjudg'd good.

If Baron and Feme levy a Fine, and the Conuzance is taken ſix Days before Term *Paſch.* and the Writ of Covenant is returnable *quindena Paſch.* which is the third of *May*, and

and the Husband dies the ninth of *May*, the King's Silver not being enter'd; yet if upon Examination it appears that the Clerk had enter'd the King's Silver in Paper, before any Exception taken to it, and that now he had enter'd the King's Silver on the back of the Writ of Covenant, as it ought to be, the Fine ſhall not be ſtayed; for when this is enter'd, it ſhall have Relation to the Writ of Covenant. *Paſch.* 7 *Jac.*

A Man and his Wife acknowledg'd a Note of a Fine 26 *Mar.* by *Dedimus poteſtatem*, and the Wife died the 27th of the ſame Month; the 28th Day Compoſition was made in the Alienation Office, on a Writ of Covenant returnable in *Hillary* Term before; and the Kings Silver was enter'd in the Office as of the ſame *Hillary* Term, and ſo the Fine was paſs'd and Engroſs'd; and in *Eaſter* Term the Heir of the Wife moved againſt this Fine; but the Court reſolv'd the Fine ſhould ſtand. *Hob.* 330.

A Feme Covert is to be examin'd upon a Fine, when ſhe and her Husband paſs ſome Eſtate or Intereſt, or make a Grant and Render to another, or Releaſe her Right by a Fine of Lands or Tenements. 1 *Inſt.* 353.

The Examination of a Feme Covert ought to be ſecret, and the Effect is, to Examine her whether ſhe be Content to levy a Fine of ſuch Lands, naming them particularly and diſtinctly, and the Eſtate that paſſeth by the Fine, of her own voluntary free Will, not by Menaces or compulſory Means: But where nothing is contain'd in the Fine, but only that the Husband and Wife do take an E-

ſtate

ſtate by the Fine, this ſhall not conclude the Wife; becauſe in ſuch caſe ſhe is not to be examin'd.

A Fine which paſſeth an Eſtate, ought not to be receiv'd, if the Feme be not examin'd; but if the Fine be receiv'd and recorded, the Feme Covert or her Heirs ſhall not be permitted to aver that ſhe was not examin'd, nor aſſented; for this would be againſt the Record of the Court, and tend to weaken the general Aſſurances of the Realm. 2 *Inſt.* 515.

Fine and Non-claim of the Wife's Land ſhall Bar the Husband, who ſuffer'd five Years to paſs, and all claiming under him, and the Wife herſelf during the Coverture; but ſhe ſhall have a new five Years after the Death of her Husband. *Cro. Car.* 200.

A Man ſeized of Lands in Fee takes a Wife, and after levies a Fine, and the Proclamations are made, and the five Years paſs in his Life; then he dies, and after his Death other five Years paſs, and afterwards the Wife brought her Writ of Dower; ſhe ſhall be barred; for as ſhe had Title at the Time of the Fine levied, ſhe ſhall be bound by Non-claim for five Years after her Title conſummate. *Moor* 53.

Feme Covert is Tenant for Life, Remainder in Fee to the Son, which ſhe ſhall have; and he in Reverſion before the Birth of the Son bargains and ſells the Land, and levies a Fine of it to the Baron and Feme, the particular Eſtate of the Wife is drowned in the Reverſion, and the contingent Remainder is deſtroy'd. 2 *Sand.* 386.

If the Husband ſeized in Tail of Land for valuable Conſideration, bargain and ſell this to another in Fee, and Covenant, that he and his Wife ſhall levy a Fine for better Aſſurance; and it is agreed, that 30 *l.* Part of the Conſideration Money ſhall be paid to the Husband upon the Cognizance of the Fine by the Baron and Feme; and after they acknowledge a Fine before the Judge in the Circuit, and the 30 *l.* is paid to and receiv'd by the Wife, the Husband being ſick in Bed, and the Husband dies before the Term, and upon this the Wife ſtays the paſſing of the Fine, and after brings a Writ of Dower; the Bargainee ſhall not have any Remedy in Equity againſt the Dower, for that it is a Maxim in Law, that the Feme Covert ſhall not be bound without a Fine. But the Court agreed, if the Wife had any perſonal Eſtate, as Executrix or Adminiſtratrix to her Huſband, ſhe ſhall be liable for this; and thereupon a Commiſſion was granted to enquire of Aſſets. 1 *Rolls Abr.* 375.

If Baron and Feme levy a Fine of Lands, whereof the Husband is ſeized in Right of his Wife, this ſhall not be receiv'd with Warranty by them and the Heirs of the Huſband; but it ſhall be receiv'd by them and the Heirs of the Wife, becauſe it is the Inheritance of the Wife. 44 *Ed.* 3.

Baron and Feme by Fine Grant Land to *A.* for 99 Years, if he ſo long live, and by the ſame Fine Warrant the Lands to *A. contra omnes homines toto termino prædicto*; the Baron dies. *Per Curiam*, a good Action of Covenant lies againſt the Wife upon her

4 Warranty

Warranty in the Fine, altho' ſhe was Covert Baron: For when the Warranty is only annex'd to an Eſtate for Years, it is no more than a Covenanr for Damages perſonal; and they are bound to Warrant the Land, and to anſwer in Value of their own proper Eſtates. 2 *Saund.* 180.

A. makes an Eſtate to Friends in Truſt, for the Uſe of his Wife, to Commence after his Death, the Wife joins in a Fine with her Husband of the Land leaſed in Truſt; this Fine ſhall Dock the Truſt, and there being an Extent upon the Land leaſed, this Truſt ſhall not prevent the Extent by reaſon of the Fine.

If *A. B.* with the Wife of another Perſon levy a Fine by the Name of *A. B.* and *E.* his Wife, of the Inheritance of the Feme, and he who is the Husband comes into Court and ſhews the Matter, and prays that the Fine may not paſs; yet the Court will Proceed; for the Court ſhall not determine the Loyalty of Matrimony; but if the Truth be ſo, that ſhe is not the Wife of *A. B.* it ſhall not injure the Husband. *Trin.* 7. *Jac.*

A Man ſeized in Fee levies a Fine to the uſe of himſelf for Life, and after to the Uſe of ſuch a Wife as he ſhall Marry, and ſhall ſurvive him; he and his Wife levy a Fine to a Stranger; the Baron dies, and the Feme ſurvives; ſhe by her Fine hath bar'd her poſſibility by Eſtoppel. *Moor.* 557.

Tenant for Life, Remainder to Baron and Feme, and their Heirs, the Baron and Feme ſuffer a Recovery: The Queſtion was, if the Heirs of the Wife are bound by this Recovery; for the Feme being Covert, it was con-

 ceiv'd

ceiv'd she was not Tenant to the Præcipe, because it appears not that she was examin'd. Adjudg'd that it is not necessary to examine a Feme Covert upon a Recovery, tho' it be prudential to do it; but in a Fine it is otherwise, because there is no Recompence in Value; and the Feme here is Tenant to the Præcipe, and she shall be estopped to speak against the Recovery, for she joins in it with her Husband, and there is no Default made by the Baron; and now the Record is perfect, and a Thing contrary to it is not to be averr'd; but before the Record was perfect she might have pleaded; also the Recompence in Value in this Case shall go to the Heirs of the Wife, and the Tenant for Life is bound by this Recovery, and the Feme is privy thereto: If a Stranger had been Tenant to the Præcipe, and the Baron and Feme had been vouch'd, the Feme had been bound. *Stile* 319. But it was the Opinion of Chief Justice *Bridgman*, that a Feme Covert ought to be privately examin'd in a common Recovery, tho' the Practice was otherwise, which was a Fault, and ought to be corrected; *Sid.* 11. And so is my Lord *Coke*'s Opinion. 10 *Co.* 45.

If the Baron seized in Right of his Wife for Life, the Remainder in Tail to *B.* Remainder to *C.* and the Husband bargains and sells the Land to another, against whom a Præcipe is brought, who voucheth him in Remainder, and so a common Recovery passeth; this shall bind the Remainder, but not the Wife, because the Bargainee was a good Tenant to the Præcipe. 2 *Rolls Abr.* 394.

Baron and Feme ſeized to them and the Heirs Males of the Body of the Baron, Remainder in Tail to another, the Reverſion to the right Heirs of the Baron; the Baron levies a Fine, the Conuzee ſuffers a Recovery, and vouches the Baron, who vouches the common Vouchee: This Recovery by the Privity ſhall bind the Tail. Here, altho' the Wife was not vouch'd, who had an Eſtate for Life with her Husband; and tho' the Eſtate of the Wife is not recontinu'd, yet the Husband as Voucher, ſhall be in Judgment of Law in Privity of the Eſtate-Tail which he once had; and the Eſtate of the Wife by the Husband's Fine is put to a Right, ſo that the Husband comes in as ſole Tenant in Tail: It would be otherwiſe if the Baron and Feme were ſeized to them and the Heirs of their two Bodies, with Remainders over. 3 *Co. Rep.* 6.

But an Eſtate is made to Baron and Feme jointly, and to the Heirs of the Body of the Husband, &c. and a common Recovery is had againſt the Baron, who vouches the common Vouchee; the Baron ſurvives his Wife, and dies without Iſſue; this is not good to Bar the Remainders: For the Baron had not Power to ſever the Jointure, nor is he, during the Life of his Wife, ſeized by Force of the Tail, ſo that the Præcipe being brought againſt him only, the Conveyance cannot for any Part Enure to the Eſtate-Tail, or to the Remainder; to all the Eſtate it cannnot Enure, becauſe the Wife had a joint Eſtate with him who was no Party to the Recovery; and for a Moiety it cannot be good, for there are no Moieties between Baron and Feme. 3 *Co.* 5.

Where Baron and Feme are vouch'd, it ſhall

be intended to be in the Right of his Wife. Four Husbands and their Wives are vouch'd in a Recovery, and the Plaintiff brought his Writ of Error as Heir to one of the Husbands; it was adjudg'd ill; he ought to have brought it as Heir to one of the Wives.

If a common Recovery be suffered, and the Baron and Feme, as in Right of the Wife, (the Feme being within Age) are vouch'd, and they appear by Attorney, and vouch over, and so a Recovery is had, this is Error; for tho' the Husband be of full Age, yet the Wife being within Age, she ought to appear by Guardian. *Hill.* 17 *Jac. Rolls* 1 *Abr.* 288. By *Dyer* 290, 366. The Appearance of a Feme Covert, in a Recovery, within Age by Attorney is Error; and tho' it may be objected, that the Husband is of full Age, and he may make Attorney for himself and his Wife, the Law is not so; for the Rule is, that the Husband cannot give away or lose the Inheritance of the Wife; but it must be given or lost by herself or her own Act, and she ought to appear by Guardian notwithstanding the full Age of the Husband, who is to be join'd for Conformity with her. *Sid.* 322.

If a Man seized of Lands in the Right of his Wife, Lets the same to another for Term of Life, now the Husband has the Reversion of the Fee-simple, being a Discontinuance to the Wife: But if the Husband dies, leaving the Wife and Tenant for Life, and the Reversion descend to the Heir of the Baron, and he grants the Reversion to another in Fee, and the Tenant attorns, and then the

Te-

Tenant for Life dies, and the Grantee of the Reversion enters; this is no Discontinuance to the Wife, but she may well enter upon the Grantee, because the Grantor had nothing at the Time of the Grant, in the Right of the Wife. *Lit. Sect.* 639. Though if the Baron and Feme, in such Case join in a Lease by Deed, the Reversion is not discontinued, but remains in the Wife; and yet it was at Common Law, a Discontinuance for Life. 1 *Co. Inst.* 339.

To a Lease of the Wife's Land, which may be made for three Lives, or twenty-one Years, or under, reserving the ancient Rent, or more, she must be a Party, and seal the Indenture; and the Rent must be reserved to Husband and Wife, and the Heirs of the Wife; and the Husband cannot alien, discharge, or grant away the Rent, but during the Coverture only. Stat. 32 *H.* 8. *Co. Lit.* 44, 45.

Leases made with these Qualifications, shall bind the Wife and her Heirs; and if they are not warranted by this Statute, yet they shall be good against the Husband.

But the Husband purchased Lands to him and his Wife, and their Heirs, and afterwards he let those Lands to two Persons for sixty Years, if they lived so long, rendring Rent, without making the Wife a Party to the Lease, this Lease shall bind the Wife by the Stat. 32 *H.* 8. for it is not within the Proviso, as the sole Inheritance of the Wife. *Cro. Car.* 22.

A. possessed of a Term for an hundred Years by Deed indented, mentioned to be made between him and *B.* his Wife, of the one Part; but ſhe never ſealed the Deed. *A.* and *B.* grant and aſſign the Term to *C.* yielding and paying, during the Term to *A.* and *B.* and the Survivor of them, and the Aſſigns of the Survivor of them, 10*l.* Rent *per Annum*; upon Condition that if the Rent be not paid, it ſhall be lawful for him and his Wife, and the Survivor of them, and the Aſſigns of the Survivor of them to re-enter, and after *A.* dies, neither his Adminiſtrator nor *B.* the Wife, ſhall have the Rent, or enter for the Condition broken. The Wife ſhall not have the Rent, becauſe ſhe ſealed not the Deed, and ſo the Rent cannot be reſerved to her, being a Stranger; ſo it is void as to her; and the Adminiſtrator of *A.* ſhall not have this as Aſſignee of *A.* during the Life of *B.* inaſmuch as this was not intended as a Limitation to determine by the Death of *B.* but to be reſerved to *B.* herſelf, and ſo the Aſſignee in Law of the Husband cannot claim it, becauſe he did not ſurvive the Wife. And the Condition in this Caſe, runs with the Rent; therefore the Rent being gone, the Condition is gone alſo; and although the Rent be reſerved during the Term, yet the Words *To A. B.* reſtrain it. 2 *Roll. Abr.* 450. See 2 *Saund.* 386.

A Man poſſeſſed of a Term for Years, in the Right of his Wife, made a Leaſe for Years, rendring Rent to him, his Executors and Aſſigns, and died, the Rent is gone; but by *Montague*, the Wife may be relieved in Chancery. *Godb.* 279.

In this Caſe it was held, that the Wife ſhould have the Reſidue of the Term, but the Executors of the Husband ſhall have the Rent;

Rent; for it was not incident to the Reversion, the Wife not being a Party to the Lease. A Man possessed of a Term of twenty Years, in Right of his Wife, made a Lease for ten Years, rendring Rent to him, his Executors and Assigns, and then died. By *Houghton* and *Crook*, the Rent is gone; though it was agreed, if the Husband, after the Lease made, had granted over the Reversion, the Grantee should not have it. *Blackstone* and *Heath*'s Case.

The Baron, by the Intermarriage, hath full Power over the Wife's Term, to alien it; and if the Wife dies, the Term survives to the Husband; and if the Husband dies, it survives to the Wife, unless he dispose thereof; but the Husband can make no Disposition thereof by Will. *Plowd.* 416.

A Man possessed of a Term for Years, in Right of his Wife, made a Lease for Years of the same Land, to begin after his Decease; and afterwards he died, and the Wife survived him; the Question was, If the Wife shall have this, or the Lessee? And adjudged, that the Lessee shall have it; for as the Husband,. during his Life, might contract for the Land, for the whole Term which the Wife had in it, so might he do for any Part of the Term at his Pleasure; for if he may demise the Land for twenty-one Years, to begin presently, he may also make it to begin at any Time to come after his Death, if the Term of the Wife be not expir'd. *Pop.* 5.

A Woman conveys a Lease in Trust for her Use, and afterwards marries, in such Case it lies not in the Power of the Husband to dispose of it; and if the Wife die, the Husband

band ſhall not have it, but the Executor of the Wife. *March Rep.* 45. A Leaſe for Years was granted to the Leſſee, to the Uſe of the Grantor's Siſter, whom he afterwards ſhould marry; who married her accordingly, and then died. The Feme takes the Plaintiff to Husband, and afterwards ſhe died; the Defendant takes Adminiſtration of the Plaintiff's Wife's Goods, and the Plaintiff ſued the Defendant in Chancery, to have the Term; and it was decreed, by Advice of all the Judges in *England*, that neither the Term nor the Uſe belonged to the Huſband. *Cro. El.* 466.

The Wife having aſſigned her Term, in Truſt for herſelf, before Marriage, the Huſband, without joining with the Truſtees, mortgages the Truſt; and the Husband being dead, the Mortgagee exhibits his Bill to have the Lands conveyed to him, or that they ſhould redeem, and the Court diſmiſſed the Plaintiff's Bill; for it has been the conſtant Practice of the Court, ever ſince Queen *Elizabeth*'s Time, to ſet aſide all Incumbrances, and Acts of the Husband, upon the Truſt in the Wife's Term, and that he ſhall not charge or grant it away. *Chanc. Caſes* 225.

Baron and Feme mortgage their Intereſt in the Wife's Term; and before the Day of Payment the Wife died, and the Husband paid the Money at the Day, in Redemption of the Mortagage, and then enter'd and took another Wife, and made her Executrix, who enter'd. *R.* took Adminiſtration to the Goods of the firſt Wife, and entered upon the Leſſee, on whom the ſecond Wife entered, and made

made the Leaſe to the Plaintiff, and Judgment was given for the Plaintiff. Here, tho' the Leaſe was at firſt the Wife's, and the Husband was poſſeſſed in her Right, ſo that if he had purchaſed the Fee-ſimple, the Leaſe had not been extinct; yet by the Intermarriage he hath full Power to alien it; and if he ſurvive the Wife, he is to enjoy it againſt her Executors and Adminiſtrators. 1 *Roll. Abr.* 344.

Feme Executrix hath a Term, and takes Husband, and the Husband purchaſes the Reverſion, in this Caſe, the Term is extinct, as to her, if ſhe ſurvive; but as to all Strangers it ſhall be accounted Aſſets in her Hands. *Moor* 54.

A. and his Wife were poſſeſſed, in Right of the Wife, of a Term, which ſhe had as Adminiſtratrix to her firſt Husband *C.* and being indebted, by Contract, granted the Term to *D.* to the Uſe of *A.* and his Wife, for their Lives, and after to the Uſe of *D.* himſelf; *A.* ſued for this Debt, and Recovery againſt him; and the Sheriff, by *Fieri fac'* ſold the Term to the Defendant. The Grant of the Term is not void by Stat. 3 *H.* 7. as made to defraud Creditors; for this Grant is not to avoid Creditors, the Term being in Right of the Wife, as Adminiſtratrix, if it ſo continued in the Hands of *A.* and had never been granted; this was not extendible for the Debt of *A.* and if *A.* himſelf had it as Executor, it would not have been extendible for his proper Debt; and Fraud ſhall not be intended, except expreſly found. *Coleman*'s Caſe.

A Feme

A Feme Covert Executrix, may have a Term, Goods or Chattels Real. And in Debt the Husband is charged in Right of his Wife, as Executrix; and when Judgment is given against them, it shall be *De bonis suis propriis*. Cro. Car. 519.

Lease was granted to *J. S.* who assigned it over to *K.* and *K.* by his Will, devised the same to his Wife, and made her Executrix also; and she aftewards took one *W.* to Husband, and died, *W.* takes out Letters of Administration of the Goods and Chattels of his Wife, and leased it to the Plaintiff; the Question was, If the Wife be in as Executrix, or Legatee; for until Election made, she shall not have it as Legatee. But it was proved that the said Wife, as Executrix to her Husband, had made a Lease by Deed, reciting thereby, that the Husband was possessed in Right of his Wife, as Executrix of her first Husband. *Per Curiam:* This is an express Claim, as Executrix; and then when the Wife dies, if the Husband would have Advantage of it, he ought to take out Letters of Administration of the Goods of the first Husband. 1 *Leon.* 215.

Two Femes are Jointenants of a Lease for Years, one of them takes Husband and dies, the Term shall survive; for though all Chattels Real are given to the Husband, if he survive, yet the Survivor between Jointenants is the elder Title, and after the Marriage, the Wife continued sole possessed, and if the Husband die, the Feme shall have it, and not the Executors of the Husband; *aliter* of Personal Goods. 1 *Inst.* 185.

Baron

Baron and Feme Jointenants for eighty Years; the Baron by Indenture, lets all the Land for ſeventy Years, to commence immediately after his Death; the Baron died, and the Wife ſurvived: It was held to be a good Leaſe, and did bind the Feme. *Cro. El.* 287. But where the Baron and Feme are Joint Leſſees for their Lives, Remainder to the Survivor of them for Years, the Baron grants over this Term, and dies; this Grant is void, becauſe there was nothing in either of them to grant over, until there was a Survivor. *Poph.* 5.

The Baron and Feme (in Right of the Feme) and a third Perſon, were Jointenants for the Lives of the Wife, and of the third Perſon; the Baron and Feme by Indenture, let the Moiety for twenty-one Years, the Feme dies, and the ſurviving Jointenant enters; Leſſee brings Treſpaſs, and recovers; for the Leaſe is good, and is as a Leaſe made by her, until ſhe after Coverture, or one who claims in Privity by her, avoids it by Entry. It is not void by the Death of the Baron, but voidable only; and the Avoidance ought to be by Entry; and this cannot be by the Jointenant's Survivor, he being Paramount to the Wife, and ſo the Leaſe ſhall bind as long as any Jointenant is alive. *Cro. Jac.* 417.

Baron and Feme ſeiſed of Lands in the Right of the Wife, levied a Fine to the Uſe of themſelves for their Lives, and afterwards to the Uſe of the Heirs of the Wife; proviſo that it ſhall and may be lawful for the Baron and Feme, at any Time during their Lives, to make Leaſes for one and twenty Years,

Years, or three Lives. The Wife being Covert, made a Leaſe for one and twenty Years, and adjudged a good Leaſe againſt the Huſband; though it was made when ſhe was a Feme Covert, and by her alone; and this by Virtue of the Proviſo. *Godb.* 327. *ſed Quære.*

The Husband makes a Leaſe of the Wife's Land, and dies, the Leaſe is voidable by the Entry of the Wife after his Death. *Cro. Jac.* 332.

A Leaſe is made by Baron and Feme, *in jure Uxoris*, and he dies; if ſhe accepts the Rent, it is good againſt her; for by her own Act ſhe hath affirm'd it, and the Eſtate continues. *Cro. Jac.* 563.

Baron and Feme make a Leaſe by Indenture, for Term of Years, rendring Rent, the Leſſee enters, the Husband before the Day of Payment of the Rent, dies; and the Wife alſo, before the Day of Payment, takes a ſecond Husband, who accepts the Rent at the Day, and dies; the Wife may not ouſt the Termor: She might have avoided the Term before the Day, at her Pleaſure; but that Liberty ſhe had aſſigned to her ſecond Husband. *Dyer* 159.

A Man ſeiſed in Fee, in the Right of his Wife, had Iſſue by her, and ſo is Tenant by the Curteſy; and after makes a Leaſe for Years, reſerving Rent, and then the Wife dies, the Husband likewiſe dying before the End of the Term; this Leaſe is void and ended in the Law, before any Entry of the next Heir of the Wife; foraſmuch as he cannot make this good by any Acceptance of the

the Rent, the Leaſe being made only by the Husband. 1 *Roll. Abr.* 380.

Baron and Feme ſeiſed of Land in Right of the Wife, the Husband alone makes a Leaſe for Years, and afterwards Baron and Feme levy a Fine, and they after that both die, the Conuſee ſhall avoid the Leaſe. 1 *Leon.* 247.

If a Feme Sole, being a Widow ſeiſed of Lands, ſecretly takes Husband, and conceals her Marriage, and ſo continuing under the Notion of a Widow, makes Leaſes of divers Parcels of Land, and afterwards the Time of her Marriage is publiſhed; the Husband in Equity ſought to avoid the Leaſes, but was denied Relief, and decreed to confirm the Leaſes during the Term. *Chanc. Rep.*

When a Feme Covert receives from a Leſſee any Rent, the Leſſee not having Notice of the Coverture, there being no Countermand of Payment to the Wife; *per Curiam*, This Payment of Rent to the Wife, is no Payment, but the Husband may well demand it, and recover the ſame again: Though this ſeems to be hard upon Tenants, that they ſhould refuſe to pay the Rent, and ſo forfeit their Bonds of Covenants; and it is next to an Impoſſibility for them to Divine whether ſhe be married. *Cro. Jac.* 621.

Land was demiſed to Baron and Feme for their Lives, the Remainder to the Survivor of them for Years; the Husband granted over this Term for Years, and died, the Wife ſhall have it, and not the Grantee; for there was nothing in the one or the other to grant over, but the Survivor. So if the Wife had died

died after the Grant, and the Baron ſurvived, he ſhall have the Term againſt his own Grant. *Poph.* 4, 5. And if a Leaſe be made to Baron and Feme, for their Lives, the Remainder to the Executors of the Survivor of them; and the Husband grants the Term and dies, this ſhall not bar the Wife, becauſe ſhe had but a Poſſibility, and no Intereſt. *Co. Lit.* 46.

But if a Leaſe is made to Baron and Feme for their Lives, with Remainder to the Heirs of the Survivor, it is a good Remainder, notwithſtanding the Uncertainty; and in that Caſe the Husband, after the Death of the Wife, ſhall have Judgment to recover the Land. *Godb.* 139.

A Leaſe is granted to Baron and Feme, during the Coverture, and the Baron ſows the Land, and after they are divorced *cauſa præ-contractus*, the Baron ſhall have the Corn, becauſe the Judgment is an Act of Law. 5 *Coke* 116.

If an Husband, ſeiſed in Fee, or for Life, in the Right of his Wife, ſows the Land, and dies, or his Wife dies before Severance, yet he or his Executors ſhall have the Corn. 1 *Inſt.* 55.

A Feme ſeiſed in Fee, or for Life, of Land, ſows it, and after takes Husband, who dies before Severance, the Wife ſhall have the Corn, and not the Executor or Adminiſtrator of the Husband. And where Baron and Feme are Jointenants, and the Baron ſows the Land, the Wife ſurviving ſhall have the Emblements. *Godb.* 189.

A Feme Covert is Tenant for Life, Remainder to another, and Hops are growing

out

out of the ancient Roots on the Land, the Feme dies a little before the gathering of the Hops; the Queſtion was, Whether theſe Hops appertain to the Husband of the Feme, or to him in Remainder? The Court held, that they are like Emblements, which ſhall go to the Husband or Executor of the Tenant for Life, and not to him in Remainder; for they are ſuch Things as accrue by Manurance and Induſtry of the Owner, and not to be compared to Apples and Nuts, which grow of themſelves. *Cro. Car.* 515.

If a Man poſſeſſed of a Manor for ninety-nine Years, makes his Will, and deviſes it to *A.* his Wife, for her Life, to ſet Leaſe, or make Eſtates out of it, in as ample Manner as if the Deviſor were living, during the ſaid Term; and after the Death of *A.* deviſes it to *B.* his Daughter, and to the Heirs of her Body begotten, and dies: *A.* being Executrix, conſents to the Legacy, and after makes a Leaſe of a Tenement, Parcel of the Manor, to *C.* for ninety-nine Years, if three Lives ſhall ſo long live, and dies; this is a good Leaſe againſt *B.* the Daughter, altho' it was objected, that by this Clauſe, ſhe had only Power to diſpoſe of it during her Life. 2 *Roll. Abr.* 261.

A Man may deviſe Lands to the Wife, though they are but one Perſon in Law; for the Deviſe taketh not Effect, till after his Deceaſe. But though a Laſt Will doth not take Effect till after Death; yet if a Feme Covert be ſeiſed of Land in Fee, ſhe cannot deviſe the ſame to her Husband; becauſe at the Time of the making her Will, ſhe was *ſub poteſtate viri*, and the Law ſhall intend it to be done by the Coercion of the Huſband. 1 *Inſt.* 112.

If a Man deviſe a Term to his Wife, if ſhe ſo long live unmarried; and if ſhe marry, then the Wife ſhall have a Rent out of the Land, and make his Wife Executrix, and die, and the Wife conſents to the Legacy of the Term, and enters upon it, and after takes Husband, this Conſent to the Legacy of the Term, is alſo a Conſent to the Rent, when the Contingent happens. *Mich.* 13 *Jac. B. R.*

But it has been held, that a Feme Covert cannot aſſent to a Legacy; for if ſhe ſhould have Power to aſſent, or diſaſſent to a Legacy, then if a Term be deviſed to a Feme for Life, (who is alſo Executrix) Remainder to *A. B.* if the Feme takes *A. B.* to Husband, it would be in her Power to affirm or deſtroy this Deviſe, which would be miſchievous. *Sid.* 188.

A Feme Covert may make a Will, if her Husband agree to it after her Death. *Mich.* 8 *Jac.*

And a Feme Covert may not deviſe Things in Action, which ſhe hath, without the Conſent or Agreement of the Husband. 4 *H.* 6.

A Feme Covert, Executrix, cannot deviſe any Goods ſhe has as Executrix, without her Husband's Aſſent or Agreement afterwards, although ſhe may make an Executor without his Aſſent. *Mich.* 8 *Jac.*

Regularly a Feme Covert may not make a Will; and therefore where a Feme Covert made her Will, by which ſhe deviſed 30 *l.* *per Annum* out of her own Eſtate, to a Charitable Uſe; the Heir ſubmits himſelf to an Award, and is bound to perform it; the Arbitrators award Payment of it, yet by Decree of Chancery, the Heir was Diſcharged of the Payment, and the Deviſe declared void *ab initio*. *Cro. Eliz.* 27.

But though a Wife cannot make her Will, without her Husband's Aſſent, ſhe may make a Writing or Declaration, in the Nature of her Will, and it ſhall be good. And the Husband may bind himſelf by Covenant or Bond, to permit his Wife, by Will, to diſpoſe of Legacies, &c. Debt upon Bond conditioned; whereas the Defendant was to eſpouſe *A. B.* a Widow, if the Marriage took Effect, and he ſhould ſurvive the ſaid *A. B.* there was to be paid to the Obligee 300 *l.* to and for ſuch Uſes and Purpoſes as ſhe the ſaid *A. B.* by any Writing under her Hand and Seal, ſubſcribed and publiſhed in the Preſence of two Witneſſes, ſhould nominate, declare and appoint, &c. The Defendant pleads ſhe did not limit, declare or appoint any Uſe or Purpoſe for the Employment of the Money. The Plaintiff replies, that ſhe, by her Will in Writing, ſealed and and publiſhed by her, in the Preſence of two Witneſſes (naming their Names) did appoint ſuch Sums to be paid, and that the Defendant had not paid them; and on Arreſt, Judgment *pro Quer.* *Tilley* and *Pierce*'s Caſe. *Cro. Car.* 376.

The Condition of a Bond was, Whereas *A. B.* had taken *C. D.* to Wife, being poſſeſſed of divers Goods, if he ſhould permit his ſaid Wife to make a Will, and diſpoſe in Legacies, as much as ſhe would, not exceeding 100*l.* and pay and perform what ſhe appointed; That then, *&c.* the Defendant pleads ſhe made not any Will; and upon Iſſue it was found that ſhe made a Will, and did diſpoſe of divers Legacies, not exceeding 100*l.* but that ſhe was Covert at the Time of making the Will; and Judgment *pro Quer.* for it is a Will within the Intent of the Condition, and it is her Appointment, which the Husband is bound to perform. *Cro. Car.* 219.

The like Caſe is in *Cro. Car.* 597. The Condition was to permit his Wife to make a Will of her firſt Husband's Goods, to the Value of 100*l.* to be paid within one Year after her Deceaſe, *&c.* And the Defendant pleaded that he permitted his Wife to make a Will; but did not plead that he paid the Money accordingly; and the Plea was adjudged ill. *Sherman* and *Lilly.*

Articles of Agreement were made before Marriage, That the Wife ſhall make a Will, and the Husband pay the Legacies deviſed. *Per Curiam*, Her Will is void, and the Husband bound only by the Articles. *Mod. Rep.* 211.

If a Feme Covert make a Will, and deviſe Goods to another, and the Husband after her Death, deliver the Goods to the Deviſee accordingly; this ſhall bind him. 26 *E.* 3.

A Feme Sole makes her Will, and deviſes her Land to a certain Perſon, whom ſhe afterwards marries, if ſhe dies in his Life-time, the Will is void. 4 *Rep.* 60.

Of Divorces, separate Maintenances, Elopements, &c.

AS to Divorce, it is where a Man and his Wife, lawfully espoused, are adjudged by Law to live separate, for sufficient Reasons plainly proved.

And the Causes of Divorces, which dissolve Matrimony, are the five following:

1. *Causa Præcontractus*,
2. *Causa Frigiditatis*,
3. *Causa Consanguinitatis*,
4. *Causa Affinitatis*,
5. *Causa sævitiæ sive Metus.*

These Divorces declare the Marriage void *ab initio*, and Bastardise the Issue. But if two are divorced for Consanguinity, and they were Ignorant of it, the Issue shall be Legitimate. 1 *Roll. Rep.* 212.

If a Man contract with a Woman to marry her, and after he marries another Woman, the first Woman sues in the Spiritual Court, and it is by Sentence adjudged that the Man and first Woman are Baron and Feme. *Sid.* 13. Sir *Robert Paine*'s Case. And *Noy* held, that if the Wife be divorced from her Husband, *causa præcontractus* made with another by *verba de præsenti*; that in this Case, immediately by Sentence given in Court, the Marriage shall be Consummate between the

Woman and her first Husband, without any Rites *in facie Ecclesiæ*.

Two were pre-contracted, one after is espoused to a Stranger, and afterwards sued in the Spiritual Court, and Sentence is there given, that they shall marry according to the Precontract, and the Woman marries; this is good without Divorce or Consent of the Husband, and their Issue is not a Bastard. *Moor* 169.

A Man contracts to marry with *A.* and marries *B.* *A.* sues him in the Spiritual Court, and Sentence is given, That he shall espouse *A.* and cohabit with her, which he doth, and they have Issue, then he dies; and adjudged that the Issue shall inherit, though there was no Divorce from the Marriage of *B.* *Moor* Case 303.

Causa Frigiditatis, is in Case of Impotency, where a Man hath *perpetuam Impotentiam generationis.*

Sentence of Divorce was given against one *Bury*, *causa frigiditatis naturalis*, *ad sectam Uxoris suæ*; and the Wife was after married to *Carey*, by whom she had Issue; and she gave all her Inheritance to *Carey*, her second Husband; and *Bury* was also married to another Woman, by whom he had Issue. In this Case, the Opinion of the Doctors was, That then the Persons shall be compelled to cohabit together as Man and Wife; *Eo quod sancta Ecclesia decepta fuit in priori judicio.* Dyer 179. And 37 *El.* A Feme sues a divorce for Frigidity, and after the Husband marries another Wife, by whom he had Issue;

ſue; adjudg'd, that the ſecond Marriage was void. *Stafford*'s Caſe.

Cauſa affinitatis & conſanguinitatis, relates to Marriages with Kindred and Relations; as where a Man marries his Siſter, Daughter, Father's Siſter, Son's Daughter, his Brother's Wife, *&c.* prohibited by Law.

One *Mann* married h's Wife's Siſter's Daughter; for whiich he was ſued before the High Commiſſioners; and though this was not expreſly forbidden, yet becauſe Degrees, more remote are forbidden, they gave Sentence of Divorce. *Cro. Eliz.* 298.

Cauſa ſævitiæ ſive Metus; If the Husband take from his Wife Apparel, and other Neceſſaries, it is a good Foundation to ſue a Divorce, *cauſa ſævitiæ.*

And if one of them be in Danger of Poiſoning from the other, this is good Cauſe to pronounce Sentence of Separation.

A Woman lawfully eſpouſed to her Huſband, ſued a Divorce, *propter ſævitiam*, and it was *ſeparamns a Menſa & Thoro*; but no Word of *Divorciamus*. She married again, and was proſecuted for *Poligamy*; and it was clearly agreed by the Civilians, that the ſecond Marriage was unlawful, and ſhe might be in Danger of the Stat. 1 *Jac.* 1. but it was not adjudged. Though in my Lord *Roſs*'s Caſe, it was the Opinion, that they might marry again. *Cro. Car.* 461.

A Divorce *a Menſa & Thoro*, or *Cauſa Adulterii*, doth not diſſolve the Marriage; for it is ſubſequent to the Marriage, as the others are precedent. And in Caſe of Divorce *cauſa Adulterii*, the Coverture continues between the Parties; if the Husband after ſuch Divorce releaſe an Obligation, or any other Duty due to the Wife before Coverture, it hath been held a good Releaſe; which proves the Continuance of the Marriage.

And therefore, in *Littleton*'s Caſe, if a Leaſe is made to the Husband and Wife, to have and to hold to them, during the Coverture between them, they have an Eſtate for their two Lives, upon Condition, (*viz.*) If one of them die, or there be a Divorce between them, then it ſhall be lawful for the Leſſor and his Heirs to enter. *Lit. Sect.* 380. *Littleton* here ſpeaks of ſuch Divorce as diſſolves the Marriage *a vinculo Matrimonii*, for though the Husband and Wife are divorced *cauſa Adulterii*, yet the Freehold continues, becauſe the Coverture continueth. *Co. Lit.* 235.

Baron and Feme are divorced *a vinculo Matrimonii*, Dower ceaſes; and if it be by Reaſon of *Precontract*, Conſanguinity or Affinity, the Children begotten between them are Baſtards. But if the Divorce be only *a Menſa & Thoro*, it doth not debar the Woman of her Dower, or Baſtardiſe the Iſſue, *&c.* 1 *Inſt.* 235. 7 *Rep.* 43.

If a Marriage *de facto*, be voidable by Divorce, in Reſpect of Conſanguinity, Precontract, or the like, whereby the Marriage might have been diſſolved, and the Parties freed *a vinculo Matrimonii*; yet if the Husband die before any Divorce, in this Caſe, becauſe it cannot be avoided, the Wife *de facto* ſhall be endowed;

endowed; for this is *Legitimum Matrimonium quoad dotem.* 1 Inst. 33.

A Sentence of Divorce may be repealed in the Spiritual Court, by Suit, after the Death of the Parties. But if any of them die before the Sentence of Divorce is given, they cannot sue to declare the Marriage void, and Bastardise the Issue; for the Trial belongs originally to the Common Law, where there is no Disability by Sentence in the Spritual Court. 7 *Rep.* 44.

A Divorce shall continue so long as the Sentence is in Force, and unrepealed; and the Issue of that Marriage shall be Bastards. Also the Issue of the second Marriage may inherit, until the Sentence be repealed. 2 *Leon.* 207.

Where a Man and his Wife are divorced, and she is an Inheritrix, in this Case, mean Acts done shall not be reversed by the Divorce, as Receipt of Rent, Presentation to a Benefice, Gift of the Goods of the Wife, &c. though it is otherwise of Inheritances, if the Husband had discontinued or charged the Land. *Baron and Feme, p.* 379.

A Woman was divorced *Causa Adulterii* in the Husband; the Wife sued in the Spiritual Court for a Legacy given to her by a Stranger; and the Defendant pleaded a Release made by the Husband, after the Divorce. *Per Curiam*; This Divorce is not a *Dissolutio a vinculo Matrimonii*; so as that either of them may marry again; but it is a Separation only, and they are not compellable to cohabit; but if they will they may. And in regard this Separation doth not avoid the Marriage

Marriage absolutely, but they still remain Man and Wife, the Release of the Husband is good to extinguish the Duty. And the Books which say that the Feme shall have her Goods after a Divorce, are to be intended of an absolute Divorce *ab initio*. *Cro. El.* 908.

On a Divorce *a vinculo Matrimonii*, the Parties may marry again. Where a Man was divorced for the Incontinency of his Wife, and after married another, this was adjudged a void Marriage; for the Divorce was only *a Mensa & Thoro*, not *a vinculo Matrimonii*. *Moor* 942. But in Divorces for Adultery, several Acts of Parliament have allowed the innocent Party to marry again.

If a Feme *post annos nubiles*, *i. e.* at Twelve Years of Age, contract Matrimony with *A. B.* and afterwards marry with *C. D.* and after she has passed the Age of Sixteen, her Marriage with *C. D.* is dissolved *Causa praecontractus*; by this Divorce there is a Nullity of the Marriage from the Beginning: And if she had any Goods or Personal Estate, she ought to have the same again; for *Cessante causa cessat effectus*. But if he had given them away or sold them before, without Collusion, then there could be no Remedy; though if it were by Collusion, the Wife might have averred the same. And she may recover her Goods, whereof the Property may be known by Action of Detinue; and the rest that are in Money, she may sue for by the Spiritual Law, or in the Chancery. *Dyer* 13. 1 *Nels. Abr.* 675.

If

If the Husband aliens the Land of the Wife, and after they are divorced *Caufa præcontractus*, or any other Caufe which diffolves *a vinculo*, the Wife, during the Life of the Baron, may enter and have her Lands by the Stat. 32 *H.* 8.

And if Baron and Feme purchafe Lands jointly, and are differfed, then the Baron releafes, and after they are divorced; here in this Cafe, the Feme fhall have a Moiety, although there were not Moieties before; for the Divorce converted it into Moieties. By Divorce, an Eftate-Tail of Baron and Feme may be extinct. *Godb.* 18.

If a Man be bound in an Obligation to a Feme Sole, and after fhe marries him, and after that fhe is divorced, fhe may then have an Action, which by the Marriage was fufpended.

A Feme Covert may fue without her Hufband, for her feparate Maintenance. And a Woman, under Separation from her Hufband, muft fue by her next Friend. She may fue her Husband in her own Name, for Alimony. *Mod. Cafes* 35. *Wood's Inft.* 62.

Alimony is that Allowance for Maintenance, which a married Woman is entitled to upon any occafional Separation from her Husband; except in the Cafes of Elopement and Adultery; and the Spiritual Court is the proper Court to fue in for it; where a Man may be fued for ill Ufage of his Wife, and be ordered to pay her fo much *per* Week Alimony, which was anciently called *Rationabile Eftoverium.* 12 Rep. 30. Moor 874.

Baron

Baron and Feme by Agreement ſeparated and liv'd apart, and it was Agreed that the Wife ſhould have 150*l.* *per Ann.* ſeparate Maintenance; and out of which ſhe had ſav'd ſome Money, put it out to Intereſt taking Bonds in a Friend's Name, and afterwards diſpoſed thereof by Will: This was in Chancery eſtabliſh'd a good Diſpoſition. *Chan. Caſ.* 118.

The Lord *Holles's* Lady lent 100*l.* to a Perſon, and in the Note which was firſt given for it, was written that the Money ſhould be diſpos'd as the ſaid Lady *Holles* ſhould direct: An Action at Law being brought for this Money, it was barr'd by the Statute of Limitations; then a Bill in Equity was exhibited for Relief, and in regard the Money was look'd upon as a *Depoſitum*, and a Truſt thereupon for the Lady, a Decree was obtained for the ſame. 2 *Ventr.* 345.

Covenant to pay the Defendant's Wife, or whom ſhe ſhould appoint, 50*l.* a Year, as a ſeparate Maintenance, provided ſhe lived at ſuch a Place as ſhould be directed: The Defendant Pleads ſhe did not live at the Place appointed; and the Plaintiff replies, that ſhe was ready to live at any ſuch Place, but that no Place was appointed; to which the Defendant demurred, as being a Condition precedent. *Per Curiam*; the Defendant ſhould have alledg'd that ſhe lived at ſuch a Place, and another was appointed; for this is a Condition ſubſequent, the Covenant being in Purſuance of a former abſolute Agreement to paſs ſo much; and it is like the Aſſent of the Husband, which is intended 'till the contrary appears. 3 *Keb.* 363.

In

In Covenant: The Defendant covenanted with the Plaintiff, that *A.* Wife of the Defendant, ſhould be permitted to live ſeparate from him, until he and the ſaid *A.* by Writing ſigned by them ſeverally, and atteſted by two Witneſſes, ſhould give notice to each other that they would Cohabit: And further, that the Defendant during the Coverture, and until ſuch Notice be given of their Deſires to Cohabit as aforeſaid, would pay to the Plaintiff 300 *l. per Ann.* for Maintenance of the ſaid *A.* at four quarterly Payments; and ſets forth, that the ſaid *A.* from the Date of the Indenture of Covenants, to the Time of the Suit commenced, did live ſeparate from the Defendant; and no Notice of Cohabitation had been given during that Time of either Side, and Sues for 75 *l.* one Quarter's Payment.

The Defendant pleads in Bar, that after the Indenture aforeſaid, and before the Action, another Indenture was made between the Defendant and *A.* his Wife of the one Part, and the Plaintiff of the other Part; reciting the firſt Indenture, and alſo that the Defendant and *A.* did intend to Cohabit, and did ſo at that Time; and expreſſing, that it was the true Intent and Meaning of all the Parties to the ſaid Indenture produc'd *ut ſupra*, that ſo long as the Defendant and *A.* ſhould agree to Cohabit, the ſaid annual Payment ſhould ceaſe: And the Plaintiff by the laſt Indenture covenanted, that ſo long as they cohabited, the Defendant ſhould be indemnified from the Payment of the 300 *l. per Annum.* The Plaintiff replies, they did not Cohabit *modo & for-*

ma

ma prout: The Defendant demurs. Judgment was given for the Plaintiff, for the last Deed had not taken away the Effect of the former; and the Cohabitation was not according to the first Indenture, by Writing mutually signed, *&c.* *Gawden* and *Draper.* 2 *Ventr.* 217.

Bond conditioned, that whereas the Defendant should Marry a certain Widow, who was possess'd of divers Goods of her first Husband's, and the Goods of his Children, which the second Husband was not to meddle with; but that she and the Children should be permitted to Enjoy them, without Interruption of the Defendant. The Defendant pleads Performance: And the Plaintiff assigns for Breach, that the first Husband was possess'd of such a Shop and Goods, and that the Wife had them before her second Marriage; and that such a Day after the Marriage, the Defendant her second Husband took the said Goods into his Hands, and them detained: Verdict *pro Quer.* *Cro. Car.* 204.

The Wife of an improvident Husband had unknown to him, by her great Frugality, rais'd a large Sum of Money for the good of their Children; which she had dispos'd of for that Purpose, being no otherwise provided for: And this Disposition of the Wife the Lord Chancellor confirm'd by Decree; but afterwards upon Review, and Assistance by the Judges the Decree was reversed, as being dangerous to give a Feme Power to dispose of her Husband's Estate. *Scot* and *Brograve*'s Case, *Anno* 1639. In *George*'s and *Chancey*'s Case, a Disposition by Feme Covert, of Money

ney

ney raised out of a separate Maintenance, was adjudg'd good against the Husband. *Vide supra.*

A Feme Covert purloin'd her Husband's Goods and Money, and put the Money into other Men's Hands, who bought Lands to her Use therewith: The Heir and Executor of the Husband, sued in Equity to have the Land or Money restored. But *Egerton* Chancellor denied Relief: He said he would not Relieve the Husband, were he Living, *for he sate not there to give Relief to Fools or Buzzards, who would not keep their Money from their Wives.*

I now proceed to *Elopements* of Feme Coverts, the last Head of my Treatise.

Elopement, says a Writer of Antiquity, by the Sound of the Word and Nature of the Offence seems to be derived *a Lopex* a Fox; for it is when a Woman goes away from her Husband, and seeks her Prey far from Home, which is the Fox's Quality.

If a Woman Elope from her Husband, and live in Adultery with another, she shall lose and forfeit her Dower; unless the Husband of his own free Will suffer her to Cohabit with him, and be reconciled to the Wife: But to prove the Reconciliation, lying together several Nights, at several Places, shall not avail. Against this it was objected, that the Husband and Wife never were resident or abiding in one House together; and that the Feme continued in Adultery with one or other, as long as her Husband lived. *Et non allocatur*; for there may be many Elopements with many Reconciliations; and the Defendant

ant at his Peril must take Issue upon one. *Dyer* 170. Lord *Powis*'s Case.

A Wife elopes from the Husband, and has a Child by another Person; if the Husband be within the four Seas at the Time, it is no Bastard by the Laws of *England*. *Hill.* 14. *Jac.* 1.

But if a Woman Elopes from her Husband, and the Husband gives publick notice of it, and declares he will not pay any Debts of hers she Contracts; if any Persons Trust her afterwards, the Husband is not liable to satisfy the Debt. 1 *Sid. Rep.* 109.

Tho' according to the Opinion of Chief Justice *Holt*, if a Wife run away and Elope from her Husband, and contract Debts, and after the Husband comes after her, and lies with her, tho' but for a Night, that will make him chargeable for the Debts of the Wife. *Pasch.* 3. *Ann. Mod. Cas.* 171.

Vide more, under *Actions against Husband and Wife.*

The

The Argument *of* JUDGE HIDE *in the Exchequer Chamber*, Term. Trin. 15. Car. 2. *in the Case of* Manby *and* Scot, *whether and in what Cases, the Husband is bound by the Contract of the Wife.*

A Feme Covert departs from her Husband against his Will, and continues absent from him divers Years; afterwards the Wife desires to Cohabit with her Husband, but he refuseth to admit her, and from that Time the Wife lives separate from him: During this Separation, the Husband forbids a Tradesman of *London* to Trust his Wife with any Goods or Wares; and yet for some Years before and afterwards he allows his Wife no Maintenance: The Tradesman contrary to the Prohibition of the Husband, sells and delivers Wares to the Wife upon Credit, at a reasonable Price; and the Wares so sold to the Wife are necessary for her, and suitable to the Degree of her Husband: The Wares are not paid for; wherefore the Tradesman brings an Action upon the Case against the Husband, and declares that the Husband was indebted to him in 40 *l.* for Wares and Merchandizes formerly to the Husband sold and deliver'd; and that the Husband in Consideration thereof, did promise to pay the said

Money: That the Husband hath not paid the same, tho' thereunto requir'd; and for that Money the Action is brought. Now, whether this Action will lie against the Husband for the Wares thus sold and delivered to the Wife, contrary to the Prohibition of the Husband, or not, is the Question?

This Case is the meanest that ever received Resolution in this Place; but as the same is now handled, it is of as great Consequence to all the King's People as any Case can be; it concerns every individual Person of both Sexes, that is, or hereafter shall be Married within this Kingdom, in the first and nearest Relation betwixt Man and Wife: It toucheth the Man in point of his Power and Dominion over his Wife, and it concerns the Woman in point of her Substance and Livelihood; and I will deliver my Opinion plainly and freely, according as I conceive the Law to be, without favouring the one, or courting the other Sex.

First, I hold, that the Husband shall not be charged by such a Contract, tho' he do not allow any Maintenance to his Wife. *Secondly*, admit the Husband were chargeable generally by such a Contract; yet I conceive, that this Action doth not lie for the Plaintiff, as the Declaration is, and as the Verdict is found against the Defendant in this particular Case.

For the first, every Gift, Contract or Bargain, contains an Agreement on the Behalf of the Contractor or Bargainor, that the Donee or Bargainee shall have the Things contracted for; and the other is content to take them, and so in every Contract there is a mutual Assent of the Minds of the Parties, which mu-

tual

tual Assent is an Agreement. *Plowd.* 17. *Fogasse's* Case. But a Feme Covert cannot give a mutual Assent of her Mind, nor do any Act without her Husband; for her Will and Mind (as also her self) is under and subject to the Will or Mind of her Husband; and consequently she cannot make any Bargain or Contract of her self, to bind her Husband.

In the Beginning when GOD created Woman an Help meet for Man, he said *They Two shall be one Flesh*; and thereupon our Law says, that Husband and Wife are but one Person in the Law: Presently after the Fall, the Judgment of GOD upon Woman was, *Thy Desire shall be to thy Husband, for thy Will shall be subject to thy Husband, and he shall Rule over Thee.* 3 Gen. 16. Hereupon our Law puts the Wife *Sub potestate viri*, and says, *Quod ipsa Potestatem sui non habeat, sed vir Suus*; and she is disabled to make any Grant, Contract or Bargain, without the Allowance or Consent of her Husband. *Bract. lib.* 3. *cap.* 32. 1 *Roll.* 351. *pl.* 45, 46. The Words of the Books and Authorities of our Law to prove this Point are observable; namely, if a Feme Covert make a Contract, or buy any Thing in the Market, or elsewhere, without the Consent of her Husband, tho' it come to the Use of the Husband, yet the Contract is void, and shall not charge the Husband; but if a Man command or Licence his Wife to by Things necessary, or Agree that she shall buy, he shall be bound by this Command or Licence. Old *Nat. Br.* 62. 21 *H.* 7. 70 *Fitz. N. B. R.* 120. Which proves, that it is not the Buying or Contract of the Wife, which Binds or Charges the Husband, (for that is void in itself) but the Command or Licence of the Husband, which makes it the Contract or Bargain of the Husband.

As to my Brother *Twisden*'s Argument for the Woman's Power, when he says, that all those Books are where the Wife deals or trades as a Factor to her Husband, and all grounded upon that Reason, the Words themselves prove the Contrary; for the Difference taken by all the Books is, between the Buying and Contract of the Wife, without the Knowledge or Consent of her Husband; and a Buying or Contract had by the Wife, with Allowance or Command of the Husband. In the first Case, the Buying or Contract is void; in the other, the Allowance or Command makes it good, as the Contract or Bargain of the Husband: Besides, weigh the Inconveniences which would follow, if the Law were otherwise.

Judges, in giving their Judgments and Resolutions in Cases depending before them, are to judge of Inconveniencies as Things illegal; and an Argument *ab inconvenienti* is very strong to prove that it is against Law. *Plowd.* 279. Then examine the Inconveniencies which must ensue, if the Law were according to my Brother *Twisden* and *Tyrrel*'s Opinions: If the Contract or Bargain of the Wife, made without the Allowance or Consent of the Husband, shall bind him upon Pretence of necessary Apparel, it will be in the Power of the Wife (who by the Law of God and of the Land, is put under the Power of the Husband, and is bound to live in Subjection to him) to Rule over her Husband,

and

and undo him, and it ſhall not be in the Power of the Husband to prevent it. For here the Wife ſhall be her own Carver, and Judge of the Fitneſs of her Apparel, of the Time when it is neceſſary for her to have new Cloaths, and as often as ſhe pleaſes, without asking the Advice or Allowance of her Huſband: And will Wives depend on the Kindneſs and Favours of their Husbands, or be obſervant towards them as they ought to be, if ſuch a Power be put into their Hands?

Then admitting, that the Wife in Truth wants neceſſary Apparel, and thereupon ſhe goes into *Ludgate Street* to a Mercer and takes up Stuff, and makes a Contract for neceſſary Clothes; thence ſhe goes into *Cheapſide*, and takes up Linen there in like Manner; and alſo goes into a third Street, and fits herſelf with Ribbonds, and other Things ſuitable to her Occaſions, and her Husband's Degree: This done ſhe goes away, diſpoſeth of the Commodities to furniſh herſelf with Money to go Abroad to *Hide-Park*, or to Play at Gaming, or the like. Next Morning, this good Woman goes Abroad into ſome other Part of *London*, makes her Neceſſity and want of Apparel known, and takes more Wares upon Truſt, as ſhe had done the Day before; after the ſame Manner ſhe goes to a third and fourth Place, and makes new Contracts for freſh Goods; none of theſe Tradeſman knowing or imagining ſhe was formerly furniſh'd by the Others, and each of them ſeeing and believing her to have great need of the Commodities ſold her; ſhall not the Husband be chargeable and liable to pay every one of these, if the Contract of the Wife doth bind him? Certainly he is, and where this will End no Man can foresee.

As for my Brother *Tyrrel's* Saying, we may alter the Law because an Inconvenience may follow thereon, that is True: But we ought to provide against such Inconveniencies as may arise, before we adjudge or declare the Law in a particular Case in Question, whether the Law be so or not? And that is the Case here: It is objected, that the Husband is bound of Common Right, to provide for and maintain his Wife; and the Law having disabled the Wife to bind herself by her Contract, therefore the Burden shall rest upon the Husband, who by Law is bound to Maintain her: Generally the Antecedent is most true, but apply this general Proposition to our particular Case, and then see what Logick there is in the Argument. I am bound to maintain and provide for my Wife: Therefore my Wife departing from me against my Will, shall be her own Carver, and take up what Apparel she pleaseth upon Trust, without my Privity or Allowance, and I shall be bound to pay for it.

Besides, altho' it be true, that the Husband is bound to maintain his Wife, yet that is with this Limitation, *viz.* So long as she keeps the Station wherein the Law hath placed her, and she continues a Help meet unto him; for if a Woman of her own Head, without the Allowance or Judgment of the Church, which hath united them in the State of Matrimony (and which only can separate or dissolve this Union) depart from her Husband against his Consent,

Consent, be the Pretence what it will, she doth thereby put herself out of the Husband's Protection; so that during such unlawful Separation, she is no Part of her Husband's Care, Charge or Family.

The Husband is Head of the Wife, as fully as the King is Head of the Commonwealth; and the Wife by the Law is put *sub potestate viri*, and under his Protection, tho' he hath not *Potestatem vitæ & necis* over her, as the King hath over his Subjects. When the Wife goes away from her Husband against his Will, she forsakes and deserts his Government, and assumes to govern herself contrary to the Law of God and of the Land; and therefore it is but just, that the Law for this Offence, should put her into the same Condition in the petit Commonwealth of the Houshold, that it puts the Subject for the like Offence in the great Commonwealth of the Realm; as the one shall be out of the King's Protection, so the other shall be out of the Protection of the Husband.

But 'tis objected by my Brother *Tyrrell*; that it appears not in whose Default this Departure was, whether in his, or her Default? To this I answer, that the Law doth not allow a Wife to depart from her Husband in any Case, or for any Cause whatsoever, of her own Head: An express Command is laid upon her by the Law of God to the contrary. *Cor*. 7. 10. And the Provision which our Law hath made for the Safeguard of the Person of a Woman, in Case of Cruelty by her Husband, and for her Maintenance, if the Husband refuses to allow it, proves that it is not lawful for the Wife to go from her Husband upon any Pretence whatsoever.

If the Wife be in Fear or Doubt of her Husband, that he will beat or Kill her, she may have a *Supplicavit* out of the Chancery against her Husband, and cause him to find Sureties that he will not beat or Use her otherwise than in a Civil Manner, and for to Order and Rule her, *&c.* *F. N. B.* 179. And if the Husband refuse to give or allow necessary and fitting Maintenance unto his Wife; the Law hath provided a Remedy for her by Complaint to the Ordinary and Proceedings in the Ecclesiastical Court.

Next it is said, that the Wife in our Case did return, and desire to Cohabit with her Husband again, which he refus'd; and so she is remitted to her former Condition. Admit that be True, her Return hath not put her in a better Condition than she was before her Departure; in which Case, she could not be her own Carver, and have charged her Husband (according to her Pleasure) with Apparel, but was to be clothed in such Sort as her Husband thought fit. Besides, in our Case the Wife departed from her Husband, and liv'd from him divers Years, before the Wares Sold or the Action brought; then she desired to Cohabit with him, which he refused to admit, and from that Time she liv'd from him: This is what appears in the present Case; and is this Offence so easily purged, with a bare Desire to Cohabit, without some other Submission and Satisfaction given of her better Carriage for the Future.

The

The Church declares, that one of the principal Ends for which Marriage was ordained, is for the mutual Society, Help and Comfort, which the one ought to have of the other, in Prosperity and Adversity: The Woman of her self in contracting of Marriage, makes a solemn Vow *in facie Ecclesiæ*, to live together with her Husband, in the holy State of Matrimony; to Obey him and Serve him, to Love him and keep him in Sickness and in Health, 'till Death them do part. Now the Wife in our Case, by departing from her Husband against his Will, breaks all the Commands of the Law of God, and her own Vow: She makes a voluntary Separation, and temporary Divorce between herself and her Husband; she deprives him of that mutual Society, Help and Comfort which she owes to him for many Years; and are all these Offences wash'd away with a Desire only to Cohabit with him, without any Contrition? No certainly, Confession and Promise of future Obedience, ought to precede her Remitter or Restitution to the Privileges of a Wife: And it is the Rule in the *Civil Law*, that the Wife ought to be a Penitentiary before the Husband is bound to receive her, or to give her any Maintenance; and no such Thing appears in this Case.

It is said by my Brother *Twisden*; altho' the Wife departs from her Husband, yet she continues his Wife, and she ought not to Starve. If a Woman be of so haughty a Stomach, that she will chuse to Starve, rather than Submit and be reconciled to her Husband; she may take her own Choice:

The

The Law is in no Default, which doth not provide for ſuch a Wife. And if a married Woman who can have no Goods of her own to Live on, will depart from her Husband againſt his Will, and not ſubmit herſelf unto him, let her live on Charity, or Starve in the Name of God; for in ſuch Caſe the Law ſays, her evil Demeanor brought it upon her, and her Death ought to be imputed to her own Wickedneſs.

As to the Objection, that it were ſtrange if our Law, which gives Relief in all Caſes, ſhould ſend a Woman unto another Law or Court to ſeek Remedy to have Maintenance: I Anſwer, it is not ſending the Wife to another Law, but leaving the Caſe to it's proper Juriſdiction, it being of Eccleſiaſtical Cognizance. Is it any Strangeneſs or Diſparagement to the Common Pleas, to ſend a Felon taken in the Court, to the King's Bench to be indicted? Or to the King's Bench, to ſend a Woman to the Common Pleas to recover her Dower? Why is it more ſtrange for the Common Law to ſend a Woman to the Ordinary to determine Differences betwixt her and her Husband, touching Matters of Matrimony, than for our Courts at Common Law to write unto the Ordinary, to certify Loyalty of Marriage, or the like, where Iſſue is join'd on theſe Points in the King's Courts? For altho' the Proceſs in the Eccleſiaſtical Courts be in the Names of the Biſhops, yet theſe Courts are the King's Courts, and the Law by which they proceed is the King's Law. 5 *Rep.* 39. *Cawdrie's* Caſe.

And

And as in Temporal Causes, the King by the Mouth of the Judges in his Courts of Justice, determines them by the Temporal Law; so in Causes Ecclesiastical and spiritual, the Cognizance whereof belongs not to the Common Law, they are determined by the Ecclesiastical Judges, according to the King's Ecclesiastical Laws: And that Causes of Matrimony, and the Differences between Husband and Wife, relating to Alimony or Maintenance for the Wife, (which are dependant upon or incident unto Matrimony) are all of Ecclesiastical, and not secular Cognizance, is evident by the Books and Authorities of our Laws. *De Causa Testamentaria, sicut nec de Causa Matrimoniali, curia Regia se non intromittat, sed in foro Ecclesiastico debet placitum terminari. Bract. lib.* 2. *c.* 20. All Causes Testamentary, and of Matrimony, by the Laws and Customs of the Realm, do belong to the spiritual Jurisdiction. *Stat.* 24 *H.* 8. *cap.* 2.

The Words of the Writ of Prohibition granted in such Cases, are, *Placita de Catallis, & Debitis quæ sunt de Testamento vel Matrimonio, Spectant ad forum Ecclesiasticum.* In a Suit commenced by a Woman against her Husband, before the Commissioners for Ecclesiastical Causes for Alimony, a Prohibition was prayed and granted, because it is a Suit properly to be brought and prosecuted before the Ordinary; in which, if the Party find himself grieved, he may have Relief by Appeal unto the superior Court, and that he cannot have upon a Sentence given in the high Commission Court. 1 *Cro.* 220. *Drake's* Case.

But

But then it is objected by my Brothers *Tyrrell* and *Twisden*, that the Remedy in the Ecclesiastical Court is not sufficient: For if the Husband will not obey the Sentence of the Ordinary, it is but Excommunication for his Contumacy, and that will neither Feed nor Cloath the Wife. Are the Censures of the Church grown of so little Account with us, or is the Separation *a Communione Fidelium*, become so contemptible, as to be slighted with *but Excommunication?* Hath our Law provided any Remedy so penal, or can it give any Judgment so fearful as this? With us the Rule is, *committitur Marescal.* or *Prison.* de, &c. *Traditur Satanæ*, i.e. Take him Gaoler 'till he pay the Debt, or take him Devil 'till he obey the Church: And this Judgment is warranted by the Rule of St. *Paul, whom I have delivered unto Satan.* 1 Cor. 5. 5. And it is said by our Law, *Excommunicato interdicitur omnis actus Legitimus, ita quod agere non potest, nec aliquem convenire cum ipso, nec orare, nec loqui, nec palam, nec abscondite vesci licet.* Bracton lib. 5. cap. 23.

Where a Man is excommunicated by the Law of the Church, he is disabled to maintain any Action; if he sue an Action real or personal, the Tenant or Defendant may Plead, that he is excommunicated, and demand Judgment if he shall be answered. *Litt.* 201. He who is rightfully cut off from the Unity of the Church and Excommunicate, ought to be taken by the whole Multitude as a Heathen and a Publican, until he be openly reconciled by Penance. *Act.* 33. Confirm'd by 13 *Eliz.* *If he neglect to hear the Church, let him be as*

an

an Heathen and Publican. Matt. xviii. 17. Shall a Man be accurs'd, barred of the Company or Society of Christians, cut off from the Body of Christ, and accounted as a Heathen and Publican, for not allowing Maintenance to his Wife, when the Church enjoins him so to do; and shall not this be accounted a sufficient Remedy for the Wife? I fear it is the want of Religion, and due Credence to the Censures of the Church, which occasions this Objection, rather than a real want of sufficient Remedy in Law for her Relief.

The last Matter to be answered, is rather the Opinion of my before mentioned Brothers in their Arguments, than an Objection in this Case; namely, If an Action upon the Case doth not lie against the Husband upon the Contract of the Wife for necessary Apparel, an Action of Trover and Conversion lieth against him for the Stuff; and so one way or other the Husband must pay the Reckoning. If the Law should be so, it were a Conversion with a Witness; for then the Husband would seem to be *Sub potestate Fœminæ*: He might say with St. *Paul*, *that the Head of the Woman is the Man*; but if the Wife shall lay his Headship in the Gaol, it will not be in the Power of the Husband to prevent or avoid it.

One kind of Divorce between Husband and Wife is, when an Action of Trespass is brought against them, and the Husband only appears, and Process issues against the Wife, until she be waved and outlawed, she can never purchase her Pardon, or reverse the Outlawry, unless the Husband will appear; so that if the Husband please he is Divorced: If the Wife be outlawed by erroneous Process, and the Husband will not bring a Writ of Error; he may by this way be rid of his Wife, and that doth countervail a Divorce. 14 *H.* 6. 14. *a.* 18 *Ed.* 4. 4. *a.* *See* 1 *Lev.* 51. 1 *Keb.* 194, 637.

By these Books it appears, that the Law puts a Power in the Husband to get rid of the Wife, and provides a Remedy to tame a Shrew; but I never heard before, that the Law hath left it in the Power of the Wife to do so by her Husband: And I do not remember that my Brothers did vouch any Authority, or give any Reason for Maintenance of their Opinions; and therefore, I may with Freedom deny the Law to be as they have said. Besides, the Nature of an Action of Trover, proves that it lies not in this Case: The Count is, that the Plaintiff was possess'd of such Goods, as of his own proper Goods, and casually lost them; that the Goods came to the Defendant's Hands by finding, yet he knowing them to belong to the Plaintiff refuseth to deliver them to him, but hath converted them to his own Use. So that an Action is grounded upon a Wrong supposed to be done by the Defendant, in converting the Goods of the Plaintift knowingly to his own Use, against the Will of the Plaintiff: And that is the Reason why the Plaintiff in that Action, must prove a Demand of the Goods, and an actual Conversion by the Defendant, or else he fails in the Action.

In an Action of the Case, for that the Defendant did find the Goods of the Plaintiff, and

and delivered them to Persons unknown, *non deliberavit modo & forma* is no Plea, without saying *Not Guilty*, where the Thing rests in Feasance: And if the Action be, that the Plaintiff was possess'd, *ut de bonis propriis*, and the Defendant did find and Convert them to his own Use, it is no Plea, that the Plaintiff was not possess'd, *&c.* but he must Plead *Not Guilty* to the Misdemeanor, and give the other Matter in Evidence. 33 *H.* 8. *Bro. Act. Cas.* In Trover, the Plaintiff declares, that he was possess'd of the Goods, and lost them, and that the Defendant found them, and converted them to his own Use: The Defendant pleaded, that the Plaintiff did gage the Goods unto him for 10 *l.* and that he detained the Goods for the Same; this is no Plea, but he ought to Plead *Not Guilty*, and give this Matter in Evidence; for the Action doth suppose a wrong, which the Defendant ought to Answer. 4 *E.* 6.

Now what wrong is done to the Plaintiff in our Case, when he himself sells and delivers the Goods? Put the Case of Sale made to a Man upon Credit, and the Vendee promis'd to pay for the Goods at *Michaelmas*, but fails to do it; shall the Salesman have Trover against the Vendee, because he pays not the Money at the Day? And will the Sale to this Feme Covert, alter the Case, or the Law, as to the Action? It is True, that for a Conversion by the Woman before Coverture, or by the Wife during the Coverture, an Action of Trover lies against the Husband and Wife; but this is for a Conversion by wrong, when she takes the Goods, and Coverts them against the

the Will of the Owner. 1 *Cro.* 254. *Remis* and *Humfrey's* Case. In Case a Man comes to buy Goods, and offers Money for them, which the Owner agrees to accept; if the Buyer takes the Goods away without Payment or Delivery by the Owner, there an Action of Trespass or Trover lies, notwithstanding the Bargain. 21 *H.* 7. 6. Otherwise it is, if they agree upon a Price, and the Vendor taketh the Vendee's Word for Payment, and delivers the Goods unto him; for there the Vendor is put to his Action for the Money upon the Contract, and shall not bring Trover for the Goods. 14 *H.* 8. 22.

If an Infant gives or sells Goods, and delivers them with his own Hand, he shall have no Action of Trespass against the Donee or Vendee, by reason of the Delivery. 21 *H.* 7. 39. But if an Infant give or sell Goods, and the Vendee or Donee takes them by Force on the Gift or Sale, the Infant may have an Action of Trespass against him. *Hob.* 77. 2 *Rol. Rep.* 408. *Latch* 10. So in this Case; if a Feme Covert takes Wares of a Shopkeeper against his Will, upon Pretence of Buying them, an Action lies against the Husband: Tho' if the Owner sell the Goods to the Wife upon Trust, and delivers the Goods unto her; he shall not have an Action of Trespass against the Husband, because of this Delivery.

A Man takes my Wife and Cloaths her, this amounts to a Gift of the Apparel unto her: And I may take my Wife, with the Apparel, and no Action lies against me. 11 *H.* 4. 83. 1 *Cro.* 344. By the same Reason, when

when a Man delivers Stuff, or other Wares to my Wife, knowing her to be a Feme Covert, to make Apparel, without my Privity or Allowance; this ſhall be conſtrued to be a Gift of the Stuff unto her, and I ſhall not be charged in any Action for it. And if an Action of Trover ſhould be brought againſt the Husband, in our Caſe; then he would be barred of all thoſe Helps which my Brothers (who maintain that Opinion) have allowed unto him, and have made Reaſons, for which an Action of the Caſe ſhould lie againſt him on the Contract; namely, the Jurors are to Examine and Set the Price or Value, and the Neceſſity and Fitneſs of Things, with Relation to the Degree of the Husband, whereby Care is taken that the Husband ſhall have no wrong; for in an Action of Trover, the Jury cannot Examine any of thoſe Matters, but are to inquire only of the Property of the Plaintiff, and the Converſion by the Defendant, and to give Damages according to the Value of the Goods: And ſo it ſhall be in the Power of the Wife to take up what ſhe pleaſeth, and to have what ſhe liſts, without Reference unto the Degree, or reſpect to the Eſtate of her Husband, and he ſhall be charged with it *Nolens volens*.

It is objected, that the Jury is to Judge what is fit for the Wife's Degree, that they are truſted with the Reaſonableneſs of the Price, and are to Examine the Value; and alſo the Neceſſity of the Things or Apparel. Alas, poor Man! What a Judicature is ſet up here, to decide the private Difference between Husband and Wife? The Wife will have a Velvet Gown, and a Sattin Petticoat; and the Husband thinks Mohair is as Fashionable, and fitter for his Quality: The Husband says, that a plain Lawn Gorget of 10 *s.* pleaseth him and suits best with his Condition; but the Wife takes up at the *Exchange* a *Flanders* Lace or Point-handkerchief of 40 *l.* A Jury of Mercers, Silkmen, Sempsters and Exchange-men are very excellent and indifferent Judges to decide this Controversy: It is not for their Support to be against the Wife, but to be for her; that they may put off their braided Wares to the Wife upon Trust, at their own Price, and then Sue the Husband for the Money. And are not a Jury of Drapers and Milleners bound to favour the Mercer or Exchange-men to Day, that they may do the like for them to Morrow?

Besides, what Matter of Fact (and of that only the Law hath made Jurors the Judges) is there in the Fitness of the Commodities, with respect to the Degree of the Husband? And whether this or that Thing be the most necessary for the Wife? The Matter of Fact is, to find that the Wife wanted necessary Apparel, and that she bought such and such Wares of the Plaintiff, at such a Price, to Cloath herself; and leaves the Fitness of the one, and the Reasonableness of the other to the Court, for that is Matter of Law, whereof the Jurors have no Cognizance. In Cases of Fines, Customs and Services, if the Question be, whether the same be reasonable or not? This shall be adjudg'd by the Discretion of the Justices, upon the true State of the Matter, and not by the Jury: For Rea-

sonableness

ſonableneſs belongs to the Cogniſance of the Law. 4 *Rep.* 27. *Co. Lit.* 56. Leſſee for Life, makes a Leaſe for Years, and dies within the Term; in an Action of Treſpaſs brought by the firſt Leſſor againſt the Leſſee for Years, he ought by his Plea to ſet forth what Day his Leſſor died, and at what Place, where the Land lies, and when he left the Poſſeſſion; and ſo leave it to the Diſcretion of the Court, whether he did quit the Poſſeſſion in reaſonable Time or not? 22 *E.* 4. 18.

The Fitneſs or Neceſſity of Apparel, and the Reaſonableneſs of the Price, ſhall be judged by the Court, on the Circumſtances of the Matter, as the ſame appears by the Pleadings, or is found by the Jury; but the Jurors are not Judges thereof. Again, there is a twofold Neceſſity, *Neceſſitas ſimplex, vel abſoluta*; and *Neceſſitas qualificata, vel convenientiæ.* Of a ſimple and abſolute Neceſſity in the Caſe of Apparel or Food for a Feme Covert, the Law of the Land takes Notice, and provides a Remedy for the Wife, if the Husband refuſe or neglect to do it. But if it be only *Neceſſitas convenientiæ*, whether this or that Apparel, this or that Meat or Drink be moſt convenient for any Wife, the Law makes no Perſon Judge thereof, but the Husband himſelf; and in theſe Caſes, no Man is to put his Hand between the Bone and the Fleſh.

I ſhall conclude the general Queſtion, or firſt Point, with the Judgment of Sir *Thomas Smith*, in his Book of the *Common-wealth of* England, lib. 1. c. 11. fol. 23. *The Natural-*

lest Conjunction of two towards the making a further Society of Continuance, is of Husband and Wife, each having Care of the Family, the Man to get, to travel abroad, to defend; the Wife to save, to stay at home and distribute that which is gotten for the Nurture of the Children and Family, is the first and most natural Apparence of one of the best Kind of Commonwealths, where not one always, but sometimes, and in some Things, another bears Rule; which to maintain, GOD hath given the Man greater Wit, Strength and Courage to compel the Woman to obey, by Reason or Force; and to the Woman Beauty, fair Countenance and sweet Words, to make the Man obey her again for Love. Thus each obeyeth and commandeth the other; and they two together Rule the House, so long as they remain together in One. I wish that the Women of this Age would learn thus to obey, and thus to command their Husbands; then would they want for nothing that is fitting.

I am now come to this particular Case, as it stands before us on the Record. Admit that the Husband were chargeable by Law, by the Contract of his Wife, yet Judgment ought to be given against the Plaintiff, upon this Declaration, as this Verdict is found. For first, the Declaration is, That the Defendant was indebted to the Plaintiff in 40*l.* for Wares and Merchandises, by the Plaintiff to him before that Time sold and delivered; and the Verdict finds that the Wares were not sold and delivered to the Defendant, but the same were sold to his Wife, without his Privity or Consent. So it appears, that the Plaintiff hath mistaken his Action upon the

Case

Case, for Wares sold unto him; and ought to have declared Specially, according to the Truth of the Case, for Wares sold to his Wife for necessary Apparel. The Action brought by the Plaintiff is false, and this Verdict is against his Case.

Then the Jury find, that the Defendant's Wife departed from him against his Will, and and lived from him; and that the Defendant, before the Wares were sold to his Wife, did forbid the Plaintiff to trust her with any Wares; and that the Plaintiff, contrary to his Prohibition, did sell and deliver those Wares to the Wife upon Credit; and I conceive, that this Prohibition doth so far bind and bar the Plaintiff, that he shall never have any Action against the Defendant for Wares sold and delivered to his Wife, after he was prohibited by the Husband. It is agreed by all, that a Feme Covert cannot generally make any Contract, which shall charge or discharge her Husband, but by the Authority or Consent of the Husband, precedent or subsequent. And when the Husband forbids a particular Person to trust his Wife, this Prohibition is an absolute Revocation or Countermand, as to that Person, of the general Authority which the Wife had before, and puts him in the same Condition, as if the Wife had never any Authority given her.

It is said by my Brothers *Twisden* and *Tyrrel*, That the Prohibition of the Husband is void; for (says *Tyrrel*) the Husband is bound to maintain his Wife, notwithstanding her Departure from him; and therefore he cannot prohibit others to do it. And

Twisden ſays, it is a Right veſted in the Wife by the Law; therefore the Prohibition of the Husband ſhall not deveſt or take it away from her. I have already anſwered theſe Reaſons, on which they ground their Opinions, and will not repeat them. But admit that the Husband be by Law bound to maintain his Wife, notwithſtanding her Departure from him againſt his Will; and that the Law doth give or veſt a Right in the Wife to bind or charge the Husband by her Contract, for neceſſary Apparel; will this be a good Conſequence thereupon; therefore the Husband cannot forbid this or that particular Perſon to truſt his Wife?

A Man makes a Deed of Feoffment in Fee, upon Condition that the Feoffee ſhall not alien, this Condition is void. *Lit. Sect.* 360. But would it not be a ſtrange Concluſion to ſay thereupon, If a Man makes a Feoffment in Fee, upon Condition that the Feoffee ſhall not alien to *J. S.* that this Condition is likewiſe void? The Reaſon given by *Littleton*, why the Condition is void in the former, and not in the latter Deed, is applicable to this Caſe, namely, the Condition in the firſt Caſe ouſts the Feoffee of all the Power which the Law gives unto him, which ſhould be againſt Reaſon, wherefore the ſame is void; but in the latter Caſe, the Condition doth not take away all the Power of aliening from the Feoffee; and therefore it is good. So in our Caſe, if the Prohibition were ſo general, that the Wife were thereby diſabled altogether to cloath herſelf, perhaps it might be reaſonable to ſay, that the Prohibition was void;

void; but it being a Reſtriction only to one particular Perſon, there is no Colour to ſay that it is not good.

It is true, as my Brother *Tyrrel* ſays, that I cannot diſcharge others to deal with my Wife, although I may forbid my Wife to deal with them; but it follows not thereon, but that my Prohibition to a particular Man doth make his dealing with, or truſting my Wife, to be at his own Peril; ſo that he ſhall not charge me thereby in any Action; as in Caſe of a Servant, who buys Proviſion for my Houſhold by my Allowance. If I forbid a Butcher, or other Victualler, to ſell to my Servant without ready Money, and he delivers Meat to my Servant afterwards upon Truſt, 'tis at his Peril; he ſhall have no Action againſt me for it.

It appears not by this Declaration or Verdict, That the Defendant's Wife did want Apparel; that ſhe ever deſired her Husband to ſupply her therewith; that he refuſed to allow her what was fit; that the Wares ſold her by the Plaintiff were for neceſſary Apparel, or of what Nature or Price the Wares were; ſo that the Court may judge of the Neceſſity or Fitneſs thereof: But only that the Plaintiff did ſell and deliver, upon Credit, divers Wares unto the Wife, for 40 *l.* that this was a reaſonable Price for theſe Wares, and the ſame were neceſſary for her, and ſuitable to the Degree of her Husband; and for theſe Reaſons the Defendant ought to have Judgment in this particular Caſe againſt the Plaintiff, be the Law in general what it will.

I will conclude all, as the seven Princes of *Persia* (who knew Law and Judgments) did in the Case of Queen *Vasthi*, Esther cap. i. ver. 16. &c. *This Deed that this Woman hath done, in departing from her Husband against his Will, and taking of Clothes upon Trust, contrary to his Prohibition, shall come abroad to all Women; and if it shall be reported that her Husband (by the Opinion of the Judges) must pay for the Wares which she took up, whilst she lived from him, then shall their Husbands be despised in their Eyes: But when it shall be known throughout the Realm, That the Law doth not charge the Husband, in this Case, all the Wives shall give to their Husbands Honour, both great and small.*

This is the full Substance of the learned and very remarkable Argument of Judge *Hide*, in this Case. And according to his Opinion, Judgment was given in the Exchequer Chamber, for the Defendant; *Tyrrell*, *Twisden* and *Mallet* dissenting. See 1 *Sid.* 109, 110. and 1 *Mod. Rep.* 124, 125, &c.

And See also 1 *Vent.* 24, 42. 2 *Vent.* 155. 1 *Lev.* 4, 5, 6. 1 *Keb.* 69, 80, 87, 206. *Aleyn* 61. *March* 60, 82. *Latch* 126. *Stile* 18. *Yelv.* 166. *Palm.* 343. *Cro. Car.* 254, 355, 494. *Cro. Jac.* 661. 1 *Leon.* 312. 1 *Roll. Abr.* 6. *Pl.* 6. *Noy* 79, 126. 1 *Salk.* 113, 116, 119. 2 *Show* 283. 6 *Mod.* 171, 239. *Skinn.* 323.

PRECEDENTS of Deeds and Conveyances, concerning Feme Coverts, and other Women.

A Deed of Partition *of Lands made by Coparceners.*

THIS *Indenture*, Tripartite, made the—— Day of——, in the Year, &c. *Between* *E. B.* of, &c. of the first Part, *M. B.* of, &c. of the second Part, and *S. B.* of, &c. of the third Part. *Whereas W. B.* late of, &c. Father of the said *E. B. M. B.* and *S. B.* being seised in his Demesne as of Fee, of and in one Messuage or Tenement, situate, &c. and of and in one other Messuage or Tenement and certain Lands, situate, lying and being in, &c. is dead, without any Heir Male of his Body, lawfully begotten, and not making any Disposition of the said Premisses, whereby all and singular the said Messuages and Lands, with the Appurtenances, are descended and come unto the said *E. B. M. B.* and *S. B.* *Now this Indenture witnesseth*, that the said *E. B. M. B.* and *S. B.* *have* agreed to make Partition; and by these Presents do make a full, perfect and absolute Partition of the said Messuages or Tenements, and Lands to and amongst them the said *E. B. M. B.* and *S. B.* in three Parts, in Manner following (that is to say) That she the said *E. B.* her Heirs and Assigns, shall have, hold and enjoy

enjoy, To the only proper Uſe and Behoof of the ſaid *E. B.* her Heirs and Aſſigns for ever, *All* that Meſſuage or Tenement, *&c.* for the full Part, Share and Proportion of her the ſaid *E. B.* of and in all and every the Meſſuages, Tenements, Lands and Premiſſes above-mentioned, deſcended to them the ſaid *E. B. M. B.* and *S. B.* as aforeſaid; and that the ſaid *M. B.* her Heirs and Aſſigns, ſhall have, hold and enjoy, to the only proper Uſe and Behoof of the ſaid *M. B.* her Heirs and Aſſigns for ever, *All* that other Meſſuage or Tenement, *&c.* for the full Part, Share and Proportion of her the ſaid *M. B.* of and in all and every the Meſſuages, *&c.* And that the ſaid *S. B.* her Heirs and Aſſigns, ſhall have, hold and enjoy, to the only proper Uſe and Behoof of the ſaid *S. B.* her Heirs and Aſſigns for ever, *All* thoſe Lands, *&c.* above-mentioned, for the full Part, Share and Proportion of her the ſaid *S. B.* of, and in, *&c.* *And* the ſaid *M. B.* and *S. B.* do by theſe Preſents grant, aſſign, releaſe and confirm to the ſaid *E. B.* and her Heirs, the ſaid Meſſuage or Tenement, *&c.* above-mentioned; and all the Eſtate, Right, Title and Intereſt, which they the ſaid *M. B.* and *S. B.* or either of them, have or hath, or may or ought to have, of, in and to ſaid Meſſuage, *&c.* *To have and to hold* the ſaid Meſſuage and Premiſſes, with the Appurtenances, to the ſaid *E. B.* her Heirs and Aſſigns, to the only Uſe and Behoof of the ſaid *E. B.* her Heirs and Aſſigns in Severalty for ever. *And* the ſaid *E. B.* and *S. B.* do by theſe Preſents, grant, aſſign, releaſe and confirm to the ſaid

M. B.

M. B. and her Heirs, the ſaid other Meſſuage or Tenement, *&c.* and all the Eſtate, Right, Title and Intereſt, *&c.* *To have and to hold* the ſaid other Meſſuage or Tenement and Premiſſes, to the ſaid *M. B.* her Heirs and Aſſigns, to the only Uſe and Behoof of the ſaid *M. B.* her Heirs and Aſſigns, in Severalty for ever. *And* the ſaid *E. B.* and *M. B.* do by theſe Preſents, grant, aſſign, releaſe and confirm to the ſaid *S. B.* and her Heirs, the ſaid Lands and Premiſſes in, *&c.* and all the Eſtate, Right, *&c.* *To have and to hold* the ſaid Lands and Premiſſes, with the Appurtenances, to the ſaid *S. B.* her Heirs and Aſſigns, to the only Uſe and Behoof of the ſaid *S. B.* her Heirs and Aſſigns in Severalty for ever. *And* the ſaid *M. B.* and *S. B.* for themſelves ſeverally and apart, and not jointly, and for their ſeveral Heirs, Executors, Adminiſtrators and Aſſigns, do ſeverally and apart, and not jointly covenant and grant, to and with the ſaid *E. B.* her Heirs and Aſſigns, that ſhe the ſaid *E. B.* her Heirs and Aſſigns, ſhall and may from henceforth for ever hereafter, peaceably and quietly have, hold, occupy, poſſeſs and enjoy the ſaid Meſſuage or Tenement, *&c.* before allotted and granted for the Part of the ſaid *E. B.* free and diſcharged of and from all other Eſtates, Rights, Titles, Intereſts, Charges and Incumbrances whatſoever, had, made, or ſuffered, or hereafter to be had, made or ſuffered, of or by the ſaid *M. B.* and *S. B.* or either of them, their or either of their Heirs or Aſſigns; and that without any Let, Hindrance, Interruption or Denial of them the ſaid *M. B.*

and

and *S. B.* or either of them, their or either of their Heirs or Aſſigns, or of any other Perſon or Perſons lawfully claiming by, from or under them or any of them. *And* the ſaid *E. B.* and *S. B.* ſeverally and apart, and not jointly, and for their ſeveral Heirs, Executors, *&c.* do ſeverally and apart, and not jointly covenant and grant, to and with the ſaid *M. B.* her Heirs and Aſſigns, that ſhe the ſaid *M. B.* her Heirs and Aſſigns, ſhall and may from henceforth for ever hereafter, peaceably and quietly have, hold, occupy, poſſeſs and enjoy the ſaid other Meſſuage or Tenement, *&c.* before allotted and granted for the Part of the ſaid *M. B.* free and diſcharged of and from, *&c.* and that without any Let, Hindrance, or Interruption, *&c.* *And* the ſaid *E. B.* and *M. B.* ſeverally and apart, and not jointly, *&c.* do covenant and grant to and with the ſaid *S. B.* *&c.* that ſhe the ſaid *S. B.* her Heirs and Aſſigns, ſhall and may from henceforth for ever hereafter, peaceably and quietly have, hold, *&c.* the ſaid Lands and Premiſſes before allotted and granted for the Part of the ſaid *S. B.* free and diſcharged from, *&c.* *ut ſupra.* [Here might be added a Covenant for further Aſſurance to each other.] *In witneſs*, &c.

A Partition

A Partition *of Lands among Parceners, by Way of casting Lots.*

THIS *Indenture*, Tripartite, made, *&c.* *Between A. M.* of, *&c.* of the firſt Part, *T. S.* of, *&c.* Eſq; and *J.* his Wife, of the ſecond Part, and *L. G.* of, *&c.* Widow, of the third Part. *Whereas* by one Indenture, bearing Date, *&c.* made or mentioned to be made between *W. M.* and, *&c.* he the ſaid *W. M.* covenanted and agreed to levy a Fine of All thoſe his Manors and Farms, and Lands called, *&c.* (by Way of Settlement) to the Uſe of, *&c.* and a Fine in, *&c.* Term, was levied accordingly. *And whereas* the ſaid *W. M.* is ſince dead, without any Heir Male of his Body lawfully begotten, whereby the ſaid Manors, Farms, Lands, Hereditaments and Premiſſes, are deſcended and come to the ſaid *A. M. J. S.* and *L. G.* *Now this Indenture witneſſeth*, That for a Partition of all and ſingular the ſaid Manors, Farms, Meſſuages, Lands, Tenements, Hereditaments and Premiſſes before-mentioned, to be made between the ſaid Parties to theſe Preſents, that every of them may hold and enjoy their Part in Severalty to them, their Heirs and Aſſigns: It is hereby covenanted, granted, concluded and agreed, by and between all the ſaid Parties to theſe Preſents, for them and their Heirs, in Manner and Form following; (that is to ſay) That all the ſaid Manors, Farms and Lands, *&c.* ſhall be, and are hereby divided and ſet forth into three Parts, Diviſions

visions or Allotments; and that for the first of the said three Parts, Divisions or Allotments, there shall be, and is hereby set forth and allotted the said Manor of, *&c.* with the Rights, Members and Appurtenances, and also, *&c.* and that for the second of the said three Parts, Divisions or Allotments, shall be and is hereby set forth and allotted, All that the said Manor of, *&c.* situate, lying in, *&c.* and that for the third of the said three Parts, Divisions or Allotments, there shall be and is hereby set forth and allotted, All those the Farms of, *&c.* with the Lands thereto belonging, and every Part thereof, with their Appurtenances; being all the Manors, Farms, Messuages, Lands, Hereditaments and Premisses, in the said recited Indenture and Fine comprised or settled as aforesaid. *And it is hereby further* covenanted, granted, concluded and agreed, by and between all the said Parties to these Presents, for them, their Heirs and Assigns, That all the said Premisses being so hereby set forth and divided into the said three Parts, Divisions or Allotments, as aforesaid; it shall be determined by Way of Lot, to which of them the said Parties each several Part, Division or Allotment shall belong, in Manner following; (*viz.*) In one small Scroll of Parchment, shall be written these Words, *Manor of*, &c. or, *The first Division*, which Scroll shall be inclosed in Wax, to be made up round, in the Form of a Ball, and the said Ball shall stand for and be the Lot for the first Part, Division or Allotment of the Manors and Lands, set out as aforesaid. In one other like Scroll of Parchment shall be be written these Words, *Manors of*, &c. or the second Division, which Scroll shall be enclosed in Wax, made up round in Form of a Ball, &c. and in one other like Scroll of Parchment shall be written these Words, *Farms of*, &c. or, *The third Division*, &c. *And* all the said three Scrolls of Parchment, or Balls, shall be put together in a Bag; and first, the said *A. M.* shall put her Hand into the said Bag, and take out one of the said Balls; and afterwards the said *T. S.* for himself and the said *J.* his Wife, shall put his Hand into the said Bag, and take out another of the said Balls; and afterwards the said *L. G.* shall put her Hand into the said Bag, and take out another of the said Balls; and that Lot which shall be taken by the said *A. M.* shall stand and be for the Part and Share of the said *A. M.* her Heirs and Assigns, of all the said Manors and Lands, &c. And that Lot which shall be taken by the said *T. S.* shall stand and be for the Part and Share of the said *J.* his Wife, her Heirs and Assigns, of all the said Manors, &c. And that Lot which shall be taken by the said *L. G.* shall stand and be for the Part and Share of the said *L. G.* &c. *And* that every of them the said *A. M. T. S.* and *J.* his Wife, and *L. G.* and their several Heirs and Assigns, and all other Persons claiming by, from or under them, or any of them, or by any Grants or Conveyances made by them, or any of them, shall and will for ever abide and stand to such Determination by Way of Lot, as aforesaid; and that after such Determination made by Lot, Assurances and Conveyances shall be made of the said several Parts and Divisions accordingly, (that is to say

say) such of the said Parties to these Presents, and his, her and their Heirs and Assigns, to whom the said Manor of, &c. hereby allotted and set forth for the said first Division or Allotment, that shall fall or happen by Way of Lot, as aforesaid, shall and will from Time to Time, and at all Times, within the Space of seven Years next ensuing the Date hereof, at and upon the reasonable Request, and at the Costs and Charges in the Law of the said other Parties to these Presents, their Heirs and Assigns respectively, make and execute such Assurances and Conveyances for the assuring, releasing and conveying of all the rest of the said Manors of, &c. set forth and allotted for the said second Division, and for the said third Division respectively; and of all his, her and their Estate, Interest, Claim and Demand in or to the same, unto such of the said Parties, and their Heirs and Assigns, to whom they shall respectively happen or fall, by such Lot as aforesaid, as by the said Parties and their Heirs, shall be reasonably devised and required. And such of the said Parties to these Presents, and their Heirs and Assigns to whom the said Manors of, &c. hereby allotted and set forth for the said second Division or Allotment, shall fall or happen by Way of Lot as aforesaid, shall and will from Time to Time, and at all Times, within the Space of, &c. next ensuing the Date hereof, at and upon the reasonable Request, &c. make and execute such Assurances, &c. for assuring and conveying the rest of the said Manors, &c. set forth and allotted for the first Division, and for the said third Division respectively; and all his, her and their Estate, &c. *ut supra*.

And

And the like for the Party to whom the third Division shall happen, to assure to those that have the First and Second. *In witness*, &c.

A common *Marriage-Settlement*, or *Jointure* of Lands.

THIS *Indenture* Tripartite, made, &c. *Between T. D.* of, &c. Esq; of the first Part, *M. E.* of, &c. *F. T.* and *H. W.* of, &c. of the second Part, and *A. E.* Daughter of the said *M. E.* of the third Part, *witnesseth*, That the said *T. D.* for and in Consideration of a Marriage intended (by GOD's Permission) shortly to be had and solemnised, between the said *T. D.* and the said *A. E.* and of the Sum of 4000*l.* to be had and received by the said *T. D.* as a Marriage Portion with the said *A.* and that a competent Jointure may be had, made and provided for the said *A. E.* (in Case the said Marriage shall take effect) and for the settling and assuring of the Messuages, Lands, Tenements and Hereditaments, herein after mentioned, to and upon the several Uses, Intents and Purposes herein after limited and declared, pursuant to the Agreement made upon the Contract of the said intended Marriage; he the said *T.D. hath* granted, bargained and sold, aliened, released and confirmed; and by these Presents doth grant, &c. unto the said *M. E. F. T.* and *H. W.* (in their actual Possession, now being, by Virtue of a Bargain and Sale to them thereof made for one whole Year, by Indenture, bearing Date the Day next before the Day of the Date of these Presents, and by Force of the Statute for transferring of Uses into Possession) and to their Heirs and Assigns for ever, *All* that Capital Messuage, commonly called or known by the Name of, *&c.* And all those Messuages, or Tenements and Lands, *&c.* and all other the Messuages, Lands, Tenements and Hereditaments of the said *T. D.* situate, *&c.* in the County of, *&c.* and all Houses, Buildings, Gardens, Orchards, Lands, Meadows, Pastures, Feedings, Trees, Woods, Underwoods, Ways, Paths, Waters, Water-courses, Easements, Profits, Commodities, Advantages, Emoluments and Hereditaments whatsoever, to the said Messuages or Tenements belonging, or in any wise appertaining, or which now are or formerly have been accepted, reputed, taken, known, used, occupied or enjoyed, to or with the same, or as Part, Parcel or Member thereof, or of any Part thereof; and also the Reversion and Reversions, Remainder and Remainders, Rents and Services of all and singular the said Premisses above-mentioned, and of every Part and Parcel thereof, with the Appurtenances; and all the Estate, Right, Title, Interest, Claim and Demand whatsoever, as well in Equity as in Law, of him the said *T. D.* of, in and to all and singular the same Premisses, and of, in and to every Part and Parcel thereof, with the Appurtenances: *To have and to hold* all and singular the said Messuages, Lands, Tenements and Hereditaments above-mentioned, and every Part and Parcel thereof, with the Appurtenances, unto the said *M. E. F. T.* and *H. W.* their Heirs and Assigns, to and for the several Uses, Intents, Trusts and

Purpo-

Purposes herein after mentioned, limited, express'd and declar'd, (that is to say) to the Use and Behoof of the said *T. D.* and his Heirs, until the said Marriage between him and the said *A. E.* his intended Wife, shall be had and solemnised; and from and after the Solemnization thereof, to the Use and Behoof of the said *T. D.* and his Assigns, for and during the Term of his natural Life, without Impeachment of Waste; and from and after the Determination of that Estate, by Forfeiture or otherwise, to the Use and Behoof of the said *M. E. F. T.* and *H. W.* and their Heirs, for and during the natural Life of the said *T. D.* in Trust, to preserve and support the contingent Remainders herein after limited, from being defeated and destroyed, and for that Purpose to make Entries, and bring Actions, as the Case shall require; yet nevertheless in Trust, to permit and suffer the said *T. D.* and his Assigns, to receive and take the Rents, Issues and Profits thereof, to his and their own proper Use and Benefit, during his natural Life; and from and after the Decease of the said *T. D.* to the Use and Behoof of the said *A. E.* (intended Wife of the said *T. D.*) and her Assigns, for and during the Term of her natural Life, for her Jointure, and in full Satisfaction and Bar of her Dower or Thirds, which she may claim to have in any Lands, Tenements or Hereditaments, whereof or wherein he the said *T. D.* shall at any Time, during his Life, be seised of any Estate of Inheritance; and from and after the Decease of the Survivor of them the said *T. D.* and *A.* his intended Wife, to the Use and Behoof of the Heirs

Males of the Body of the said *T. D.* on the Body of the said *A. E.* lawfully to be begotten; and for Default of such Issue, to the Use and Behoof of the said *M. E. F. T.* and *H. W.* their Executors, Administrators and Assigns, for and during the Term of five hundred Years, thence next following, and fully to be compleated and ended, upon the Trusts, and subject to such Conditions as are herein after declared, of and concerning the same Term; and from and after the Expiration, or other sooner Determination of that Term, to the Use and Behoof of the said *T. D.* his Heirs and Assigns for ever. *Provided* always, and it is hereby declared and agreed, by and between the said Parties to these Presents, that the said Term of five hundred Years, so limited to them the said *M. E. F. T.* and *H. W.* their Executors, Administrators and Assigns, as aforesaid, is upon this Condition, that if the said *T. D.* shall happen to die without Issue Male, by him begotten, on the Body of the said *A.* or shall leave Issue Male, and such Issue Male shall die before he shall attain the Age of Twenty-one Years, without Issue Male; and that in either of the said Cases, there shall happen to be one or more Daughter or Daughters of their Bodies begotten, that then, and in such Case, if the Heirs or Assigns of the said *T. D.* do and shall well and truly pay, or cause to be paid, to such Daughter or Daughters respectively, at her and their respective Ages of Twenty-one Years or Days of Marriage, the several Portions following (that is to say) if it shall happen there shall be but one such

Daughter,

Daughter, then the Sum of 4000 *l.* for the Portion of ſuch Daughter, to be paid to her at the ſaid Age of Twenty-one Years, or Day of Marriage, which ſhall firſt happen, with Intereſt in the mean Time, after the Rate of 5 *l. per Cent. per Annum*; and if it ſhall happen that there ſhall be two or more ſuch Daughters, then the Sum of 6000 *l.* for the Portions of ſuch two or more Daughters, to be equally divided among them, Share and Share alike; and to be paid to them reſpectively at their ſaid reſpective Ages of Twenty-one Years, or Days of Marriage, which ſhall firſt happen, with Intereſt therefore in the mean Time, *&c.* And if any ſuch Daughter or Daughters ſhall happen to die unmarried, before her or their Portion or Portions ſhall become payable as aforeſaid, then the Portion or Portions of her or them ſo dying, ſhall go and be paid to the Survivors or Survivor of them, equally to be divided amongſt them, Share and Share alike, (to be paid at the ſame Time as the original Portions ſhould or ought to become payable, as aforeſaid, in Caſe they had been living) ſo as no one ſuch Daughter ſhall have for her Portion, by Survivorſhip, or otherwiſe, by Virtue of the ſaid Term of five hundred Years, above the Sum of 400 *l.* And in Caſe there ſhall be no ſuch Daughter, who ſhall live to be married, or attain the Age of Twenty-one Years, that then, and in either of the ſaid Caſes ſo happening, the ſaid Term ſhall ceaſe, determine and be void, any thing herein contained to the contrary, notwithſtanding. *Provided alſo*, and upon this further Condition, That in Case the said *T. D.* shall happen to die without such Issue Male, as aforesaid, and shall happen to leave one or more Daughter or Daughters, and such Daughter or Daughters, or either of them, shall happen to marry in the Life-time of the said *T. D.* and *A.* his intended Wife, or either of them, or in the Life-time of the said Trustees, or any or either of them, without the Consent of such of them the said *T. D.* and *A.* and of the said Trustees, or the greater Number of them, who shall be then living, signed and declared under their Hands; that then the Portion and Portions hereby intended for such Daughter and Daughters so marrying respectively, shall go and be paid to such other Daughter or Daughters, who shall marry with such Consent as aforesaid. And in Case all such Daughters shall happen to marry, without such Consent as aforesaid, that then the said Term of five hundred Years shall cease and be void: *Provided also*, and it is hereby further declared and agreed, that it shall and may be lawful to and for him the said *T. D.* during his Life, and after his Death, for the said *A.* his intended Wife, during her Life, in Case the said intended Marriage shall take Effect, by any Writing or Writings, under his or her Hand and Seal respectively, attested by two or more credible Witnesses, to make any Lease or Leases, Demise or Grant, of all or any Part or Parts of the said Messuages and Lands to any Person or Persons whatsoever, for the Term of twenty-one Years, or for any Term or Number of Years, not exceeding twenty-

twenty-one Years; ſo as ſuch Leaſes, Demiſes or Grants for Years, be made to commence and take Effect in Poſſeſſion within one Year after the Date thereof; and ſo as upon all and every ſuch Leaſe or Leaſes, Demiſes or Grants to be made by the ſaid *T. D.* and *A.* his intended Wife reſpectively, there be reſerved payable yearly, during the Continuance thereof, the beſt and moſt improv'd yearly Rents, which at the Time of making thereof, can or may be gotten for the ſame; and ſo that in every ſuch Leaſe there be contained a Clauſe of Re-entry for Nonpayment of the Rent or Rents thereby reſerved; and ſo as the Leſſee and Leſſees to whom ſuch Leaſe and Leaſes ſhall be made, do ſeal and deliver Counterparts of ſuch Leaſe and Leaſes. *And* the ſaid *T. D.* for himſelf, his Heirs and Aſſigns, doth covenant and grant, to and with the ſaid *M. E. F. T.* and *H. W.* their Heirs and Aſſigns, that the ſaid Meſſuages, Lands, Tenements, Hereditaments and Premiſſes above-mentioned, ſhall and may from henceforth, for ever hereafter, be, remain and continue to, for and upon the ſeveral Uſes, Intents, Truſts and Purpoſes, and under and ſubject to the ſeveral Limitations, Proviſo's and Agreements before-mentioned and expreſſed, concerning the ſame, according to the true Intent and Meaning of theſe Preſents. *And alſo*, that he the ſaid *T. D.* and his Heirs, and all and every other Perſon and Perſons, and his and their Heirs, any Thing having or claiming in the ſaid Meſſuages, Lands, Tenements and Premiſſes abovementioned, or any Part thereof, by, from or under him, them, or any of them, shall and will, at all Times hereafter, upon the reasonable Request of the said *M. E. F. T.* and *H. W.* their Heirs and Assigns, make, do and execute, or cause or procure to be made, *&c.* all and every such further and other lawful and reasonable Grants, Acts and Assurances in the Law whatsoever, for the further, better and more perfect granting and assuring of all and singular the said Messuages, Lands, Tenements, Hereditaments and Premisses above-mentioned, with the Appurtenances, to and for the several Uses, Intents and Purposes above declared, limited and appointed, and according to the true Intent and Meaning of these Presents, as by the said *M. E. F. T.* and *H. W.* and their Heirs, or their or any of their Counsel, learned in the Law, shall be reasonably devised or advised and required. *And further*, it is covenanted, granted, concluded and agreed upon, by and between the said Parties to these Presents, and the true Meaning hereof also is, and it is hereby so declared, that all and every Fine and Fines, and also all and every Recovery and Recoveries, Assurance and Assurances, Conveyance and Conveyances in the Law whatsoever already had, made, levied, suffered, executed or acknowledged, or at any Time hereafter to be had, made, *&c.* of the said Messuages, Tenements, Lands and Premisses above-mentioned, or any Part thereof, either alone, or jointly with any other Lands, Tenements or Hereditaments, by or between the said Parties to these Presents, or by or between them or any of them, and any other Person

Person or Persons, as for and concerning all and singular the said Messuages, Lands, Tenements, Hereditaments and Premisses above-mentioned, and every Part thereof, with the Appurtenances, *shall be* and enure, and shall be adjudged, esteemed and taken to be and enure, to and for the several Uses, Intents and Purposes above-mentioned, limited, expressed and declared, according to the true Intent and Meaning of these Presents, and to and for none other Use, Intent or Purpose whatsoever. *In witness*, &c.

A Settlement *by Fine and Recovery, of Manors and Lands, on the Husband for Life, Remainder to the Wife for her Jointure,* &c. *and Terms upon Trust, for the separate Use of the Wife, to raise Money to buy her Cloaths,* &c. *and for raising Portions for younger Children.*

THIS *Indenture,* Quinquepartite, made, *&c. Between B. A.* of, *&c.* Esq; and *E.* his Wife, of the first Part, *W. A.* eldest Son and Heir Apparent of the said *B. A.* on the said *E.* begotten, and *D.* Wife of the said *W. A.* (who is eldest Daughter of *D. E.* of, *&c.* and one of the Sisters and Coheirs of, *&c.*) of the second Part, *D. C.* of, *&c.* and *F. E.* of, *&c* of the third Part, the said *D. E. H. D.* of, *&c.* and *K. J.* of, *&c.* of the

the fourth Part, and *M. L.* of, *&c.* *R. O.* of, *&c.* and *P. N.* of, *&c.* of the fifth Part, *Witnesseth*, that for and in Consideration of a Marriage already had and solemnized between the said *W. A.* and *D.* his Wife, and in Pursuance and Part of Performance of certain Articles of Agreement, made on the Contract of the said Marriage, bearing Date, *&c.* and made or mentioned to be made between, *&c.* And in Consideration also of the Sum of 12000 *l.* of, *&c.* to the said *W. A.* in Hand paid by the said *D. E.* as and for the Marriage Portion of the said *D.* his Wife, and in full of her Share and Proportion of the Estate of, *&c.* deceased, the Receipt whereof he the said *W. A.* doth hereby confess and acknowledge; and for the settling and assuring of the Manors, Lands, Tenements and Hereditaments herein after mentioned, to and upon the several Uses, Intents, Trusts and Purposes herein after limited, expressed and declared, pursuant to the said Marriage-Articles above-mentioned; they the said *B. A.* and *W. A.* do, and either of them doth, for themselves, their Heirs and Assigns, covenant, grant and agree, to and with the said *D. C.* and *F. E.* their Heirs and Assigns, and the said *E.* Wife of the said *B. A.* doth hereby consent and agree, that they the said *B. A.* and *E.* his Wife, and *W. A.* shall and will on this Side, and before the End of *Michaelmas* Term next coming, in due Form of Law, acknowledge and levy, before his Majesty's Justices of the Court of Common Pleas at *Westminster*, unto the said *D. C.* and *F. E.* and their Heirs, or to the

Heirs of one of them, one Fine *sur Connu-sance de Droit come ceo*, &c. of *All* that the Manor of, *&c.* and of all those Manors and Lands, *&c.* And of the Reversion and Reversions, Remainder and Remainders, *&c.* of all and singular the said Manors and Premisses, and every Part and Parcel thereof, with the Appurtenances, by such Name and Names, *&c.* and in such Manner and Form as by the Counsel of the said *D. C.* and *E.* shall be advised and thought fit. *Which* said Fine so to be had and levied in Manner aforesaid, or in any other Manner to be had and levied of the said Manors and Premisses above-mentioned, with the Appurtenances, shall be and enure, and shall be adjudged, esteemed and taken to be and enure, to and for the only proper Use and Behoof of the said *D. C.* and *F. E.* their Heirs and Assigns, whereby to make them Tenants of the Freehold of the said Premisses; *Yet neverthelefs* to this further End, Intent and Purpose, That the said *D. C.* and *F. E.* shall and will, on this Side, and before the End of the said next, *&c.* Term, permit and suffer the said *H. D.* and *K. J.* in due Form of Law, to sue forth and prosecute, one Writ of Entry *sur Dis-seisin in le post*, returnable before his said Majesty's Justices of the said Court of Common Pleas, against the said *D. C.* and *F. E.* of all and singular the said Manors, *&c.* by such Name and Names, Quantity and Number of Messuages, *&c.* as by the said *H.D.* and *K. J.* or their Counsel learned in the Law shall be reasonably devised, or advised and required, *Unto* and upon which said Writ of Entry,

try, so to be brought, the said *D. C.* and *F. E.* shall appear and vouch to Warranty, the said *W. A.* and the said *W. A.* shall appear *gratis*, and enter into the said Warranty, and after his Entry into the said Warranty, shall vouch over the common Vouchee, who shall likewise appear and enter into the said Warranty and Imparl, and afterwards make Default, to the End one perfect Common Recovery, with double Voucher, shall and may thereof be had, prosecuted and suffered in all Things, according to the usual Order and Form of Common Recoveries, for Assurance of Lands, Tenements and Hereditaments, in such Cases used and accustomed; and the same Recovery shall also be executed in due Form of Law, by one Writ *Habere facias seisinam* accordingly. *And* it is covenanted, granted, concluded and agreed upon, by and between the said Parties to these Presents, that the said Recovery, so or in any other Manner and Form, to be had and suffered; and also all and every other Recovery or Recoveries to be hereafter executed, had or suffered of the said Manors and Premisses, or any Part thereof, by or between the said Parties to these Presents, or by or between them, or any of them, and any other Person or Persons on this Side, and before the End of, &c. Term next coming, and the full Force of them, and every of them, and all other Assurance and Assurances of the said Premisses, or any Part thereof, had, or to be had, or made between the said Parties, or any of them, shall be and enure, and shall be adjudged, esteemed and taken, and are meant and

and intended to be and enure, to, for, and upon the ſeveral Uſes, Intents, Truſts and Purpoſes, and ſubject to the ſeveral Proviſo's and Agreements hereafter particularly mentioned, limited, expreſſed and declared, (that is to ſay) *As for and concerning* all that the Manor and Capital Meſſuage of, &c. and the Reverſion and Reverſions, Remainder and Remainders, Rents and Services thereof, to the Uſe and Behoof of the ſaid *W. A.* and his Aſſigns, for and during the Term of his natural Life, without Impeachment of or for any Manner of Waſte, and with Liberty to commit Waſte; and from and after the Determination of that Eſtate, by Forfeiture or otherwiſe, then to the Uſe and Behoof of the ſaid *D. E. H. D.* and *K. J.* their Heirs and Aſſigns, for and during the natural Life of the ſaid *W. A.* to preſerve and ſupport the contingent Remainders herein after limited, from being defeated or deſtroyed; and for that Purpoſe to make Entries, and bring Actions, as the Caſe ſhall require; but nevertheleſs in Truſt to permit and ſuffer the ſaid *W. A.* and his Aſſigns, for and during his natural Life, to receive and take the Rents, Iſſues and Profits of the ſaid Manor and Premiſſes, to and for his and their own proper Uſe and Benefit; and from and after the Deceaſe of the ſaid *W. A.* then to the Uſe and Behoof of the ſaid *D.* Wife of the ſaid *W. A.* and her Aſſigns, for and during the Term of her natural Life, in full of her Jointure, and in Satisfaction and Bar of her Dower at the Common Law; and from and after the ſeveral Deceaſes of

them

them the ſaid *W. A.* and *D.* his Wife, then to the Uſe and Behoof of the firſt Son of the Body of the ſaid *W. A.* on the Body of the ſaid *D.* his Wife lawfully begotten, or to be begotten, and the Heirs Males of the Body of ſuch firſt Son, lawfully iſſuing; and for Default of ſuch Iſſue, then to the Uſe and Behoof of the ſecond Son of the Body of the ſaid *W. A.* on the Body of the ſaid *D.* his Wife, lawfully begotten, or to be begotten, and the Heirs Males of the Body of ſuch ſecond Son, lawfully iſſuing; and for Default of ſuch Iſſue, then to the Uſe and Behoof of the third Son of the Body of the ſaid *W. A.* on the Body of the ſaid *D.* his Wife, lawfully begotten, or to be begotten, and the Heirs Males of the Body of ſuch third Son, lawfully iſſuing; and for Default of ſuch Iſſue, then to the Uſe and Behoof of the fourth Son of the Body of the ſaid *W. A.* on the Body of the ſaid *D.* his Wife, to be begotten, and of the Heirs Males of the Body of ſuch fourth Son, lawfully iſſuing; and for Default of ſuch Iſſue, then to the Uſe and Behoof of the fifth, ſixth, ſeventh, eighth, ninth and tenth Son and Sons, and of all and every other Son and Sons of the Body of the ſaid *W. A.* on the Body of the ſaid *D.* his Wife lawfully to be begotten, ſeverally and ſucceſſively, and in Remainder one after another, as they and every of them ſhall be in Seniority of Age and Priority of Birth, and of the Heirs Males of the Body and Bodies of all and every ſuch Son and Sons lawfully iſſuing; the Elder of ſuch Son and Sons, and the Heirs Male of his Body lawfully iſſuing, always to be preferred and take before the younger of ſuch Son and Sons, and the Heirs Male of his and their Body or Bodies lawfully iſſuing; and for Default of ſuch Iſſue, and in Caſe the ſaid *D.* at the Death of the ſaid *W. A.* ſhall be *Enſient* and with Child, then to the Uſe of the ſaid *D.* and her Aſſigns, until the ſaid *D.* ſhall be delivered of ſuch Child; and if ſuch Child ſhall be a Son, then to the Uſe and Behoof of ſuch afterborn Son, and the Heirs Males of his Body lawfully iſſuing; and for Default of ſuch Iſſue, then to the Uſe and Behoof of the Heirs Males of the Body of the ſaid *W. A.* lawfully to be begotten; and for Default of ſuch Iſſue, then to the Uſe and Behoof of, *&c.* ſecond Son of the ſaid *B. A.* and the Heirs Males of his Body lawfully to be begotten; and for Default of ſuch Iſſue, then to the Uſe and Behoof of the third, fourth, fifth, ſixth, ſeventh, eighth, ninth and tenth Son and Sons, *&c.* of the Body of the ſaid *B. A.* on the Body of the ſaid *E.* begotten, *&c.* and for Default of ſuch Iſſue, then to the Uſe and Behoof of all and every the Daughter and Daughters of the ſaid *B. A.* on the Body of the ſaid *E.* begotten, and to be begotten, and the Heirs of the Body and Bodies of ſuch Daughter and Daughters lawfully to be begotten; and for Default of ſuch Iſſue, then to the Uſe and Behoof of the ſaid *B. A.* his Heirs and Aſſigns for ever, and to and for none other Uſe, Intent or Purpoſe whatſoever. *And as for and concerning* all that the Manor of, *&c.* to the Uſe and Behoof of the ſaid *M. L. R. O.* and *P. N.* their Executors, Administrators and Assigns, for and during the Term of 99 Years next ensuing and fully to be compleat and ended, if the said *D.* Wife of the said *W. A.* shall so long Live; upon this special Trust and Confidence, that they the said *M. L. R. O.* and *P. N.* their Executors, Administrators and Assigns, shall from Time to Time during the joint Lives of the said *W. A.* and *D.* receive and take the Rents, Issues and Profits of the said Manor, Lands and Premisses last abovementioned, and pay and answer the same unto the said *D.* for her sole and particular Maintenance for Cloaths, Apparel, and otherwise as she shall think fit, and the said *W. A.* not to intermeddle with the same; and the Acquittance and Discharge, Acquittances and Discharges of the said *D.* from Time to Time under her Hand, shall be judg'd, deemed and taken to be good and sufficient Discharges unto the said *M. L. R. O.* and *P. N.* their Executors and Administrators for the same, and every Part thereof, against the said *W. A.* his Heirs, Executors and Assigns, and against all Accounts to be to him or them given, rendred or yielded therefore: And as for and concerning the said Manor and Premisses limited for the said Term of 99 Years, immediately after the Determination of that Term; and as for and concerning all and singular other the said Manors, Messuages, Lands, &c. whereof no Use or Estate is herein before limited, to the Use and Behoof of the said *B. A.* and *E.* &c. *Provided always*, and it is further covenanted and agreed, by and between the said Parties to these Presents, and hereby so declared, that in in Caſe the ſaid *D.* Wife of the ſaid *W. A.* ſhall happen to die in the Life-Time of the ſaid *W. A.* without Iſſue Male of her Body by the ſaid *W. A.* begotten, or having Iſſue Male, and ſuch Iſſue ſhall all happen to die in the Life-Time of the ſaid *W. A.* without Iſſue Male; that then and in ſuch Caſe, it ſhall be lawful for the ſaid *W. A.* with the Conſent of the ſaid *B. A.* and *E.* his Wife, if both of them ſhall be living, otherwiſe with the Conſent of the Survivor of them; and if both of them ſhall be dead, then for the ſaid *W. A.* without ſuch Conſent, and at his Will and Pleaſure, by any Writing or Writings by him to be ſigned and ſealed in the Preſence of two or more credible Witneſſes, to revoke, alter and make void all and every the Uſe and Uſes herein before limited and appointed, ſubſequent to the Limitation to him for his Life; and by the ſame Writing or Writings, or by any other Deed or Deeds, Writing or Writings, to create, limit or appoint any other new Uſe or Uſes of the ſaid Premiſſes, or any Part thereof, ſo as ſuch new Uſe and Uſes ſo to be created or appointed, be to the Heirs Males of his own Body, or to ſome Heir Male and his Iſſue of the Family of the ſaid *B. A.* and not otherwiſe. *Provided alſo*, and it is further agreed and declared, by and between the ſaid Parties to theſe Preſents, that in Caſe the ſaid *W. A.* ſhall have more than one Son, or a Son or Sons, and one or more Daughter or Daughters by him begotten on the ſaid *D.* his Wife, then it ſhall and may be lawful to and for the ſaid *W. A.* by any

Deed or Deeds, Writing or Writings, or by his last Will and Testament in Writing, to be duly executed, &c. to charge the said Manors and Premisses, or any Part thereof, by creating or limiting a Term of 100 Years or otherwise on the said Premisses abovementioned, and to be defeazible on Payment of the Sum of 10, 000 *l.* for the Portion or Portions of such younger Son or Sons, Daughter and Daughters by such Proportions, and in such Sort, Manner and Form, as the said *W. A.* by such Deed or Deeds, Writing or Writings, or by his last Will and Testament in Writing, to be executed, as aforesaid, shall direct, limit and appoint: And further, that in such Case, it shall be lawful for the said *W. A.* at any Time during his Life, by such Writing or Will as aforesaid, to charge the said Premisses, or any Part thereof, with any Annuity or Annuities, to and for such younger Son or Sons, not exceeding in the whole the Sum of 1000 *l. per Annum*, as the said *W. A.* shall by such Deed or Deeds, Writing or Writings, or by his last Will in Writing, to be duly executed as aforesaid, direct, limit or appoint; so as the said Charge, Term of 100 Years, or the said Annuity or Annuities, do not commence or take Effect 'till after the Deceases of the said *B. A.* and *E.* his Wife, any Thing herein contained to the contrary thereof in any wise notwithstanding. *Provided also*, and it is hereby further agreed and declared, that it shall and may be lawful to and for the said *B. A.* during his Life, and the said *E.* after his Death, during her Life; and also for the said *W. A.* during his Life,

Life, and for the ſaid *D.* after his Death, and during her Life, as they ſhall reſpectively become Owners, and be in Poſſeſſion of the Premiſſes by the reſpective Limitations in theſe Preſents herein before mentioned, by Indenture under their reſpective Hands and Seals, to Demiſe and Leaſe to any Perſon or Perſons whatſoever, all and every, or any of the ſaid Manors and Premiſſes abovementioned to them ſeverally limited in Uſe, as aforeſaid, for any Term or Number of Years not exceeding the Term of 21 Years in Poſſeſſion, and not in Reverſion, Remainder or Expectancy; ſo as no ſuch Leaſe or Leaſes be made diſpuniſhable of Waſte, and ſo as upon every ſuch Leaſe, there be reſerved the greateſt and moſt improved yearly Rent that can or may be had and obtained for the ſame, without taking any Money or other Thing, by way of Fine or Conſideration for ſuch Leaſe or Leaſes, and ſo as the Perſon or Perſons to whom ſuch Leaſe or Leaſes ſhall be granted, do Seal and Execute Counterparts of the ſame Leaſes. *And* the ſaid *B. A.* and *W. A.* for themſelves ſeverally and apart, and not jointly, and for their reſpective Heirs and Aſſigns, do ſeverally and apart, and not jointly, Covenant and Grant, to and with the ſaid *D. E. H. D.* and *K. I.* their Heirs and Aſſigns, that all and ſingular the ſaid Manors, Meſſuages, Lands, Tenements, Hereditaments and Premiſſes abovementioned, ſhall and may from Time to Time, and at all Times, for ever hereafter, Remain, continue and be, to, for and upon the ſeveral Uſes, Intents, Truſts and Purpoſes herein before mentioned, limit-

 ed,

ed, expressed and declared, according to the true Intent and Meaning of these Presents, and to and for none other Use, Intent, Trust, or Purpose whatsoever. *And* that free and clear, and freely and clearly acquitted and discharged of and from all former and other Bargains, Sales, Gifts, Grants, Leases, Jointures, Dowers, Uses, Wills, Intails, Fines, &c. And all other Charges, Estates, Rights, Titles, Troubles and Incumbrances, had, made, committed, done or suffered by them the said *B. A.* and *W. A.* or either of them, their or either of their Heirs or Assigns, &c. *And also*, that they the said *B. A.* and *W. A.* and their Heirs, and all and every other Person and Persons, and his and their Heirs, any Thing having or claiming in the said Manors and Premisses abovementioned, &c. shall and will upon the reasonable Request of them the said *D. E. H. D.* and *K. I.* their Heirs and Assigns, &c. (Covenant to make further Assurance, as in the preceding Settlement) *And lastly*, it is covenanted, granted, concluded and agreed upon, by and between all the said Parties to these Presents, &c. that all and every Fine and Fines, Recovery and Recoveries, Assurance and Assurances, &c. shall Enure to the Uses, &c. (*ut ante.*) *In Witness*, &c.

4

A Mar-

A Marriage Settlement *made by the Wife of her own Estate, so as to be entirely at her Disposition after Marriage; except a Part for the Husband*, &c.

THIS *Indenture* Tripartite, made, *&c.* *Between E. A.* of, *&c.* of the first Part, *S. T.* of, *&c.* Esq; of the second Part, *B. W.* of, *&c. H. S.* of, *&c.* and *W. E.* of, *&c.* of the third Part. *Whereas* the said *E. A.* is and standeth seized in Fee-simple of and in the several Manors, Messuages, Lands, Tenements and Hereditaments herein after mentioned. *And whereas*, there is a Marriage intended shortly to be had and solemnized between her the said *E. A.* and the said *S. T.* upon the Contract of which Marriage it is agreed, that she the said *E. A.* shall and may have and receive out of her said Estate, during the joint Lives of them the said *S. T.* and *E. A.* the yearly Sum of 1500*l.* clear of all Reprizes to her own separate Use, and to be paid in manner herein after express'd; and the Residue of the Rents and Profits of the same, is to be receiv'd, paid, applied and disposed of, upon such Trusts, and for such Ends, Intents and Purposes, as are herein after declared. *Now this Indenture witnesseth*, That as well in Consideration of the said intended Marriage, as for the Settling and Assuring of the Manors, Lands, Tenements and Hereditaments herein after mentioned, to the several Uses, Intents and Purposes, and Subject to the Powers, Proviso's, and Agreements herein after declared, touching and concerning the ſame; and for and in Conſideration of the Sum of 10 *s.* of, *&c.* in Hand paid to the ſaid *E. A.* by the ſaid *B. W. H. S.* and *W. E.* at and before the Sealing and Delivery of theſe Preſents, the Receipt whereof is hereby acknowledged; and for divers other good Cauſes and Conſiderations her the ſaid *E. A.* hereunto moving; ſhe the ſaid *E. A.* with the Conſent and Approbation of the ſaid *S. T.* teſtified by his being a Party to and Signing and Sealing of theſe Preſents, *Hath* granted, bargained, ſold, aliened, enfeoffed, releaſed and confirmed, and by theſe Preſents doth Grant, *&c.* unto the ſaid *B. W. H. S.* and *W. S.* (in their actual Poſſeſſion now being, *&c.*) and to their Heirs, *All* that the Manor of, *&c.* with the Rights, Members and Appurtenances thereof in the County of, *&c.* and alſo all that Meſſuage or Tenement, *&c.* and all Lands, *&c.* and the Reverſion and Reverſions, Remainder and Remainders, Rents, Iſſues and Profits of the ſaid Premiſſes; and all the Eſtate, Right, Title, Intereſt, Property, Claim and Demand of her the ſaid *E. A.* in and to the ſame. *To have and to hold* the ſaid Manors, Lands, Tenements, Hereditaments, and all and ſingular the Premiſſes hereby granted, or intended to be hereby granted, with their and every of their Rights, Members and Appurtenances, unto the ſaid *B. W. H. S.* and *W. E.* and their Heirs, to the ſeveral Uſes, Intents and Purpoſes, and Subject to the Eſtates, Powers, Proviſo's and Limitations herein after in theſe Preſents limited and expreſs'd, (that is to ſay) to the Uſe of the ſaid

ſaid *E. A.* her Heirs and Aſſigns until the ſaid Marriage between her and the ſaid *S. T.* her intended Husband ſhall be had and ſolemnized; and from and after the Solemnization thereof, to the Uſe of the ſaid *B. W. H. S.* and *W. E.* their Executors, Adminiſtrators and Aſſigns, for the Term of 99 Years from thence next enſuing, and fully to be compleat and ended, if the ſaid *S. T.* and *E. A.* ſhall jointly ſo long live, upon the Truſts herein after mentioned, touching and concerning the ſaid Term; and after the Determination of that Eſtate, to the Uſe and Behoof of the ſaid *E. A.* her Heirs and Aſſigns for ever; with and under ſuch Powers, Privileges, Advantages and Authorities, as are herein after mentioned and expreſs'd, (*viz.*) that it ſhall and may be lawful to and for the ſaid *E. A.* at any Time or Times during her natural Life; jointly with the ſaid *S. T.* her intended Husband, or for her alone and without the ſaid *S. T.* notwithſtanding her Coverture, and as if ſhe were ſole and unmarried, as often as ſhe ſhall ſee Occaſion, and at her own Will and Pleaſure, by any Deed or Deeds, Writing or Writings, to be by her ſealed and executed in the Preſence of three or more credible Witneſſes, or by her laſt Will and Teſtament duly made and publiſh'd, and which he the ſaid *S. T.* as much as he may or can, doth hereby empower her to make, or by any Writing purporting her laſt Will and Teſtament ſealed and executed as aforeſaid, to limit and appoint any new or other Uſe or Uſes, Eſtate or Eſtates, of, in and concerning the ſaid Manors, Lands, Tenements, Hereditaments and Premiſſes above-mentioned, or of in and concerning any Part or Parts, Parcel or Parcels thereof, to any Perſon or Perſons whatſoever, either in Fee-ſimple, Fee-tail, or for Life or Lives; or for any Term or Number of Years, abſolute or determinable upon the Death of any one or more Perſon or Perſons; and by the ſame Deed or Deeds, Writing or Writings, laſt Will and Teſtament, at the like Will and Pleaſure of the ſaid *E. A.* to charge the ſaid Manors, Lands, *&c.* or any Part or Parcel thereof, with the Payment of any Sum or Sums of Money in Groſs, or with any Annual Sum or Sums of Money, to be paid at ſuch Days and Times, and in ſuch Manner and Form as the ſaid *E. A.* ſhall in and by ſuch Deed or Deeds, Writing or Writings, laſt Will and Teſtament, or Writing purporting her laſt Will and Teſtament, direct, limit or appoint; with Power of Revoking all or any ſuch Uſe or Uſes, Charges, Eſtate or Eſtates, or any other the Appointments hereby reſerved to be made, and of appointing any new Uſe or Uſes, Eſtate or Eſtates, of and in the ſaid Manors, Lands, Tenements, *&c.* or otherwiſe of charging the ſame, or any Part or Parcel thereof, after ſuch Revocation made, with the Payment of any Annual Sum or Sums of Money as the ſaid *E. A.* ſhall in her Diſcretion think fit. *Provided* always, that ſuch Eſtate or Eſtates, Charges, Limitations or Appointments ſo to be made limited or appointed, be not made to commence 'till after the Death of the ſaid *E. A.* or to prejudice the Eſtate and Term of 99 Years, de-

determinable

terminable as aforesaid, hereby limited to the said *B. W. H. S.* and *W. E.* their Executors, Administrators and Assigns, any Thing herein contained to the contrary Notwithstanding. *And* as for, touching and concerning the said Term and Estate of 99 Years, limited to the said *B. W. H. S. &c.* their Executors, Administrators and Assigns, it is hereby covenanted and agreed, by and between all the said Parties to these Presents, and the true Intent and Meaning of them and every of them is, and is hereby declared to be, that the same is on the Trusts, and to the Intents and Purposes following, (that is to say) *Upon Trust*, in the first Place, that they the said *B. W. H. S.* and *W. E.* and the Survivors and Survivor of them, their Executors, Administrators and Assigns, shall yearly and every Year during the Joint Lives of them the said *S. T.* and *E. A.* out of the Rents, Issues and Profits of the said Manors, Lands, Tenements, Hereditaments and Premisses hereby granted, raise any Sum or Sums not exceeding 1500*l.* a Year, over and above all Charges and Reprizes whatsoever, as the said *E. A.* notwithstanding her Coverture, shall by any Writing signed with her own Hand, in the Presence of three or more credible Witnesses direct and appoint, and pay the same yearly during the joint Lives of them the said *S. T.* and *E. A.* to the said *E. A.* or to such Use and Uses, and to such Person and Persons as she the said *E. A.* notwithstanding her Coverture, shall by any Writing executed as aforesaid, direct and appoint: And upon this further Trust, that they the said *B. W. H. S.* and

W. E.

W. E. and the Survivors and Survivor of them, their Executors and Administrators, shall and will from Time to Time and at all Times hereafter, during the Continuance of the said Term of 99 Years, permit and suffer the said *S. T.* and his Assigns, yearly to receive and take all the Rest and Residue of the Rents, Issues and Profits of all and every the Premisses aforesaid. *Provided always*, and it is hereby declared and agreed by and between all the said Parties to these Presents, that it shall and may be lawful to and for the said *E. A.* by and with the Consent of the said *S. T.* from Time to Time and at all Times during the joint Lives of them the said *S. T.* and *E. A.* by any Writing or Writings indented under both their Hands and Seals, attested by two or more credible Witnesses, to make any Lease or Leases, Demises or Grants, of all such Part and Parts of the said Manors, Messuages, Lands, Hereditaments and Premisses, as now are or have been anciently leased for one or more Life or Lives, or for any Term or Number of Years determinable upon one or more Life or Lives, to any Person or Persons for one, two, three or four Lives, or for any Term or Number of Years determinable on one, two, three or four Lives in Possession, Reversion or Remainder, or by way of future Interest; yet so as there shall never be above four Lives at any one Time in Being in any one Lease; and so as upon such Lease or Leases, Demises or Grants, there be reserved payable yearly, during the Continuance thereof, the ancient accustom'd yearly Rent or Rents, Heriots, and other

ther Things uſually paid for the ſame Premiſſes, ſo to be leaſed or granted; and ſo as ſuch Leaſes be not made diſpuniſhable of Waſte, and in every ſuch Leaſe or Leaſes there be contain'd a Condition of Re-entry on Nonpayment of the Rents, Heriots, and other Things, thereby reſerved; and ſo as the Leſſee and Leſſees, to whom ſuch Leaſe and Leaſes ſhall be ſo made, do Seal and deliver Counterparts of ſuch Leaſe and Leaſes; and ſo as the Fine or Fines, Sum or Sums of Money, agreed to be paid by the Leſſees for ſuch Leaſes, be paid into the ſaid *E. A.*'s own Hands, or to ſuch Perſons as ſhe ſhall appoint by any Writing under her Hand, *&c.* any Thing in theſe Preſents contained to the contrary notwithſtanding. *And* it is hereby declared and agreed, by and between the ſaid Parties to theſe Preſents, and the ſaid *S. T.* for himſelf, his Heirs, Executors and Adminiſtrators, doth Covenant and Agree to and with the ſaid *B. W. H. S.* and *W. E.* their Executors, *&c.* that it ſhall be lawful for the ſaid *E. A.* during the joint Lives of them the ſaid *S. T.* and *E. A.* to take, have and receive to her own Uſe, notwithſtanding her Coverture, and as if ſhe were ſole and unmarried, all ſuch Sums of Money as ſhall be raiſed by any Fine or Fines, or any Leaſe or Leaſes, that ſhall at any Time or Times hereafter be made by Virtue of the ſaid Power abovementioned, and to diſpoſe thereof, and of every Part thereof, to ſuch Perſon and Perſons, and to ſuch Uſes, Intents and Purpoſes as ſhe ſhall think fit, without the Hindrance, Diſturbance or Controul of the ſaid *S. T.* and

as

as if ſhe were ſole and unmarried; it being the true Intent and Meaning of all the ſaid Parties to theſe Preſents, and ſo hereby declared to be, that the ſaid *E. A.* notwithſtanding her Coverture, ſhall have the full, ſole and abſolute Diſpoſal of all ſuch Sum and Sums of Money, as ſhall be raiſed by leaſing all or any Part of the ſaid Premiſſes for Life or Lives as aforeſaid. *In Witneſs,* &c.

A Settlement *of a Wife's Real and Perſonal Eſtate to her own ſeparate Uſe, with a Covenant from the Husband to permit her to make a Will thereof, as ſhe ſhall think fit.*

THIS *Indenture* Tripartite, made, *&c.* *Between* G. *H.* of, *&c.* of the firſt Part, *M. B.* of, *&c.* of the ſecond Part, and *J. L.* of, *&c.* and *R. T.* of, *&c.* of the third Part. *Whereas D. B.* late of, *&c.* in and by his laſt Will and Teſtament, bearing Date, *&c.* did Give, Deviſe and Bequeath unto the ſaid *M. B.* all that his Freehold Meſſuage and Lands, lying and being in, *&c.* and to her Heirs and Aſſigns for ever; and alſo all his Leaſehold Eſtate in, *&c.* for and during the Term of the Leaſe or Leaſes whereby he then held and enjoy'd the ſame; and he did thereby likewiſe give to the ſaid *M. B.* divers Debts and Sums of Money, *&c.* as in and by the ſaid recited Will proved in the Prerogative Court of, *&c.* more at large may appear: By Virtue of which ſaid Will of the ſaid

D. B.

D. B. ſhe the ſaid *M. B.* is entitled unto, and ſeized and poſſeſſed of all and ſingular the Premiſſes abovementioned. *And whereas* a Marriage is intended to be ſhortly had and ſolemnized between the ſaid *G. H.* and the ſaid *M. B.* and it is agreed by and between the ſaid *G. H.* and *M. B.* that if the ſaid Marriage ſhall take Effect, then notwithſtanding the ſaid Marriage, he the ſaid *G. H.* his Heirs, Executors, Adminiſtrators or Aſſigns, ſhall not, nor will intermeddle with, or have any Right, Title or Intereſt, either in Law or Equity, in or to any Part of the Rents, Iſſues, and Profits of the ſeveral Eſtates given and bequeathed to her the ſaid *M. B.* in and by the ſaid recited Will, as aforeſaid; nor ſhall he the ſaid *G. H.* his Executors, Adminiſtrators or Aſſigns, intermeddle with, or have any Right, Title or Intereſt, in or to any of the ſaid Sums of Money, *&c.* or the Intereſt thereof; But the ſame ſhall be and remain to and for the ſole and ſeparate Uſe and Benefit of the ſaid *M. B.* *Now this Indenture witneſſeth*, That for the making the ſaid Agreement good and effectual in the Law, and for the keeping and preſerving the Rents of the ſeveral Eſtates, and the Intereſt of the ſaid Money, *&c.* abovementioned, to and for the ſeparate Uſe of her the ſaid *M. B.* and ſo that the ſame ſhall not be in the Power or Diſpoſal of the ſaid *G. H.* or liable to the Payment of any of his Debts, or any Incumbrances; *He* the ſaid *G. H.* doth for himſelf, his Heirs, Executors and Adminiſtrators, and for every of them, Covenant, Promiſe and Agree, to and with the ſaid *J. L.* and *R. T.* and

and the Survivor of them, and the Executors and Administrators of the Survivor of them, by these Presents, that notwithstanding the said intended Marriage shall take Effect, all the Rents of the said Freehold and Leasehold Estates abovementioned, as shall from Time to Time become due and payable to her the said *M. B.* by virtue of the recited Will aforesaid; and also the Interest due, or to grow due for the said, *&c. Shall be* accounted, reckoned and taken as a separate and distinct Estate, of and from the Estate of him the said *G. H* and no ways liable or subject to him, or to the Payment of any of his Debts; but shall, with the Profits or Increase that shall hereafter be gotten, gained or made of the same, be ordered, disposed, and employed to such Person and Persons, and to and for such Use and Uses, Intents and Purposes, and in such Manner and Form as is herein after mentioned and declared; (*that is to say*) that the ready Money arising or accruing out of the said separate and distinct Estate abovementioned, shall from Time to Time be placed out at Interest, on such Securities as she the said *M. B.* shall think fit; which Securities, during the Coverture, shall be taken and made in the Names of the said *J. L.* and *R. T.* or the Survivor of them, or in the Name or Names of such other Person or Persons as the said *M. B.* shall order, direct and appoint, in Trust for her the said *M. B. And* that all the said separate and distinct Estate before declared and allotted for the said *M. B.* and the Produce and Increase thereof, shall be had, taken, held, possessed and en-

joyed

joyed, by ſuch Perſon and Perſons, and for ſuch Uſe and Uſes, as the ſaid *M. B.* ſhall at any Time or Times hereafter, during her Life, Limit, Give, Deviſe, Order, Appoint or Diſpoſe of the ſame, or any Part or Parts thereof, either by her laſt Will and Teſtament in Writing, or by any Writing purporting or intending to be her laſt Will and Teſtament, or by any other Writing to be ſigned with her Hand, ſubſcribed in the Preſence of two or more credible Witneſſes. *And* the ſaid *G. H.* doth for himſelf, his Heirs, Executors and Adminiſtrators, Covenant, Promiſe and Agree, to and with the ſaid *J. L.* and *R. T.* &c. that if the ſaid Marriage ſhall take Effect, that then he the ſaid *G. H.* ſhall and will permit and ſuffer the ſaid *M. B.* to Give, Grant, and diſpoſe of the ſaid ſeparate Eſtate, as ſhe ſhall think fit, in her Life-Time; and to make ſuch Will, or other Writing as aforeſaid, and thereby Give, Order, Deviſe, Limit and appoint her ſaid ſeparate Eſtate to any Perſon or Perſons, for any Truſt, Uſe, Intent, or Purpoſe whatſoever; and that he the ſaid *G. H.* ſhall and will permit and ſuffer ſuch Will hereafter to be made, to be duly proved by the Executors in ſuch Will named or to be named, and *Probat* to be had and taken thereof, as is uſual; and that the Perſon or Perſons to whom the ſaid *M. B.* ſhall give or diſpoſe any Part of her ſaid ſeparate Eſtate by her Will, or any other Writing, that ſhall be ſigned, ſealed and executed by her, in the Preſence of two or more credible Witneſſes as aforeſaid, ſhall and lawfully may peaceably and quietly have, hold, occupy, possess and enjoy the same, according to the true Intent and Meaning of such Gift, Devise, or Appointment, without any Let, Suit, Trouble, Denial, Hindrance or Interruption, of or by the said *G. H.* his Executors, Administrators or Assigns, or any of them. *And also*, That it shall and may be lawful to and for the said *I. L.* and *R. T.* and the Survivor of them, and the Executors and Administrators of the Survivor, at any Time from and after the said intended Marriage shall take Effect, to commence any Action or Suit in Law or Equity, in the Name or Names of the said *G. H.* and *M. B.* his intended Wife, against any Person or Persons for the Recovery of any Sum or Sums of Money due or to grow due to the said *M. B.* on her said separate Estate as aforesaid; and that the said *G. H.* shall not, nor will Release or Discharge any such Action or Suit, nor Receive, Release or Discharge any Sum or Sums of Money now due, or hereafter to grow due or owing to the said *M. B.* on Account of her said separate Estate, without the special Licence and Consent of them the said *J. L.* and *R. T.* or the Survivor of them, or the Executors or Administrators of the Survivor of them, in that Behalf first had and obtained in Writing, under their or some of their Hands and Seals: But that he the said *G. H.* shall and will avow, justify and maintain all lawful Actions and Suits that shall be so commenced for Recovery of the Premisses; and also that he the said *G. H.* shall and will as often as thereto desired by the said *J. L.* and *R. T.* or the Survivor

of

of them, &c. join with the said *M.* his intended Wife in any Receipt, Release, Discharge or Assignment necessary to be given and made on receiving in any of the Monies due or to grow due to the said *M.* as aforesaid; or in the Transferring of, &c. aforesaid. *And further*, that he the said *G. H.* shall and will from Time to Time, and at all Times, from and after the said Marriage shall take Effect, upon every reasonable Request, and at the proper Costs and Charges of the said *J. L.* and *R. T.* or the Survivor of them, or the Executors or Administrators of the Survivor of them, make, do and execute all and every such further Act and Acts, Thing and Things, for the better settling, recovering and receiving the Money, Goods and Estate of the said *M. B.* allotted and declared to be for her separate Use, Benefit and Disposal, as aforesaid, as by the said *J. L.* and *R. T.* or the Survivor of them, or the Executors, &c. or their or any of their Counsel learned in the Law shall be reasonably devised, advised or required: And that he the said *G. H.* his Executors or Administrators, shall not nor will, at any Time or Times hereafter, do, commit or suffer, or cause to be done, committed or suffered, any Act, Matter, or Thing whatsoever, whereby or wherewith, or by Reason or Means whereof, the said *M.* shall or may be any ways frustrated or hindred in the having, holding and enjoying her said Estate for her own separate Use, or in the giving or disposing of the same, according to the true Meaning of these Presents. *Provided always*, and it is declared, concluded and agreed, by and between all the ſaid Parties to theſe Preſents, and it is the true Intent and Meaning hereof, and of the ſaid Parties hereunto, that they the ſaid *J. L.* and *R. T.* and the Survivor of them, *&c.* ſhall and may from Time to Time reimburſe, ſatisfy and pay themſelves out of the ſaid Eſtate, all ſuch neceſſary and reaſonable Charges as they ſhall ſuſtain or be put unto, by reaſon of their being made Parties to theſe Preſents, and tranſacting any Truſt or other Thing purſuant thereto; and that neither of them the ſaid *J. L.* and *R. T.* ſhall be any ways accountable for the Act of the other, or liable to make good any more of the ſaid Eſtate than what ſhall really and *bona fide* come to his Hands or Cuſtody. *Provided alſo*, and it is declared, concluded and agreed, *&c.* that the ſaid *G. H.* his Executors and Adminiſtrators, ſhall from Time to Time and at all Times hereafter, be indemnified and ſaved harmleſs out of the ſeparate Eſtate of the ſaid *M. B.* of and from all manner of Coſts, Charges, Damages or Trouble, that he or they ſhall or may ſuſtain, incur or be put unto, for or by Reaſon or Means of his the ſaid *G. H.*'s joining or being made a Party in any Action or Suit for recovering any Part of the ſeparate Eſtate of the ſaid *M.* or joining or being made a Party in any Receipt, Releaſe or Aſſignment, to be made and given upon receiving any Part of the ſeparate Eſtate of her the ſaid *M. B.* as aforeſaid; or on any other Account whatſoever relating to the ſaid ſeparate Eſtate. *In Witneſs*, &c.

Marriage Articles to place the Wife's Fortune out at Intereſt, in Nature of a Settlement; and Covenant for the Husband to lay out 1000 *l.* on a Purchaſe, and ſettle the Lands on his Wife, *&c.*

Articles of Agreement *Tripartite, indented, made, concluded and agreed upon, this Day and Year,* &c. Between T. N. *of,* &c. *of the firſt Part,* G. M. *of,* &c. *of the ſecond Part, and* L. W. *of,* &c. *and* A. W. *of,* &c. *of the third Part.*

IMprimis, Whereas there is a Marriage intended (by God's Permiſſion) ſhortly to be had and ſolemnized between the ſaid *T. N.* and *A. M.* Spinſter, Daughter of the ſaid *G. M.* with whom he the ſaid *T. N.* is to have and receive the Sum of 1000 *l.* as and for a Marriage Portion: But foraſmuch as the ſaid *T. N.* is not as yet ſeized or poſſeſſed of any real Eſtate, whereby to make the ſaid *A. M.* a competent Jointure and Settlement, equivalent to her Fortune; it is therefore covenanted, agreed and declared, by and between the ſaid Parties to theſe Preſents, in Manner and Form following, (*viz.*)

Firſt, The ſaid *G. M.* for himſelf, his Executors and Adminiſtrators, doth Covenant, Promiſe and Agree, to and with the ſaid *T. N.* his Executors and Adminiſtrators, that he the ſaid *G. M.* his Executors or Adminiſtrators, ſhall and will within three Months after the

Solemnization of the ſaid intended Marriage between the ſaid *T.* and *A. M.* pay and depoſite into the Hands of the ſaid *L. W.* and *A. W.* the Sum of 1000 *l.* being the full Portion agreed to be given in Marriage with her the ſaid *A. Which* ſaid Sum of 1000 *l.* is hereby agreed by and between the ſaid Parties to theſe Preſents, ſhall from Time to Time be put out at Intereſt on the beſt Security or Securities that can be gotten and procured therefore, in the Name of the ſaid *L. W.* and *A. W.* by and with the Conſent and Approbation of the ſaid *T. N.* and the Intereſt thereof ſhall from Time to Time be paid to and received by the ſaid *T. N.* during his Life; and after his Death, by the ſaid *A.* his intended Wife during her Life; and after the Deceaſes of them the ſaid *T. N.* and *A.* then the ſaid Sum of 1000 *l.* ſhall be paid to and amongſt ſuch Child or Children of the ſaid *A.* by the ſaid *T. N.* her intended Husband to be begotten, by ſuch Proportions, and in ſuch Manner as they the ſaid *T. N.* and *A.* his intended Wife, or the Survivor of them, ſhall by any Deed or Deeds, Writing or Writings, by them or the Survivor, to be ſealed and executed in the Preſence of two or more credible Witneſſes, direct and appoint; and for Default of ſuch Direction and Appointment, then to be equally divided amongſt all and every ſuch Child or Children, ſhare and ſhare alike. *And* if there ſhall happen to be no ſuch Child or Children of the ſaid *A.* by the ſaid *T. N.* to be begotten, then the Sum of 500 *l.* Part of the ſaid Sum of 1000 *l.* ſhall and ought to be paid to the ſaid *G. M.* his Executors and Adminiſtrators, and the remaining 500 *l.* to the ſaid *T. N.* his Executors and Adminiſtrators.

Provided always, and it is hereby further agreed and declared by and between the ſaid Parties to theſe Preſents, that in Caſe the ſaid *T. N.* ſhall at any Time, during his Life, be minded and deſirous to call in the ſaid 1000 *l.* or any Part thereof, and inveſt the ſame in his Trade, or to lay out the ſame in a Purchaſe of any Lands, Tenements or Hereditaments, and ſhall procure the Conſent of the ſaid *A.* his intended Wife and of the ſaid *G. M.* for ſo doing, to be declared in Writing under Hand and Seal, *&c.* that then and in ſuch Caſe it ſhall and may be lawful to and for the ſaid *G. M. L. W.* and *A. W.* and the Survivor of them, and the Executors and Adminiſtrators of ſuch Survivor, to call in the ſaid 1000 *l.* and to pay the ſame to the ſaid *T. N.* who may either inveſt the ſame in the Trade which he the ſaid *T. N.* now uſeth, or Lay out the ſaid Money in the Purchaſe of any Lands, Tenements or Hereditaments, to be ſettled on the ſaid *A.* and the Iſſue of her Body, by the ſaid *T. N.* to be begotten, as by the Purport of ſuch Writing, ſo to be ſealed and executed as aforeſaid, ſhall be declared, agreed and directed, concerning the ſame.

Item, It is further covenanted, agreed and declared, by and between the ſaid Parties to theſe Preſents, that the ſaid *L. W.* and *A. W.* their Executors or Adminiſtrators, ſhall not be chargeable with, or liable to make good any bad Debt or Debts that ſhall or may happen by any insufficient Security or Securities; and that each of them shall be accountable for no more than what shall actually come to each of their Hands respectively, and not for the Receipts of each other. And that it shall and may be lawful to and for the said *L. W.* and *A. W.* their Executors and Administrators, to have, take and receive out of the said 1000*l.* and the Interest and Profits thereof, sufficient Money to reimburse themselves all Costs, Damages and Expences, which they, or either of them shall expend, sustain, or be put unto, in relation to the Trust hereby in them reposed.

Item, The said *T. N.* in Consideration of the said intended Marriage and Marriage-Portion, doth for himself, his Heirs, Executors and Administrators, covenant and grant, to and with the said *G. M.* his Heirs, Executors and Administrators, that he the said *T. N.* (in Case the said intended Marriage shall take Effect) shall and will, with the Approbation of the said *G. M.* and the said *L. W.* and *A. W.* or the Survivor of them, lay out the Sum of, *&c.* in a Purchase of Lands and Tenements in Fee-simple, in the County of, *&c.* and settle the same, as the Counsel of the said *G. M.* and the said Trustees, or the Survivor of them shall direct and advise, in such Manner as the same may be held and enjoyed by the said *T. N.* and his Assigns, for and during the Term of his natural Life, without Impeachment of Waste; and after his Decease, by the said *A.* his intended Wife, and her Assigns, for and during the Term of her natural Life; and after

after both their Deceases, by the Issues of their Bodies, between them to be begotten, by such Proportions, and in such Manner and Form as they the said *T. N.* and *A.* his intended Wife, or the Survivor of them, by any Deed or Deeds, Writing or Writings, by them or the Survivor of them, to be sealed and executed in the Presence of two or more credible Witnesses, shall direct, limit or appoint; and in Default of making such Appointment, then by the Heirs of the said *A.* by the said *T. N.* to be begotten, in such Manner as it shall not be in the Power of the said *T. N.* to defeat such Issue of the same; and in Default of such Issue, then by the Right Heirs of the said *T. N.* for ever. *In witness*, &c.

Articles of Marriage for settling a Wife's Estate, and paying the Wife a Sum of Money, in Lieu of a Jointure.

Articles of Agreement *Tripartite, indented, made,* &c. *Between* W. E. *of,* &c. *of the first Part,* J. D. *Spinster, Daughter of,* &c. *of the second Part, and* A. L. *of,* &c. *and* B. M. *of,* &c. *of the third Part, as followeth,* viz:

WHereas the said *J. D.* by Virtue of the Will of, &c. or otherwise, is seised to her and her Heirs in Fee-simple, of and in certain Messuages or Tenements, with the Appurtenances, situate, lying and being in, &c. *And whereas* the said *J.* is also possessed or interessed for the Remainder of a Term of ninety-nine Years, if, &c. or either of them shall so long live, of and in all that Messuage or Tenement, with the Appurtenances, situate in, &c. by Virtue of one Indenture of Lease thereof granted to the said *J. D.* by, &c. *And whereas* a Marriage is intended (by GOD's Grace) shortly to be had and solemnized between the said *W. E.* and *J. D.* with whom the said *W. E.* is to have and receive 500*l.* in Money, over and besides the Houses above-mentioned, as and for her Marriage-Portion : *It* is therefore covenanted and agreed, by and between the said Parties to these Presents, in Manner following, (that is to say).

Imprimis,

Imprimis, The said *W. E.* for himself, his Heirs and Assigns, doth covenant and grant, to and with the said *A. L.* and *B. M.* their Heirs and Assigns, That they the said *W. E.* and *J.* his intended Wife, in Case the said Marriage shall take Effect, shall and will within six Months after the said Marriage shall be had and solemnized, by Fine and other good and sufficient Conveyances in the Law, settle and assure all such Messuages and Tenements whereof she the said *J. D.* is seised as aforesaid, with the Appurtenances, to the Use and Behoof of the said *W. E.* and his Assigns, during the Term of his natural Life; and from and after the Determination of that Estate, then to the Use and Behoof of the said *A. L.* and *B. M.* their Heirs and Assigns, during the natural Life of the said *W. E.* in Trust to preserve and support the contingent Remainders herein after limited: And from and after the Decease of the said *W. E.* then to the Use and Behoof of the said *J.* his intended Wife, for and during the Term of her natural Life; and from and after her Decease, then to the Use and Behoof of the Heirs of the Body of the said *J.* by the said *W. E.* lawfully to be begotten; and for Default of such Issue, then to the Use and Behoof of the said *J.* her Heirs and Assigns for ever, and to and for none other Use, Intent or Purpose whatsoever.

Item, The said *W. E.* doth for himself, his Heirs, Executors, Administrators and Assigns, further covenant and grant, to and with the said *A. L.* and *B. M.* their Heirs, Executors, *&c.* that he the said *W. E.* and the

the said *J.* his intended Wife, shall and will, by like good and sufficient Conveyances in the Law, settle and assure the said Messuage or Tenement, with the Appurtenances abovementioned, to be situate in, *&c.* in the Possession of, *&c.* in such Manner as that the same may be held and enjoyed, and the Rents and Profits thereof may be had, received and taken by the said *W. E.* and his Assigns, during so many Years of the said Term as he shall happen to live; and from and after his Decease, then by the said *J.* his intended Wife, and her Assigns, for and during so many Years of the said Term, as she shall happen to live; and from and after her Decease, then by such Children of the said *J.* by the said *W. E.* lawfully to be begotten, and so as it may not be in the Power of the said *W. E.* to defeat such their Issue; and for Default of such Issue, then by the Executors and Administrators of the said *J.* during the Residue of the Term, and upon none other Trust, and to or for none other Intent or Purpose whatsoever.

Item, Forasmuch as the said *W. E.* is not at present seised of an Estate sufficient to make a Jointure for the said *J.* his intended Wife, the said *W. E.* doth for himself, his Heirs and Assigns, covenant and grant, to and with the said *A. L.* and *B. M.* their Heirs, *&c.* that in Case the said intended Marriage shall take Effect, and he the said *W. E.* shall happen to die in the Life-time of the said *J.* that then he the said *W. E.* shall and will, by his Last Will and Testament, or otherwise, give and assure unto the said *J. D.* the Sum

of

of 500 *l.* or the full Value thereof in Lands, Tenements, Goods or Chattels, to be at her own Difpofal, and to be by her received and taken to her own proper Ufe and Benefit. *In witnefs*, &c.

A *Bond* on *Marriage*, with Condition to leave the Wife and Children fo much Money, at the Husband's Death; and if the Wife dies in a Year, to refund Part of the Portion.

NOverint *univerfi per prefentes me* S. J. *de* &c. *teneri & firmiter obligari* E. F. *de*, &c. G. H. *de*, &c. & J. L. *de*, &c. *in Octingentis Libris bone & leg'lis monete* Magn' Britannie *folvend' eifd'm* E. F. G. H. & J. L. *vel alicui eorum aut fuo certo Attornat' Executorib' Adminiftratorib' vel Affignat' fuis, ad quam quidem folutionem bene & fideliter faciend' obligo me heredes Executores & Adminiftratores meos firmiter per prefentes, figillo meo figillat' Dat' Primo die* Julii *Anno Regni Dom'* Georgii *Dei Gra'* Magn' Britan' Franc' & Hibern' *Regis Fidei Defenfor'*, &c. *quinto Annoq; D'ni*, 1731.

THE Condition of this Obligation is fuch, That *whereas* a Marriage is intended (by GOD's Permiffion) fhortly to be had and folemnifed between the above bound *S. J.* and *C. F.* Daughter of the above-named *E. F.* with whom the faid *S. J.* is to receive, as a Marriage

Marriage Portion, the Sum of 400*l.* in Money, or the Value thereof in Goods or other Effects; and in Consideration of the said Marriage and Marriage Portion, he the said *S. J.* hath agreed to leave to the said *C.* and her Children, to be by him begotten, the Sum of 400*l.* to be paid and applied in Manner herein after mentioned. *If therefore* the said Marriage shall take Effect, and the said *S. J.* shall die in the Life-time of the said *C.* then if the Heirs, Executors or Administrators of him the said *S. J.* do and shall, within six Months next after his Death, pay or cause to be paid, into the Hands of the said *E. F. G. H.* and *J. L.* the Sum of 400*l.* to be by them applied upon the Trusts, and to and for the Ends and Purposes following, (that is to say) That in Case the said *S. J.* shall leave any Child or Children of his Body, on the Body of the said *C.* begotten, which shall live to be married, or attain the Age of Twenty-one Years respectively, the said Trustees and the Survivors and Survivor of them, shall pay the said 400*l.* to the said *C.* and such Child or Children, equally between them, Share and Share alike: And in the mean Time, until such Child or Children shall be married, or attain their said Age of Twenty-one Years respectively, the said Trustees shall pay the Interest of the said 400*l.* to the said *C.* towards the Support and Maintenance of the said *C.* and such Child or Chlidren. And in Case the said *S. J.* shall leave no Issue of his Body, on the Body of the said *C.* begotten, or leaving Issue, and such Issue shall all die before Marriage,

or

or the Age of Twenty-one Years, then the ſaid whole Sum of 400 *l.* ſhall and ought to be paid to the ſaid *C.* her Executors and Adminiſtrators. *But* in Caſe the ſaid *C.* ſhall happen to die in the Life-time of the ſaid *S. J.* having a Child or Children of his Body, on the Body of the ſaid *C.* begotten; then if the ſaid *S. J.* his Heirs, Executors or Adminiſtrators, do and ſhall forthwith pay, or cauſe to be paid to the ſaid *E. F. G. H.* and *J. L.* for the Uſe of the ſaid Child or Children, the Part, Share and Portion of ſuch Child or Children, of and in the ſaid 400 *l.* ſo appointed above for the ſaid *C.* and her Children, in Caſe ſhe ſurvived the ſaid *S.* upon an equal Diviſion to be made thereof by the ſaid Truſtees, between the ſaid *S.* and ſuch Child or Children, Share and Share alike; and then the ſaid Truſtees ſhall pay ſuch Shares and Proportions to ſuch Child or Children on their Marriage or Age of Twenty-one Years, which ſhall firſt happen; and in the mean Time ſhall pay the Intereſt thereof to the ſaid *S. J.* towards the Support and Maintenance of ſuch Child or Children, *&c.* *And* in Caſe the ſaid *C.* ſhall die within the Space of one Year, from the Day of her Marriage with the ſaid *S. J.* leaving no Child of his Body, on the Body of her the ſaid *C.* begotten; then if the ſaid *S. J.* his Heirs, Executors or Adminiſtrators, do and ſhall within ſix Months next after the Death of the ſaid *C.* refund and pay back, or cauſe to be refunded and paid back, unto the ſaid *E. F.* his Executors or Adminiſtrators, to and for his own proper Uſe and Benefit, the Sum

of

of 200*l.* being one Moiety of the Marriage-Portion given with the said C. that then, *&c.* or else, *&c.*

A Bond *for the* separate Maintenance *of a Wife.*

J. B. & *T. W.* teneri, &c. R. *T.* in centum libris, &c.

W*Hereas* several Differences have arisen between the above bound *J. B.* and *E. B.* his Wife, whereupon the said *E. B.* hath for the Space of, *&c.* lived separate and apart from the said *J. B.* and he hath not hitherto given or made any Allowance for her Maintenance: *And whereas* the said *J. B.* hath now agreed to pay, towards the Maintenance of the said *E. B.* the weekly Sum of seven Shillings, which the said *E. B.* is contented and willing to take and accept, in full Satisfaction of what she can or may claim or demand of him the said *J. B.* for Maintenance, as aforesaid. *Now the Condition* of this Obligation is such, That if the said *J. B.* do and shall pay, or cause to be paid unto the said *E. B.* on *Saturday* in every Week, during the Life of him the said *J. B.* the Sum of seven Shillings of lawful Money of *Great Britain*, without any Fraud or Delay, for the separate Maintenance of her the said *E. B.* according to the true Intent and Meaning of the Agreement above-mentioned, Then, *&c.*

The

The Condition of a Bond *from a Woman* divorced, *that she shall not claim Dower or Maintenance*, &c.

THE *Condition* of this Obligation is such, That *whereas* great Strife and Variance hath been stirred up between the above-named *W. A.* and the above bound *M. D.* concerning a supposed Marriage had between them: *And whereas* the said Variance, by legal Sentence given, by and before the Right Reverend Father in God *B.* Lord Bishop of, &c. is now decided, and the said *W. A.* and *M. D.* are divorced. *And whereas* the said *W. A.* in Consideration of the said Divorcement, hath entered into Bond to, &c. for the Use of the said *M. D.* for the Payment of the Sum of, &c. at and upon, &c. And the said *M. D.* hath sealed and delivered unto the said *W. A.* a general Release of all Debts, Duties, Dowers, Jointures, Rights, Claims and Demands, which she hath, may, might, or ought to have, claim or demand, of, by or from the said *W. A.* or by the Death of him the said *W. A.* as by the said Release may appear. *If therefore* the said *M. D.* or any other Person or Persons for her, or by her Consent, Act, Means or Procurement, do not molest, sue, implead, or cause to be molested, sued or impleaded, or otherwise troubled or put to Charges, the said *W. A.* his Heirs, Executors or Administrators, at any Time or Times hereafter, for any Maintenance, Jointure, Dower,

Meat,

Meat, Drink or Cloaths, nor for any Lands, Tenements, Hereditaments, Goods or Chattels of the ſaid *W. A.* whereof the ſaid *W. A.* now is, or at any Time hereafter ſhall be ſeiſed or poſſeſſed, or any other Perſon or Perſons, to the Uſe of the ſaid *W. A.* or any Part or Parcel thereof; nor for any other Cauſe, Contract or Demand whatſoever, from the Beginning of the World to the Day of the Date hereof: *And alſo*, if the ſaid *M. D.* from Time to Time, and at all Times hereafter, do and ſhall, upon the reaſonable Requeſt, and at the Coſts and Charges in the Law of the ſaid *W. A.* his Heirs or Aſſigns, make, ſeal and execute unto the ſaid *W. A.* his Heirs and Aſſigns, all and every further lawful and reaſonable Act and Acts, Deed and Deeds, Device and Devices whatſoever, for the full Diſſolution of all Contracts of Marriage; and for the Diſcharge of the ſaid *W. A.* his Heirs, Executors and Adminiſtrators, of and from all other Claims, Titles, Debts, Duties and Demands whatſoever, by her the ſaid *M. D.* or any other Perſon or Perſons by her Appointment, Means or Procurement, at any Time hereafter to be asked, challenged, claimed or demanded of the ſaid *W. A.* his Heirs, Executors, Adminiſtrators or Aſſigns, by Reaſon of her being Wife to the ſaid *W. A.* or to him contracted, or for any other Cauſe, Matter or Thing whatſoever, from the Beginning of the World until the Day of the Date of theſe Preſents; and from all Dowers and Title of Dower and Jointure on the Death of the ſaid *W. A.* as by the ſaid *W. A.* his Heirs, Executors or Aſſigns, or his or their Counſel learned in the Law, ſhall be reaſonably deviſed, adviſed or required; Then, *&c.*

An Aſſignment *of* Dower *to a Widow, by the Heir of her Husband.*

THIS *Indenture* made, *&c.* *Between* *T. M.* of, *&c.* Son and Heir of *L. M.* late of, *&c.* Eſq; of the one Part, and *D. M.* Widow and Relict of the ſaid *L. M.* of the other Part. *Whereas* the ſaid *L. M.* in his Life-time, and at the Time of his Death, was ſeiſed in his Demeſne, as of Fee, of and in all thoſe Meſſuages, Lands and Tenements in, *&c.* which upon the Deceaſe of the ſaid *L. M.* deſcended to the ſaid *T. M.* *And whereas* the ſaid *D. M.* hath required of the ſaid *T. M.* her Dower or Thirds, of and in the Meſſuages, Tenements, Lands and Premiſſes aforeſaid, and of and in all the Eſtate whereof the ſaid *L. M.* died ſeiſed or poſſeſſed: *Now this Indenture witneſſeth*, That the ſaid *T. M.* *Hath* aſſigned and appointed, and by theſe Preſents doth aſſign, *&c.* unto the ſaid *D. M.* the Third Part of all the ſaid Lands, Tenements and Hereditaments, (*viz.*) *All* that Meſſuage or Tenement, ſituate, lying and being in, *&c.* *To have and to hold* the ſaid Meſſuage or Tenement, and Premiſſes, with the Appurtenances, unto the ſaid *D M.* for and during her natural Life, in the Name of Dower, and in full Satisfaction of all

Dower and Thirds which ſhe the ſaid *D. M.* ought to have, or can or may claim, of, or in any Meſſuages, Lands, Tenements or Hereditaments, which were at any Time belonging or appertaining to the ſaid *L. M.* *And* the ſaid *T. M.* for himſelf, his Heirs and Aſſigns, doth covenant and grant, to and with the ſaid *D. M.* her, *&c.* That ſhe the ſaid *D. M.* ſhall and may, from Time to Time, and at all Times during her natural Life, peaceably and quietly hold and enjoy the ſaid Meſſuage or Tenement, and Premiſſes above-mentioned, to be aſſigned in Dower, without any Moleſtation, Hindrance or Interruption, of or by the ſaid *T. M.* his Heirs or Aſſigns; and that free from all former and other Grants and Incumbrances, *&c.* *And* that he the ſaid *T. M.* his Heirs and Aſſigns, ſhall and will do any further and other Acts for the further Aſſuring of the ſaid Meſſuage or Tenement, *&c.* above-mentioned, to the ſaid *D. M.* for and during her natural Life, as by the ſaid *D. M.* or her Counſel, ſhall be adviſed and required. *In witneſs*, &c.

A Releaſe *of a Woman's* Dower.

TO *all People* to whom theſe Preſents ſhall come, *A. W.* Widow and Relict of *W. W.* late of, *&c.* deceaſed, ſendeth greeting. *Know ye*, That the ſaid *A. W.* for and in Conſiderarion of the Sum of, *&c.* to her in Hand paid by *L. W.* of, *&c.* Son of the ſaid *W. W.* *Hath* remiſed, releaſed, and for ever

ever quit-claimed, and by these Presents doth fully, freely and absolutely remise, release, and for ever quit-claim, unto the said *L. W.* all and all Manner of Dower, and Right and Title of Dower whatsoever, which she the said *A. W.* now hath, may, might, should, or ought to have or claim, of, in or out of all and every the Messuages, Lands, Tenements and Hereditaments whatsoever, which were the said *W. W.*'s, her late Husband, at any Time during the Coverture between him and the said *A. W.* situate and being in the County of, *&c.* and also all Manner of Actions and Writs of Dower whatsoever; so as neither she the said *A. W.* nor any other Person or Persons for her, or in her Name, any Dower or Writ or Action of Dower, or any Manner of Right or Title of Dower, of or in the said Messuages, Lands, Tenements and Hereditaments, or of or in any Part or Parcel thereof, at any Time hereafter shall or may have, claim or prosecute against the said *L. W.* his Heirs or Assigns, but of and from the same shall be utterly debarred, and for ever excluded by these Presents. *In Witness*, &c.

A Leafe *from Husband and Wife, of the* Wife's Land, *according to the Statute.*

THIS *Indenture* made, &c. Between *A. B.* of, &c. and *C.* his Wife, of the one Part, and *E. F.* of, &c. of the other Part. *Whereas* the faid *A. B.* is feifed in Right of the faid *C.* his Wife, of and in all that Meffuage or Tenement and Lands, fituate, &c. held in Fee-tail to her the faid *C.* and the Heirs of her Body, &c. by Virtue of a Deed of Gift and Grant thereof made by *T. H.* bearing Date, &c. as thereby may appear. *Now this Indenture witneffeth*, that the faid *A. B.* and *C.* his Wife, in Confideration of the Surrender of a former Leafe, granted unto the faid *E. F.* of the Meffuage or Tenement and Premiffes aforefaid, and herein after demifed, for the Term of, &c. as alfo for and in Confideration of the Sum of, &c. of lawful *Britifh* Money to them the faid *A. B.* and *C.* his Wife, in Hand paid by the faid *E. F.* at and before the Sealing and Delivery of thefe Prefents, the Receipt whereof they the faid *A. B.* and *C.* do hereby acknowledge, and thereof do acquit and difcharge the faid *E. F.* his Executors, Adminiftrators and Affigns, by thefe Prefents, *Have* demifed, granted and to Farm letten, and by thefe Prefents do demife, grant, &c. unto the faid *E. F.* *All* that Meffuage or Tenement, with all thofe Lands, &c. fituate and lying in, &c. above-mentioned, and all Houfes, Outhoufes, Ways, Waters, Eafements

ments and Appurtenances to the ſaid Meſſuage or Tenement, Lands and Premiſſes belonging, or any Ways appertaining; which ſaid Meſſuage, or Tenement and Premiſſes, have been commonly let to Farm, by the Space of twenty Years and more laſt paſt. *To have and to hold* the ſaid Meſſuage or Tenement, Lands and Premiſſes above granted and demiſed, and every Part and Parcel thereof, with the Appurtenances, unto the ſaid *E. F.* his Executors, Adminiſtrators and Aſſigns, from the Day of the Date of theſe Preſents, for and during, and unto the full End and Term of twenty-one Years, from thence next enſuing, and fully to be compleat and ended: *Yielding and paying* therefore yearly, and every Year, during the ſaid Term, unto the ſaid *A. B.* and *C.* his Wife, and the Heirs of the ſaid *C.* the ancient and accuſtomed Rent of, *&c.* at and upon the Feaſt-Days of, *&c.* by even and equal Portions: *And* if it ſhall happen the ſaid yearly Rent of, *&c.* or any Part thereof, ſhall be behind and unpaid, by the Space of eight and twenty Days next after either of the ſaid Feaſts or Days of Payment, on which the ſame ought to be paid as aforeſaid (being lawfully demanded) and no ſufficient Diſtreſs or Diſtreſſes, in or upon the ſaid Premiſſes, can or may be found, whereby the ſame may be levied, that then, and from thenceforth it ſhall and may be lawful, to and for the ſaid *A. B. C.* his Wife, and the Heirs of the ſaid *C.* into the ſaid Meſſuage or Tenement, Lands and Premiſſes hereby demiſed, with the Appurtenances, to re-enter, and the ſame to have again, repossess and enjoy, as in his, her or their former Right and Estate, any thing herein contained to the contrary notwithstanding. *And* the said *E. F.* for himself, his Executors, Administrators and Assigns, doth covenant and grant, to and with the said *A. B. &c.* that he the said *E. F.* his Executors, Administrators and Assigns, shall and will, during the said Term hereby granted, well and truly pay, or cause to be paid, unto the said *A. B.* and *C.* his Wife, and the Heirs of the said *C.* the said yearly Rent of, *&c.* above reserved, at the Days and Times, and in Manner and Form above expressed, according to the true Intent and Meaning of these Presents. *And also* that he the said *E. F.* his Executors, Administrators and Assigns, at his and their own proper Costs and Charges, shall and will from Time to Time, and at all Times, during the said Term hereby granted, well and sufficiently repair, maintain, sustain, uphold, amend, hedge, ditch, cleanse and keep the said Messuage or Tenement, Lands and Premisses hereby demised, and every Part and Parcel thereof, with the Appurtenances, in and with all needful and necessary Reparations and Amendments whatsoever, when, and as often as need shall require; and the same so well and sufficiently repaired, maintained, sustained, *&c.* at the End of the said Term, or other sooner Determination of this present Demise, unto the said *A. B. C.* his Wife, or the Heirs of the said *C.* shall and will peaceably and quietly leave and yield up. *And* the said *A. B.* for himself, the said *C.* his Wife, and the Heirs

of

of the ſaid *C.* doth covenant and grant, to and with the ſaid *E. F.* his Executors, Adminiſtrators and Aſſigns, by theſe Preſents, that he the ſaid *E. F.* his Executors, *&c.* paying the ſaid yearly Rent of, *&c.* above reſerved in Manner aforeſaid, and performing the Covenants and Agreements herein before contained, which on his or their Parts and Behalfs, are or ought to be paid, done and performed, ſhall and may peaceably and quietly have, hold, occupy, poſſeſs and enjoy the ſaid Meſſuage or Tenement, Lands and Premiſſes above-mentioned, and every Part and Parcel thereof, with the Appurtenances, for and during the ſaid Term hereby granted, without any Interruption or Denial of the ſaid *A. B. C.* his Wife, or the Heirs of the ſaid *C.* or of any other Perſon or Perſons whatſoever, lawfully claiming, or to claim any Right, Title or Intereſt, from, by or under him, her, them, or either, or any of them. *In witneſs*, &c.

A Will *and Appointment* by a Wife, *of Legacies to be paid after her Death, purſuant to a Power given by Marriage Articles.*

I*N the Name of GOD, Amen.* I *M. T.* Wife of *B. T.* of, *&c.* by Virtue of a Power to me given and reſerved in and by the Marriage Articles or Settlement entered into and made between me and my Truſtees *J. L.* and *G. M.* of, *&c.* and the ſaid *B. T.* bearing Date, *&c.* do this Day, *&c.* in the Year of our Lord, &c. make and publish this my Last Will and Testament, in Manner following, (that is to say) *Imprimis*, I give and bequeath, and hereby appoint to be paid to my dear Brother *L. B.* the Sum of 200*l.* to me due from, &c. by one Bond or Obligation by him given, for Payment thereof to my said Trustees, the said *J. L. G. M.* &c. for my Use, at and upon, &c. last past. *Item*, I give to my loving Sister *A. B.* the Sum of 100*l.* which lies in a Bag, sealed up in the middle Drawer of the Scrutore, in my Closet; and also my Gold Watch, and best Suit of wearing Apparel. *Item*, I give and appoint to my Cousins *T. B. E. B.* and *C. B.* &c. the Sum of 10*l.* a-piece, to buy them Mourning; to be paid out of my separate Estate, which I shall leave behind me at my Death. *Item*, I give to my Servant Maid *E. W.* the Sum of 5*l.* and all my Clothes, except my best Suit of wearing Apparel, above bequeathed to my Sister *A. B.* *Item*, All the Rest and Residue of my Goods and Chattels, and separate Estate whatsoever, whereof I shall die possessed or entitled unto, I give to the said *J. L.* and *G. M.* &c. whom I make, constitute and ordain Executors and Overseers of this my Will, to take Care and see the same performed, according to my true Intent and Meaning. *In witness* whereof, I the said *M. T.* have to this my Last Will and Testament, or Appointment for the Disposition of my Estate, set my Hand and Seal the Day and Year above-written.

THE

THE

TABLE.

A.

The TABLE.

D.

D.

E.

Estates

I. *In-*

I.

L.

O.

P.

The TABLE.

Q.

R.

When

The TABLE.

FINIS.

REPRINTS OF LEGAL CLASSICS PUBLISHED BY THE LAWBOOK EXCHANGE, LTD.

WOMEN AND THE LAW

Anthony, Susan B. *An Account of the Proceedings of the Trial of Susan B. Anthony, on the Charge of Illegal Voting, at the Presidential Election in Nov., 1872. and on the Trial of Beverly W. Jones, Edwin T. Marsh and William B. Hall, the Inspectors of Election by whom her Vote was Received.* Rochester: Daily Democrat and Chronicle Book Print, 1874. vii, 212 pp. Reprinted 2002 by The Lawbook Exchange, Ltd. LCCN 2001041397. ISBN 1-58477-187-9. Cloth. $65.

* An account of the landmark suffragist trial before the U.S. Circuit Court for the Northern District of New York, at Canandaigua, in June, 1873, that brought the cause of women's voting rights to the forefront of national attention in the United States. A group of women led by preeminent abolitionist and woman's rights advocate Susan B. Anthony [1820-1906], attempted to vote during the presidential election of 1872, claiming they were entitled to do so according to the Fourteenth Amendment. The presiding officials, Jones, Hall, and Marsh, decided by a majority to accept their ballots. The women were soon arrested for this act and indicted for "knowingly voting without having a lawful right to vote." The officials were also indicted. This volume reprints the text of the indictment and a transcript of the testimony with connecting commentary. The appendix offers an address by Anthony delivered before her trial, a speech on her behalf cause by Joslyn Gage, and a critical assessment of the trial by John Hooker.

W.H. [Heale, William]. [1581?-1627]. *An Apologie for Women. Or an Opposition to Mr. Dr.G[ager]. his assertion, Who held in the Act at Oxforde, Anno. 1608, That it was Lawfull for Husbands to Beate their Wives.* Oxford: Printed by Joseph Barnes, 1609. [iv], 66 pp. Reprint available 2002 by The Lawbook Exchange, Ltd. ISBN 1-58477-287-5. Cloth. $95.

* William Gager [fl. 1580-1619], a controversial Latin dramatist, gave a public talk at one of the universities at Oxford in which he denounced women's "capacitie for learning, themselves adjudged worthie of blows." P. 3. Disturbed by this assertion, William Heale, a chaplain-fellow at Exeter College, published this stirring response. His case is substantiated by his solid examination of civil and canon law in reference to this subject. *The Dictionary of National Biography* VII: 797 (Gager) and IX:331 (Heale). *A Short-Title Catalogue of Books Printed in England, Scotland, & Ireland, 1475-1640* 13014.

[Women's Law]. *A Treatise of Feme Coverts: Or, the Lady's Law. Containing All the Laws and Statutes relating to Women, and Several Heads: I. Of Dissents of Lands to Females, Coparceners, etc. II. Of Cosummating of Marriage, Stealing of Women, Rapes, Polygamy. III. Of the Laws of Procreation of Children, and therein of Bastards or Spurious Issue. IV. Of the Privileges of Feme Coverts, and their Power with Respect to their Husband, and all others. V. Of Husband and Wife, and in what Actions they are to Join. VI. Of Estates Tail, Jointures and Settlements, Real and Personal on Women. VII. Of what the Wife is entitled to of the Husband's, and Things Belonging to the Wife, the Husband Gains Possession of by Marriage. VIII. Of Private Contracts by the Wife, Alimony, Separate Maintenance, Divorces, Elopements, etc. To which are added, Judge Hide's very remarkable Argument in the Exchequer-Chamber, Term. Trin. 15 Car. 2 In the Case of Manby and Scot, whether and in what Cases the Husband is Bound by the Contract of his Wife: And Select Precedents of Conveyances in all Cases concerning Feme Coverts.* [London]: E. and R. Nutt, and R. Gosling, 1732. [viii], 264, [16] pp. Reprint available 2002 by The Lawbook Exchange, Ltd. ISBN 1-58477-286-7. Cloth. $125.

* Reprint of the first edition of The Lady's Law which examines the doctrines of English Common Law relating to "feme coverts" or married women, from a perspective sympathetic to women. It deals with precedents of conveyances not covered in The Law of Baron and Femme, and as such can be seen as a companion volume. Marvin, Legal Bibliography (1847) 443, citing 1737 2nd ed. *Catalogue of the Library of the Law School of Harvard University* (1909) II:764.

Woolsey, Theodore D. *Divorce and Divorce Legislation, Especially in the United States. Second Edition Revised.* New York: Charles Scribner's Sons, 1882. x, [9]-328 pp. Reprinted 2001 by The Lawbook Exchange, Ltd. ISBN 1-58477-118-6. Cloth. $75.

* Woolsey presents his viewpoints on divorce legislation with extensive statistical support for his view that, with the exception of the statutes enacted in the state of New York, the United States courts are careless in their execution of divorce legislation. He also questions their adherence to Christianity. His views on the decline of divorce legislation are supported by a scholarly examination of the roots of divorce law in Hebrew, Greek and Roman law, the doctrine of divorce as portrayed in the New Testament and in the Christian Church, and in Europe since the reformation. First published in 1868, this second edition revision includes new material in the chapter on divorce legislation in the United States that bring it up to date at the time of publication.

Woolsey [1801-1889] was a theologian, educator and scholar, a professor of classical studies whose knowledge thereof informs this work. He was also President of Yale University for twenty-five years during which the University enjoyed growth and advancement in many areas. *Dictionary of American Biography* X: 519-520.

Kitchin, S.B. *A History of Divorce.* London: Chapman & Hall, Ltd., 1912. xvi, 293 pp. Reprinted 2002 by The Lawbook Exchange, Ltd. LCCN 2001041400. ISBN 1-58477-190-9. Cloth. $75.
* A history of divorce from the early Roman era to the present. "It covers in a brief, readable way the law during the Roman period, in the Eastern Church and Eastern Europe, in the canon law and Western Europe, from the Reformation to the French Revolution, in England, the United States, and the British Colonies." Marke, *A Catalogue of the Law Collection at New York University* (1953) 758.

Reeve, Tapping (1744-1823). *The Law of Baron and Femme, of Parent and Child, Guardian and Ward, Master and Servant, and of the Powers of the Courts of Chancery; with an Essay on the Terms Heir, Heirs, Heirs of the Body. Third Edition, With Notes and References to English and American Cases by Amasa J. Parker and Charles E. Baldwin, Counselors-At-Law.* Albany: William Gould, 1862. xlvi, 677pp. Reprinted 1998 by The Lawbook Exchange, Ltd. LCCN 98-36057. ISBN 1-886363-58-7. Cloth. $75.
* Third and final edition of the first American work devoted to the law of women is chiefly valued for its description of the legal character of domestic relations. This treatise delineates the marital, parental, guardian, master and chancery authority and rights of property, debts, wills, contracts and settlements. "American text writing as a significant force in our legal development begins in 1816 with Reeve's *Baron and Femme.*" Pound, *The Formative Era of American Law* 140. In 1782 the author founded the first American law school, Litchfield Law School, where he was the only teacher until 1798 when he was appointed to the superior court bench. Marke, *A Catalogue of the Law Collection at New York University (1953)*755 (referring to 1st ed.). Marvin, *Legal Bibliography (1847)* 603 (1st ed.). Parrish, 'Law Books and Legal Publishing in America, 1760-1840' in *Law Library J.* (72:355-452) 384 (1st ed.). *Catalogue of the Library of the Law School of Harvard University* (1909) II:437.

Swinburne, Henry [1560?-1623]. *A Treatise of Spousals, or Matrimonial Contracts: Wherein all the Questions Relating to that Subject are Ingeniously Debated and Resolved.* London: Printed by S. Roycroft for Robert Clavell, 1686. [xvi], 240 pp. Reprint available 2002 by The Lawbook Exchange, Ltd. ISBN 1-58477-288-3. Cloth. $125.
* First published after his death, this unique and original ecclesiastical law treatise was hailed as "... the first written in England" on the subject of matrimonial law, the relationship between spousal contracts and marriage contracts and dissolution of those contracts. The Dictionary of National Biography XIX: 229. Swinburne was commissary of the exchequer and judge of the consistatory court at York. Sweet and Maxwell, *A Legal Bibliography of the British Commonwealth of Nations* I:501 (39).